Where Do We Migrate To?

14
Issues in Cultural Theory

Acconci Studio

Svetlana Boym

Blane De St. Croix

Lara Dhondt

Brendan Fernandes

Claire Fontaine

Nicole Franchy

Andrea Geyer

Isola and Norzi

Kimsooja

Pedro Lasch

Adrian Piper

Raqs Media Collective

Société Réaliste

Julika Rudelius

Xaviera Simmons

Fereshteh Toosi

Philippe Vandenberg

Eric Van Hove

◉ Niels Van Tomme

Where Do

◉ Svetlana Boym

◉ Amitava Kumar

◉ Aaron Schuster

We Migrate To?

Center for Art Design and Visual Culture **University of Maryland Baltimore County**

ISSN 15211223
ISBN 978-1-890761-14-1
Library of Congress Control Number 2010940891

Published by the Center for Art, Design and Visual Culture
University of Maryland Baltimore County
Baltimore, Maryland 21250

Printed by C & C Offset Printing, LTD
China

Distributed by D.A.P.
Distributed Art Publishers
New York
The D.A.P. Catalog@artbook.com

FLANDERS FITS YOU
The production of this catalogue was made possible with the support of the Flemish Government through Flanders House New York.

Concept, cover, and book design by Kelley Bell

NATIONAL ENDOWMENT FOR THE ARTS
A great nation deserves great art.

Maryland State Arts Council

Director's Note

On behalf of the Center for Art, Design and Visual Culture, it gives me great pleasure to introduce *Where Do We Migrate To?* Inspired by the title of the 2005 video work by the artist Julika Rudelius, the exhibition and its accompanying catalogue look to reflect upon and rethink this question by asking each of us to consider the migrant as the "ultimate role model" and an "agent of change" rather than the popularized figure whose activities represent only a transgression of territorial boundaries. Organized by Niels Van Tomme, Director of Arts and Media at Provisions Learning Project in Washington, DC, *Where Do We Migrate To?* exposes the prejudices produced when we tie cultural identity to geographical location. Conversely, it also offers a multitude of scenarios toward how we may successfully navigate this complicated and volatile issue to reach a more inclusive resolution.

In bringing *Where Do We Migrate To?* to its culmination, we are very proud to have the following institutions, UMBC Offices and Departments, and Maryland agencies as our supporters. We are extremely grateful to Flanders House for the key role they have assumed in supporting both the exhibition and the accompanying catalogue. Dr. Freeman Hrabowski, President of the University of Maryland Baltimore County, Elliott Hershman, Provost, and John Jeffries, Dean of the College of Arts, Humanities and Social Sciences continue to play vital roles in supporting the programming initiatives of the Center for Art, Design and Visual Culture. The CADVC Internal Advisory Board has been exemplary in supervising and advancing the CADVC's mandate both at UMBC and beyond. The Maryland State Arts Council and the Baltimore County Commission on the Arts and Sciences have also contributed greatly to the CADVC's exhibition, publications, and K-12 educational outreach programs.

Our deepest thanks go to Niels Van Tomme, the exhibition's curator, for bringing the exhibition to the CADVC. We are also grateful for his unfailing commitment to the project, supervising in all facets of its undertaking in great detail and with an open mind. We also wish to thank Sonja Simonyi, curator for the film series that accompanies the exhibition, who brought together a group of films and videos that proved both substantive and provocative in the exploration of this issue while poignantly revealing its global ramifications on a human scale.

In the production of this book, Kelley Bell, Assistant Professor in Graphic Design at UMBC, created the fully integrated and beautiful design while Antonia Gardner expertly managed the editing of the four essays as well as the myriad of devils in the details. The essayists themselves, Niels Van Tomme, Amitava Kumar, Svetlana Boym, and Aaron Schuster deserve special praise for their insightful and illuminating texts. As a collective group, they offer the reader an exceptional opportunity to travel through the multi-layered experience of recognizing and assimilating what the terms *migrate* and *migrant* mean and engender in us all.

At the Center for Art, Design and Visual Culture, continued thanks and appreciation goes to the entire staff: Sandra Abbott, Dr. Maurice Berger, Janet Magruder, Graca McKenney, and William John Tudor, for their hard work, creative problem solving, and commitment to excellence. All of these qualities typify what the CADVC is and looks to present with every exhibition, publication, and public program it undertakes.

Symmes Gardner
Executive Director

Niels Van Tomme

Where Do We Migrate To?

The twenty-first century will be a century of migrations. [...] In this age of globalization there are no leftover areas. The earth has no New Frontier as such.

- Lieven De Cauter

Roberto Bolaño, in his intentionally enigmatic and meandering magnum opus *2666*, performs a series of astonishing lateral leaps with an almost aggressive literary bravura. In doing so, he delivers a painfully accurate account of our postnational world characterized by continuous movements of migration, a universe in which fixed notions of settlement and belonging are increasingly undermined by experiences of displacement and rootlessness. Stranded across the Mexican border, one of the novel's many characters, Oscar Fate, ponders his conversation with a local cashier: "I'm American. Why didn't I say I was African American? Because I'm in a foreign country? But can I really consider myself in a foreign country when I could go walking back to my own country right now if I wanted, and it wouldn't even take very long? Does this mean that in some places I'm American and in some places I'm African American and in other places, by logical extension, I'm nobody?"[1]

Such experiences of cultural displacement contrast heavily with the novel's harsh depictions of Mexican immigrants crossing the U.S. border, Bolaño's numerous accounts bearing witness to the continuous acts of humiliation and hostility these people encounter. The ways in which the United States has transformed its border with Mexico into "a high-tech, highly militarized, low-intensity war zone" make for one of the world's most controversial, and widely discussed, immigration policies.[2] Seen against this backdrop, Oscar Fate's sense of displacement is only one of many contradictions inherent to the contemporary self. In a world of incessant globalization and markedly transnational identities, the multiplicity of migratory experiences demands an increasingly complex understanding of the human condition. Subjected to an overall sense

1 Roberto Bolaño, *2666*, New York: Picador 2000, 285.

2 Amitava Kumar, *Passport Photos*, Berkeley and Los Angeles: University of California Press, 2000, xiii.

of displacement, human nature itself is undoubtedly shifting; we are all migrating into something else, towards somewhere else. In that sense, *Where Do We Migrate To?* intends to open up a wide range of political, psychological, poetic, and pragmatic manifestations of the contemporary migrant experience. Considering the migrant as "the bravest among us, [...] the most modern among us," the exhibition asks, is it possible to imagine him as a *figure*, a conceptual entity, through which we can understand our contemporary selves?[3]

Foreigners Everywhere, 2005-ongoing, is the ambiguous statement that the artist collective Claire Fontaine has been duplicating in neon, in a diverse range of languages, except English. Reflecting on some of the most disconcerting aspects of globalization, Claire Fontaine calls for an emphatic affiliation with an adversary political subject. As they note, "[T]hey have told 'go back home' to people who have lost their homes so many times that [these people] have accepted going to look for it on the other side of the world."[4] Viewed in the light of Belgian philosopher Lieven De Cauter's argument that "the United States may have been populated by a long-term flow of immigrants, but in reality this implied the eradication of the native population," Claire Fontaine's statement that "foreigners are not those who come from elsewhere" becomes particularly significant in a U.S. context.[5] Comparably, Fereshteh Toosi's *The Only Reason,* 2006, a reproduction of a 1970s Ku Klux Klan membership card reading "The only reason you are WHITE Today Is Because Your Ancestors Believed & Practiced SEGREGATION" détourned to read "The only reason you are A CITIZEN Today Is Because Your Ancestors Believed & Practiced IMMIGRATION" relates historic issues of racism and xenophobia to various degrees of inclusion and exclusion in present day society.

Xaviera Simmons's large-scale photo installation *Superunknown (Alive In The),* 2010, embodies perhaps one of the most emblematic visual representations of the migrant subject. Featuring low-grade imagery of people floating on rafts, these appropriated images, mostly taken from the Internet and featuring different geographic contexts, reference the global media spectacle fed by our daily hunger for catastrophe. Quite paradoxically, the pictures signify our remoteness to their subject matter, questioning the photographic image's value as a political tool.

3 Richard Rodriguez, quoted by Amitava Kumar in *Passport Photos*, xiv.

4 Claire Fontaine, "Foreigners Everywhere," in *Micro-Historias y Macro-mundos*, ed. Magali Arriola and Magnolia de la Garza, Mexico City: Instituto Nacional de Bellas Artes, 2010, 87.

5 Lieven De Cauter, "The Permanent Catastrophe," in *The Capsular Civilization, On the City in the Age of Fear*, Rotterdam: NAi Publishers, 2004, 99; and Claire Fontaine, 88.

In an accompanying text to her project, Simmons asks: "Where are the migrants migrating to and at what cost to their home countries? To the new countries?" Indeed, as a result of ongoing demographic growth and environmental devastation, mass migration has become an inevitable condition. Both home countries and new countries of the migrant find themselves forced to continually renegotiate their societal structures, seemingly shaking the very foundations on which these states are built.

Société Réaliste, with their project *EU Green Card Lottery*, 2005-ongoing, address the emancipatory potential of a new emerging class of permanent migratory workers. A fictitious campaign and registration office that drives prospective migrants to a website to apply for an imaginary EU Green Card, the project is not only a sharp commentary on U.S. and European immigration management but also provides "entrance points into contemporary forms and structures of political domination."[6] Conversely, Blane De St. Croix's sculptures *Landscape Sections: Borders: United States / Mexico*, 2010, and *North Korea / South Korea*, 2007-10, provide a surprisingly earthy addition to works addressing political contexts for the migrant. His miniature constructions of a slice of land represent faithful reproductions of borders between countries in varying degrees of conflict. Although shaped and defined by different modes of migration, these desolate landscapes are significantly devoid of their prime subject—the migrant.

As Slavoj Žižek notes, it is too easy "to praise the hybridity of the post-modern migrant subject, no longer attached to specific ethnic roots, floating freely between different cultural circles."[7] Indeed, directly attaching the cosmopolitan, freely traveling, contemporary artist or businessman to the underprivileged migrant worker is not only superficial, but also an act of unproductive cynicism. For the migrant, "the celebrated 'hybridity' designates a very tangible traumatic experience of never being able to settle down properly, [...] an experience full of anxiety, and demanding great effort, [...] a traumatic shock which destabilizes his entire existence."[8] How is it possible, then, to reduce such genuine shock to an enjoyment of "the lack of fixed identity"?[9] A series of artworks in the exhibition not only engages with psychological consequences of physical migration, but also examines more internalized modes of exile and diasporic isolation.

6 Société Réaliste, quoted in Niels Van Tomme, "Siding with the Barbarians," *Foreign Policy in Focus* (June 15, 2009), http://www.fpif.org/articles/siding_with_the_barbarians, accessed September 15, 2010.

7 Slavoj Žižek, *The Ticklish Subject, The Absent Centre of Political Ontology*, London and New York: Verso, 2008, first edition 1999, 220.

8 Ibid., 221.

9 Ibid

Andrea Geyer, in her newspaper *Interim,* 2002, addresses experiences of emotional destabilization. The work deals with being an immigrant in the United States, and tells the story of a young woman's insidious entrance into an unknown urban area. The narrative is intercepted with tips from contemporary instruction books for immigrants, which narrate how to assimilate to U.S. customs and culture. "It is important for you to know that what you feel right now is a typical pattern of experience, encountered by many others before you," reads one of the instructions, as the work directly relates the "individual navigation in urban space [...] to the navigation of cultural space."[10] As such, the city becomes a "body-prosthesis," to use Elizabeth Grosz's concept, in which the human body not only navigates cultural space but "coincides with the 'shape' and space of a psyche."[11]

Experiences of profound psychological instability can also turn complexly humorous, poetic, or eerie, especially when connected to linguistic mutations, the migrant's own languages consciously abandoned and the new language never completely learned, suggesting, as Rebecca Solnit eloquently notes, "the annihilation of the world [...] and the relatives [...] left behind."[12] In *Hydrant Diaspora,* 2009-ongoing, Svetlana Boym collects dialogues, complaints, appeals, and outbursts of New York immigrants of different backgrounds. Linking urban photography to notions of loss, displacement, and a nostalgic sense of humor, the work is recorded and re-created uniquely from the hydrant's point of view, an object so closely associated with New York City's urban character. Brendan Fernandes, in his video *Homecoming,* 2008, depicts lions, bellowing low growls, while the subtitles "go home" appear at the bottom of the screen. Playing with uses of language, translation, and interpretation, Fernandes asks what it actually means to "go home," expressing the absurdity of sentiments of belonging in today's transnational context.[13]

Inward projections of exile constitute an essential element of both Adrian Piper's and Philippe Vandenberg's practice, although these artists vastly differ in cultural, aesthetic, and theoretical backgrounds. According to Kobena Mercer, it is Piper's adherence to a Kantian philosophy that "metaphorically exiles her from the major trends in [...] contemporary art," even more than her thematic preoccupation with our uncompromising attitudes about race, gender, and difference.[14] Her work *Everything #4,* 2004, a mirror on which the text "Everything will be taken away" appears, is an ominous prophecy allowing for the emergence of new possibilities of

10 Andrea Geyer, http://www.andreageyer.info/projects/interim/interim.htm, accessed September 15, 2010.

11 Elizabeth Grosz, "Bodies-Cities," in *Space, Time and Perversion*, New York and London: Routledge, 1995, 244.

12 Rebecca Solnit, *A Field Guide to Getting Lost*, London: Penguin Books, 2006, first edition 2005, 55.

13 Brendan Fernandes, http://www.brendanfernandes.ca/homecoming.php, accessed September 15, 2010.

14 Amy L. Powell, rev. of Kobena Mercer, ed., *Exiles, Diasporas & Strangers*, in *Invisible Culture, An Electronic Journal for Visual Culture*, No.14/2010, http://www.rochester.edu/in_visible_culture/Issue_14/reviews/mercer.html, accessed September 15, 2010.

existence once all the old baggage is discarded. Philippe Vandenberg, on the other hand, claims that "painting that no longer elicits displacement is nothing more than matter," therefore regarding migratory sensibilities as fundamentally enriching.[15] His sweeping, diary-like drawings are a radical act of resistance, carrying the promise to liberate oneself from a looming sense of stagnation.

Joining writers like Amitava Kumar in "the search for a new poetics and politics of diasporic protest," *Where Do We Migrate To?* argues for an enhancement of the migrant metaphor, one that demands, as Kumar suggests "genuine, transformative shifts" and "the creation of new assemblages, [...] communities."[16] As such, the exhibition asks which lessons are to be learned from migrant confrontations, and whether they allow us to imagine new forms of sociability. According to Judith Butler, Giorgio Agamben's *The Coming Community* offers a "meditation on community as a kind of linguistic belonging that moves beyond both identity and universality."[17] In this text, Agamben offers a representation of potentiality, engendering true metaphor, "[b]elonging, being-*such,* is here only the relation to an empty and indeterminate totality."[18] If new insights are to be generated through such radical poetic criticism as Agamben's, an engagement with metaphorical thinking should be essential—poetry becoming a form of protest.

Kimsooja, in her video *A Needle Woman - Paris*, 2009, is shown standing perfectly still in the crowded streets of Paris, in a kind of silent dissent. Having her back to the camera, the artist's presence brings forth reactions from passersby, who form a social web around her needlelike figure. In this video, Kimsooja becomes a void; the viewer is literally seeing and responding through a foreign entity through which he or she "project[s] the fundamental uncertainty of our own being."[19] Relating image and body in a space where they cannot be separated any longer, it appears that Kimsooja forges new modes of representation that radically call for alternative forms of being together.

Immersed in poetic contemplation, the characters in Julika Rudelius's video *Adrift*, 2007, seem relentlessly on the road, in a suspended space removed from either destination or point of origin. Markedly differing in

15 Philippe Vandenberg, *L'important c'est le kamikaze, oeuvre 2000-2006*, Charleville-Mézières Arthur Rimbaud Museum, 2006, 98.

16 Kumar, x.

17 Judith Butler, http://www.upress.umn.edu/Books/A/agamben_coming.html, accessed September 15, 2010.

18 Giorgio Agamben, *The Coming Community*, Minneapolis: University of Minnesota Press, 1993, 67.

19 Keiji Nakamura, "Kimsooja's *A Needle Woman*," in *Kimsooja, To Breathe / Respirare*, Milan Edizioni Charta, 2005, 133.

age and ethnic background, the image is filled with bodies being swung to droning waves of monotonous sound. The viewer is left with no instructions for how to read this image, the only certainty being that these characters represent a cluster of people moving toward something indefinable.

In the photographic series *Shelters of Refuge*, 2008-ongoing, Lara Dhondt conceptualizes the shelter as a site that generates distraction. Researching temporary characteristics of urban life, these "spatial demarcations" function as poetic gateways, traces of alienation that conceive "sheltered daydreaming" as a gesture of refusal and isolation.[20] Imagining acts that poetically undermine fixed situations, Isola and Norzi's sculpture *prints, finisterrea*, 2007, narrates the physical imprints that people leave behind when trespassing spaces. A discreet form of opposition, the sculpture displays the ephemeral impressions remaining from distances traveled and the ways in which movement is inscribed in its immediate environment.

Eric Van Hove, with his series of interventions *Abreaction*, 2004-ongoing, physically brings migrant poetry to the streets, injecting foreignness into a public space. The performance consists of traversing a place with a single sentence of automatic writing in a foreign language, unannounced, and often in politically charged contexts. Accompanied by a local translator, Van Hove's act is an attempt to turn antagonism into hospitality through poetry, his piece evoking the philosophy of Jacques Derrida in recognizing that hospitality is always haunted by the possibility of hostility.[21]

But, leaving aside the political, psychological, and poetic manifestations of the migrant subject, would it be possible to truly implement migratory sensibilities into everyday life? In this age of advanced globalization, a "neoliberal push towards a borderless world" seems to coexist with the construction of indestructible walls of exclusion, immigrant concentration camps, and the fencing off of entire continents by high-tech surveillance equipment.[22] Both claiming their right for mobility, what happens when the figure of the artist and the migrant coincide? Would that be an occasion "to seize the moment for what it might be, to rejoin movement and movement, [...] an encounter with the contingent and the other, [...] with the cut of difference," as Brett Nielson and Angela Mitropoulos suggest in their reflection on migrant activism?[23] A number

20 Lara Dhondt, *Lara Dhondt: Shelters of Refuge*, EXTRA, Winter 2008.

21 See Jacques Derrida, "Foreigner Question," in *Of Hospitality, Anne Dufourmantelle Invites Jacques Derrida to Respond*, Stanford: Stanford University Press, 2000.

22 Brian Holmes, "Continental Drift: From Geopolitics to Geopoetics," in *Escape the Overcode, Activist Art in the Control Society*, Eindhoven: Van Abbemuseum, 2009, 197.

23 Brett Nielson and Angela Mitropoulos, "Exceptional Times, Nongovernmental Spacings, and Impolitical Movements," in *Nongovernmental Politics*, ed. Michel Feher, New York: Zone Books, 2007, 480.

of artists in the exhibition radically imagine a future for, or reflect upon existing notions of, coexistence between migrants and the others.

A series of maps entitled *LATINO/A AMERICA*, 2003-ongoing, which Pedro Lasch calls "a monument to the epics of migration," presents the artist's collaboration with individuals who are about to cross the U.S.-Mexico border.[24] Each person receives two specially designed maps to use during the crossing, one to keep and one to mail back to the artist upon arrival at their final destination. In staging such subversive collaborations, "the attempt to violate or evade the border [...] is a politically significant act" through which "a certain elimination [...] of the lines between the interned migrant and the civil dissident" take place.[25]

An antidote to the immigrant camp, Acconci Studio's *Mobile Linear City*, 1991, is an innovative model for a transportable city stored in a truck. Displaying oppositions of mobility and immobility, hospitality and hostility, as well as public and private space, this architectural proposal consists of six housing units that are telescoped into one and hooked up to a tractor. Containing the ability to shape future urban environments, Acconci's provocative architectural model is, to cite Charlie Hailey's discussion of the camp's paradigm, "at the focus of emerging political and spatial questions of identity, residency, safety."[26]

Finally, both Nicole Franchy and Raqs Media Collective address ways in which the global acceleration of migration can be addressed from a strictly defined geographic point of view. In *Ruricancho*, 2009, Franchy starts off from the recollection of aerial photographs of San Juan de Lurigancho, a district in Lima and the most populated area of South America. The video analyzes a region marked by severe demographic changes, beginning in the forties, as populations from the Andean and Amazonian regions migrated to the Peruvian capital. Similarly, with *Ndl Jn. (New Delhi Junction)*, 2002, Raqs Media Collective considers the Indian metropolis New Delhi as a migratory platform. This sound piece about moving towards and circulating within the urban landscape signals our everyday environment "as a magnet as well as a springboard for daily migrations."[27]

24 Pedro Lasch, http://www.latinoaamerica.com/, accessed September 15, 2010.

25 Nielson and Mitropoulos, 473.

26 Charlie Hailey, Camps, *A Guide to 21st-Century Space*, Cambridge: The MIT Press, 2009, 18.

27 Raqs Media Collective, http://www.raqsmediacollective.net/newdelhi.html, accessed September 15, 2010.

Taking all of this into account, *Where Do We Migrate To?*, in lieu of being a clear-cut statement about its subject matter, allows multiple perspectives to unfold simultaneously. Whether they are political, psychological, poetic, or pragmatic, each artistic inquiry takes a deliberate step back from the daily media hysteria surrounding the topic of migration. As such, the exhibition aims to open up its own transformative potential, not by simply informing its viewers with dry objective facts but by offering an exercise in a certain "indiscreet anthropology of migration," to borrow Martin Brady and Helen Hughes's description of Ulrich Seidl's seminal film on bi-directional migration *Import Export*.[28] Like Seidl's film or Roberto Bolaño's novel, *Where Do We Migrate To?* intends to be focused but panoramic, taking full responsibility for its inconsequentiality and impulsiveness. Since "the illusion of complete belonging has been shattered," as Svetlana Boym suggests, who else but the migrant, that minor prophet entering from the outside to *re*-define the inside, would be better fit to guide us through that messy, impenetrable, and unjust world that is ours?[29]

Niels Van Tomme is a New York-based curator, researcher, and art critic who serves as the Director of Arts and Media at Provisions Learning Project. His independently curated exhibitions are shown internationally.

28 Martin Brady and Helen Hughes, "Import and Export: Ulrich Seidl's Indiscreet Anthropology of Migration," *GFL*, No. 1/2008.

29 Svetlana Boym, *The Future of Nostalgia*, New York: Basic Books, 2001, 255.

Amitava Kumar

Who is a Migrant?

Who is a migrant?

The Indian man in the business suit who is as much at home in Boston as he is in Bombay or Barcelona. No, not him. Any minute now he is going to bend over and pick up his shiny Samsonite and walk briskly away.

But consider the bulging yellow suitcase bound with a length of nylon that stays untouched on the carousel. Round and round it goes. It slowly loses the company of the Swiss Army wheeled overnighters and the Tumi nylons.

The yellow suitcase awaits the arrival of that far pair, a stocky, middle-aged man holding two passports and his wife, who has a burgundy dupatta draped over her shoulders. The two received a fair bit of attention from the immigration agent sitting in her booth.

Soon, it will be the yellow suitcase's turn. Several questions will be directed at it. The couple will stand quietly, sinking in a sea of diffidence, but the suitcase will be opened and examined.

That suitcase is a migrant.

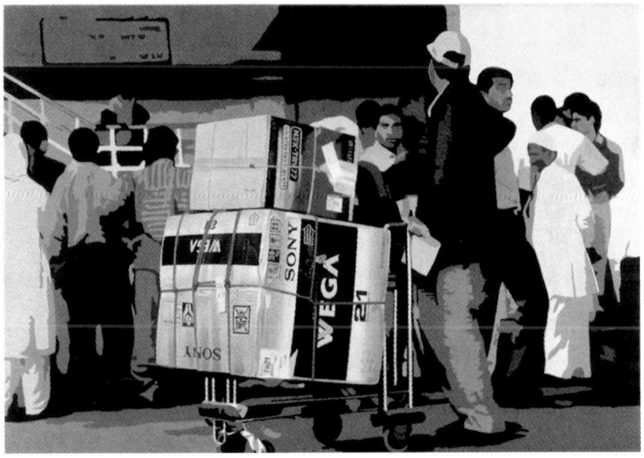

Subodh Gupta
Saat Samunder Paar VII
2003
Oil on canvas
167.4 x 228.6 cm / 65 7/8 x 90 in
Copyright: Subodh Gupta

Bags, passport, my shoes, the outline of an airplane stenciled on a sign at the airport. I had long sought an iconic image that would catch the essence of the immigrant experience. It took me a long time to realize that what I was really seeking was a way to define myself as a new arrival in the U.S. from India. I was trying to describe my loss.

I brought two bags from home, but there was a third that I left behind.

Bags, passport, my shoes crossed the yellow lines; something was left behind. Here I am, a sum of different parts; travel agents everywhere are selling ads for the parts that were left behind.

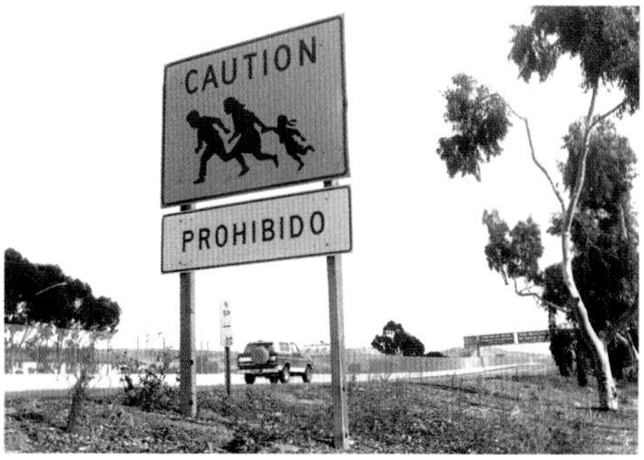

Amitava Kumar
California Road Sign
1994

For a long time, the sign in the photo above quite nicely represented for me the iconic migrant image. There is a flattening of experience in the portrayal of such marginal lives—a flattening also present in the term "alien" used to describe such persons—and that is evident in the figures of the people showing running. I was, of course, also drawn by the way in which language worked in the sign, the split between English and Spanish, one addressed to drivers who presumably only speak English, while the other, less advisory and more a warning or threat, simply delivering a prohibition. Here, in a brutal but pure form, was the truth of a society divided between those who belong and those who don't. But soon I began to suspect that my desire for a single image to represent the complex range of migrant experience mirrored the will of the State: when it lays out its implacable typologies ("Native," "Naturalized," "Alien"), the State erases all differences, all marks of individuality and diverse, overlapping histories. Instead of a singular image, or an essentialized identity, one must go looking for plurality and difference. In my personal taxonomy, it has become more important to distinguish the well-heeled migrant from the refugees, the exiled, and the masses forced to move away from their homes because of dire conditions like famine and joblessness. This would be all right, of course, were it also not a bit self-serving.

I am a border crosser, but I wasn't fleeing oppression, and the only thing that distinguishes me from my fellow frequent-flying, duty-free Indians is that they appear less troubled by irony. This doesn't stop me from heaping scorn on them. I think of them as those who carry their nostalgia in a suitcase. Rightly or wrongly, I think of them as quick to possess all that we have lost. The humid air on the road to Delhi airport, in sealed tins, they must have brought. The light dying in the eyes of a horse, frozen, they must have brought. In the dim corners of the hearts of twenty-five relatives back in India, fasting among their ragged dreams, the desire for a Parker pen, that, too, they must have brought.

Objects are like people: they can tell you where they come from.

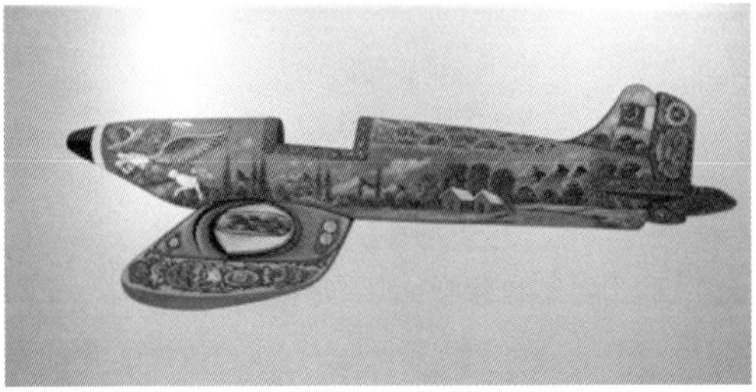

Sana Arjumand
Let's Fly First Class
2010
Image courtesy of the artist and Aicon Gallery

Look at the plane above. You have probably seen that art on trucks in places like Lahore or Ludhiana. It might be two in the afternoon. It is hot and dry around you, the man selling sugarcane juice is sleeping in the shade of a tree, and there's no one else around. Your shadow is the smallest you've ever seen in your life. And then a truck comes to a stop beside you. The exhaust pours out as if from a chimney in a brick kiln. If you look past it, however, you see, painted on the side of the truck, a landscape that includes snowy peaks, colorful huts, cool skies, fields brimming with flowers that will live longer even than plastic. Folk utopia!

Now, what happens when that painting is transposed onto the body of an airplane? I'm tempted to see in it the creative gesture of a cosmopolitan artist trying her hand at vernacular art. But there are other interpretations available. For instance, I see in this painting the wish for flight becoming literal, as a vehicle for the imagination. I imagine this make-believe airplane as a prop in one of those old-fashioned studios, the kind where couples stand in front of the backdrop of a waterfall. The painting touches me by its use of color, and its playfulness.

In a statement that I read online, Arjumand's colorful airplane was described in the following manner: "Sana covers her airplane—so often associated in a post-9/11 society with the shadow fear of terrorism—with the same religious and patriotic imagery which decorate South Asian cargo trucks, subverting the shadow paradigm with playful images that invoke a spiritual path—the term 'Mairaj' referring to the invitation from the divine to ascend the self and experience the pure essence of being...." I prefer my own reading, where I link the plane to the prop in the studio in the small town in South Asia. In my reading, the airplane is closer to the ordinary experiences of the people around the artist. In contrast, that reading, by situating the painting in the framework of post-9/11 life, makes everything that is done by Desi artists and writers only an extended conversation with the West. We begin to speak in the idioms that the West itself grants us. **I'm speaking here as an immigrant, sensitive or touchy about what people assume are my priorities.** Terror is not the sole reality of immigrant lives. The West never was, or should be, our sole interlocutor, and the readings we do of our books and our art should attempt to multiply, rather than simplify, our complexities.

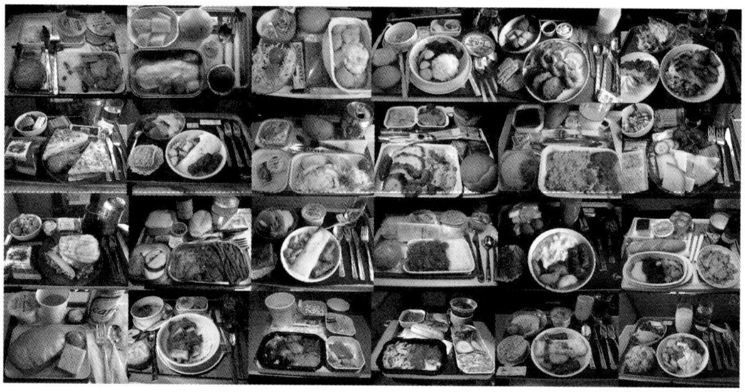

Hasan Elahi
Altitude v2.0
2006

The truth, of course, is that migrants have a more difficult time at airports than they do in art galleries. Above are the pictures of airplane meals taken by artist Hasan Elahi, who also shoots and uploads on his website pictures of the urinals he uses. Airports are sites of surveillance, especially since the attacks of 9/11, and Elahi, who is Muslim and was repeatedly interrogated by the FBI, believes he can't be too careful. On him falls the burden of presenting to the State the images that record his movements. Elahi estimates that he has more than 40,000 images on his site, making trackingtransience.net an exercise in self-surveillance. The migrant is the one who eats airplane meals and uses urinals, just like everyone else, but does so as if he is doing all this in a surveillance video produced by the State.

I no longer find it useful to speak of migrant images; a stronger case can be made for attending to migrant practices.

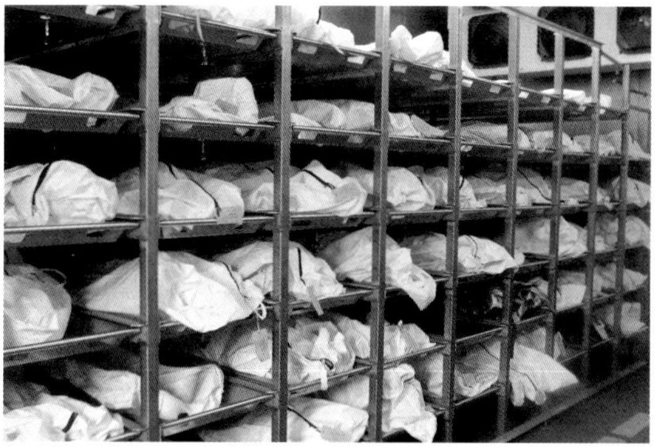

Joshua Lott
Photograph in the *New York Times*
July 28, 2010
Courtesy The New York Times/Redux

By now I have spent more years in the U.S. than I had in the country of my birth. As a new immigrant, I remember watching television with a hunger, a hunger for seeing a face that looked like mine. I would be flipping the pages of a magazine and what would arrest me would be a photograph taken in the Indian subcontinent. Even if it was a clichéd image of an elephant, or a tiger, or the Taj. The nostalgia for that kind of visual fix has now been replaced by a desire to build an inventory of acts and histories that give insight into the complexity of migrant lives. The sources for this inventory lie in art, in film, in literature, in new textbooks of sociology or ethnography, in law, in the daily record on blogs, in the news on television, and in newspapers.

Let me give you an example. During the summer this year, I came across a news story about a morgue in Pima County, Arizona, running out of space due to the number of bodies brought there of unidentified Latin American immigrants who had died in the desert. Fifty-seven corpses had been brought to the morgue during July alone, when the article appeared in the *New York Times*. The photograph accompanying the story showed white body bags on metal shelves with bright yellow, red, and orange tags. The image didn't represent art, in any conventional sense, but to me it was extraordinary. Not least because when I looked at the image and read the caption about the morgue, I thought, of course, of the vitriol swirling around in the debate over immigration and the passage of anti-immigration laws in Arizona. Intuitively, the question that arose in my mind about the photograph was, what would Brecht write about it? I remembered reading somewhere, soon after I had come to this country and was attending graduate school, that Brecht would cut pictures from the paper and write poems about them. I follow that exercise in my class sometimes, and now, at the end of this essay, am leaving this blank space below for you to write a short poem here:

Amitava Kumar is a journalist and professor of English at Vassar College. His most recent book is A Foreigner Carrying in the Crook of His Arm A Tiny Bomb *(2010).*

Svetlana Boym

Immigrant Arts, Diasporic Intimacy, and Alternative Solidarity

Polish-American artist Krzysztof Wodiczko wrote that an immigrant in today's cities is an "unintentional prophet," who dreams of a better private refuge, but also of a better public democracy that could welcome strangers like himself.[1] The immigrant's unintentional prophecy reveals something fundamental about the conditions of "native" existence in the contemporary world and sets that existence off-kilter. Such a modern immigrant, who speaks with an accent in both foreign and native languages, is a bit of a trickster, who teases us with her tongue-tied confessions that tamper with our sense of intimacy and estrangement, of cultural differences and alternative solidarities in the contemporary world.

Immigrants are no longer a minority, even though they don't often have a prominent cultural and political voice. Immigrant encounters bring forth the inconvenient histories of dissent and hardship that don't fit into news sound bytes; they complicate the conception of multiculturalism and pluralism, revealing pluralities within national traditions and multiple cultures within a single individual. Can the immigrant become a key figure for understanding the 21st -century experience of modernity—out of synch? Or does the experience of immigration complicate and embarrass our theoretical metaphors? How does art mediate across the borders and speak in immigrant tongues with multiple accents?

Russian-American writer Vladimir Nabokov compared the experience of immigration to the syncopal kick that off-centers one's life and art, and yet makes life worth living. Speaking of his own forced exile, he wrote: "The break in my own destiny affords me in retrospect a syncopal kick that I would not have missed for worlds."[2] The syncopal tale of immigration is about loss and displacement, not reconciliation. Syncopation is about the impossibility of transcendence and fusion. The syncopal tale is based on sensuous details, not symbols; it is the opposite of synthesis. Syncopation does not restore the lost home; it is present as a trace, an estranging disharmony, a foreign accent. Or even more than an accent,

1 Krzysztof Wodiczko, "Designing the City of Strangers," in *Critical Vehicles*, Cambridge, MA MIT Press, 1999, 9.

2 Vladimir Nabokov, *Speak, Memory: An Autobiography Revisited*, New York: Vintage International, 1989. Discussed in Svetlana Boym, *The Future of Nostalgia*, New York: Basic Books, 2001, 281.

the syncopation affects the syntax of the immigrant performer that resists complete assimilation into the non-immigrant metaphors of universal longing. At best, when and if an immigrant becomes an artist, she manages to transform the loss into a musical composition, a ciphering of pain into art.

In my view, this art of syncopation is at the core of the new immigrant arts. The artist doesn't have to be an immigrant, but she can encounter an immigrant/foreigner—in herself—and find new ways of mediating the experience without erasing the immigrant accent. The question, then, is not only *where* do we migrate to, but also *how* do we migrate, and what are the new medias and new metaphors for this experience?

The metaphoric connection between migration, art, and the human condition harks back to antiquity. Artistic language, at least since Aristotle's *Poetics*, has been connected to estrangement and foreignness; exile has been seen as a metaphor for the human condition since the biblical expulsion from Paradise, and the experience of modernity has frequently been compared to transcendental homelessness. Nostalgia as a modern disease was the disease of the first migrant workers, Swiss governesses, and mercenary soldiers, only later becoming a critical trope for poets and philosophers and the most manipulated emotion for nationalist politicians. I would propose different forms of mediating the experience of "immigrant arts" without fully transforming an immigrant into a metaphor or a translation of universal longing.

I will speak about three aspects of immigrant arts: double estrangement that embarrasses our theoretical assumptions, diasporic intimacy that questions conceptions of home, and alternative solidarities among artists across cultures. My figure for the immigrant arts will be an immigrant of the first generation, the one who didn't entirely assimilate herself into the native frame of reference and who keeps bilingualism alive.

Such a figure exemplifies a clash of conflicting modernities and what I call an "off-modern" experience. Off-modern art engages with the practice of double estrangement and, instead of teleologies of "post," "neo," "trans," follows the lateral move, the zigzag in the cultural evolution. Off-modern is a detour into the unexplored potentials of the modern project. It recovers unforeseen pasts and ventures into the side alleys of modern history at the margins of error of major philosophical, economic, and technological narratives of modernization and progress.[3] Critic and writer Victor Shklovsky, who had immigrant experiences himself, described the knight's move in a chess game that follows "the tortured road of the brave" as the key image for cultural evolution and alternative modern sensibility. Off-modern immigrant arts are tricksters' arts that play with multiple estrangements and belongings, redefining the conception of intimacy and nostalgia that haunts contemporary art practice.

"Intimate" refers to the "innermost," "pertaining to a deep nature," "very personal," "sexual." Yet, "to intimate" also means "to communicate with a hint or other indirect sign; to imply subtly."[4] The thirst for intimacy is thoroughly modern and new, yet it has often been accompanied by the lamentation of loss and a recognition of modern estrangement. I will speak about something now that might seem paradoxical—a "diasporic intimacy" that is not opposed to uprootedness and defamiliarization but is constituted by it. Diasporic intimacy can be approached only through indirection and intimation, through stories and secrets. It is spoken of in a foreign language that reveals the inadequacies of translation. Diasporic intimacy does not promise an unmediated emotional fusion, but only a precarious affection—no less deep, while aware of its transience. In contrast to the utopian images of intimacy as transparent and authentic belonging, diasporic intimacy is distopic by definition; it is rooted in the suspicion of a single home, in shared longing without belonging. It thrives on the hope of the possibilities of human understanding and survival, of unpredictable chance encounters, but this hope is not utopian. Diasporic intimacy is haunted by the images of home and homeland, yet it also discloses some of the furtive pleasures of exile and a concern for the fragility of worldliness and a shared world.

When we are home, we don't need to talk about it. To be "at home"—*byt' doma*—is a slightly a grammatical expression in many languages. It is as if it can't be learned; we just know how to say it in our own native tongue. To feel at home is to be comfortably unaware of things, to know that things are in their places, and so are you. It is a state of mind that doesn't depend on an actual place. The object of longing, then, is not really a place called home but this sense of intimacy with the world; it is not the past in general, but that imaginary moment when we didn't know the temptation of nostalgia.

3 On the concept of the off-modern, see Svetlana Boym, *The Architecture of the Off-Modern*, New York: Princeton Architectural Press, 2008, and www.svetlanaboym.com.

4 *The American Heritage Dictionary*, Boston: Houghton Miffin, 1985, 672.

So much has been made of the "happy homecoming" that it is time to do justice to the stories of *non-return,* or return to the place where one has never been, which can be a little off the common map. In the 21st century, millions of people find themselves displaced from their places of birth, living in voluntary or involuntary exile. Their intimate experiences occur against a foreign background. Moreover, immigrants to the United States bring with them different traditions of social interaction, often less individualistic than the one they find on arrival. In contemporary American pop psychology, one is encouraged "not to be afraid of intimacy." This presumes that intimate communication can and should be made in a plain language and consists in saying "what you mean," without irony and double speak. Immigrants—and many alienated natives as well—cannot help but dread it. It is very confining not to have a space to be "off."

An inability to return home is always a personal tragedy, but it can also become an enabling force. That doesn't mean that there is no nostalgia there, only that this kind of nostalgia precludes a restoration of the past and goes off on the diagonal, opening up of the folds of potential worlds.

The diasporic intimacy that interests me is neither the touchy-feely imperative of the breath-freshener commercial nor the fraternal/sororal warmth of a minority group. Diasporic intimacy does not promise a comforting recovery of identity through shared nostalgia for a lost home and homeland. In fact, it's the opposite. It could be seen as the mutual enchantment of two immigrants from different parts of the world or the sense of the precarious coziness of a foreign home. Just as one learns to live with alienation and reconciles oneself to the uncanniness of the world around one and to the strangeness of the human touch, there comes a surprise, a pang of intimate recognition, a hope that sneaks in through the back door. It punctuates the habitual estrangement of everyday life abroad.

A cultural genealogy of diasporic intimacy leads us away from the history of private life. We have to look for its modern beginnings in the alienating and illuminating experiences of the modern city, in the double bind of modernity and nostalgia reflected in the consciousness of urban wanderers at once estranged from and engaged with life around them.

Walter Benjamin and Charles Baudelaire discovered a "love at last sight" that produces a sexual shudder with a simultaneous shock of recognition and loss. Rather than a melancholic sorrow, love at last sight reveals itself as a miracle of possibilities. Love at last sight strikes the urban stranger when he or she realizes they are on stage, at once an actor and a spectator.[5]

Immigrants always perceive themselves as on stage, their lives resembling some mediocre fiction with occasional romantic outbursts and gray dailiness. That is, of course, when the first hardships are over and the immigrant can afford the luxury of leisurely reflection. As for sexual shock, it becomes a commonplace. What is much more uncommon is a recognition of a certain kind of tenderness, which could be more striking than a sexual fantasy. Love at last sight is the spasm of loss after the revelation; the tenderness of exiles is about a revelation of possibility after loss. It is when a loss has been taken for granted that one can be surprised that not everything has been lost. Tenderness is not about complete disclosure, saying what one really means, getting closer and closer. It excludes absolute possession and fusion. It defies symbols of fulfillment and is not very goal oriented. In the words of Roland Barthes, "Tenderness...is nothing but an infinite, insatiable metonymy" and a "miraculous crystallization of the presence."[6] In tenderness, need and desire are joined. Tenderness is always polygamous, non-exclusive. "Where you are tender, you speak your plural."[7]

Diasporic intimacy is belated and never final; objects and places were lost in the past, and one knows that they can be lost again. Yet one discovers that there is still a lot to share. The recognition of transience does not obscure the shock of intimacy, but rather heightens the intensity of surprise.

The home that one leaves and the home away from home that one creates sometimes have more in common than one would like to admit. A portable home away from home, which an immigrant ferociously guards, preserves an imprint of his or her cultural motherland. Exiles may be bilingual, but they rarely can rid themselves of an accent. A few misplaced prepositions, a few missed articles, definite or indefinite, betray the syntax of the mother tongue.

Arjun Appudarai has suggested that in light of globalization, mass immigration, and the development of electronic media, one has to redefine the notion of the "locale."[8] It is no longer a specific place where

5 Walter Benjamin, "Some Motifs in Baudelaire," in *Illuminations*, New York: Schocken Books, 1978, 169.

6 Roland Barthes, *A Lover's Discourse: Fragments*, trans. Richard Howard, New York: Hill and Wang, 1978, 224-25.

7 Ibid., 225.

8 Arjun Appadurai, *Modernity at Large: Cultural Dimensions of Globalization*, Minneapolis: University of Minnesota Press, 1996.

one belongs but rather a social context that one could export into diaspora. Yet art depends on the materiality of place, sensual perceptions, smells, and sounds. I do not know of any nostalgia for a homepage; rather, the object of nostalgia is precisely the nonvirtual, low-tech world. In this case, the locale is not a mere context, but also a remembered sensation and the material debris of the past life: things that, in the past, made one sick of home can frame the homesickness of the future.

Often the artists and theorists who speak of immigration and nostalgia are metaphorical immigrants, or sometimes immigrants of the second or third generation, who came to the new country when they were very young or were the children of immigrants. Their nostalgia became the blueprint for the discussion of longing and exile as a metaphor for the human condition and for homeless modernity. The perspective of the first-generation immigrant doesn't allow for the universalization of nostalgia but, at the same time, doesn't dwell only in cultural differences and national particularities, suggesting instead cross-cultural bridges. The immigrant of the first generation is a creature of double estrangement who carries a burden of ambivalent knowledge of culture and politics. She is aware of the complexity of everyday life and politics in the abandoned homeland, and of the strangeness of the remodeled second home. She is "off" both in her native and adopted lands, and builds new solidarities through elective affinities and across national lines. In contrast, the immigrant of the second (or second-plus) generation is actually a native who speaks the new language without an accent, while having only a limited knowledge of the utopian mother tongue. And yet he experiences a profound sense of loss. Haunted by the utopian imaginings of the other place and the other time, the immigrant of the second generation shares the frame of references and the syntax of longing with the natives, which makes his story more widely acceptable than the tongue-tied accented tale of the firsthand experiences of transplantation. These singular stories, filled with tragic and comic experiences that cannot be quite rendered in the foreign tongue, are punctuated by an untranslatable sense of humor that the immigrant trickster cannot always share with the serious natives.

Sometimes the relationship between knowledge/experience of living in the homeland and nostalgia is in inverse proportion. The immigrant of the second generation is more nostalgic for the home he has lost, precisely because he does not have adult experiences of the contradictory existence in the mother country. For him, the lost homeland is not the plural and contradictory place with internal dissent and everyday survivals, but often a mythical home to escape to from the everyday boredom of the habitual comfortable existence.

Our immigrant #1 carries with her a personal history of "syncopal kicks," their physical discomforts and embarrassments, and can offer some more unusual and radical models for artistic practice. Immigrant #1 is like a sad clown playing with multiple estrangements, as well as with multiple belongings.

What kind of new solidarities and forms of understanding can one develop through diasporic intimacy? I believe that the immigrant arts open up new forms of solidarity based on strangeness. "Solidarity" is a strange word that combines solidity and porosity in its very meaning. It was coined from the French *solidarité,* "mutual responsibility," a coinage of the *Encyclopédie* (1765) from *solidaire,* "interdependent, complete, entire," from *solide* (see *solid*). It suggests a new crystallization of relationships that combine integrity and interdependency. It is opposed both to complete individual autonomy and to the community of any kind that is based on a unified collective ethos and some kind of *volonté générale*. Solidarity combines estrangement and engagement, suggesting interdependency without the loss of singularities and multiplicities.

One can see alternative geographic connections—for example, between Latin American and East European artists, or Indians and Albanians—alternative solidarities between artists, not structures of influence, hierarchy, not even the fortuitous *hazard objectif* of curatorial intuition that places artists together, but inner artistic dialogues about multiple belongings that can open into an alternative off-modern history of avant-garde that never completely ends.

Immigrant encounters in art and beyond give space for modernities out-of-synch that don't quite fit into a single concept of globalization. The immigrant is not a marginal apparition but a key figure that walks in the off-modern zigzag, crossing black and white squares, revealing black holes and blank spots on the chessboard of contemporary art.

Svetlana Boym is a writer, theorist, and media artist who teaches in the Department of Comparative Literature and Graduate School of Design at Harvard University. Her books include The Future of Nostalgia *(2001),* The Architecture of the Off-Modern *(2008) and, most recently,* Another Freedom, The Alternative History of an Idea *(2010).*

Aaron Schuster

The Atopia of Philosophy

Modernity is often characterized by, to borrow a term from Georg Lukács, "transcendental homelessness." Isolation, alienation, and uprootedness are the hallmarks of the modern subject, who is consigned, in a tragic vein, to search for a wholeness or a presence that will forever elude it. The object of desire is lost, and by staying lost, it drives further the subject's restless wandering—a pursuit which, in the end, is nothing but a quest for one's own self. If the related figures of the migrant, the exile, the outcast, the nomad, the vagabond, and the drifter speak strongly to the contemporary imagination, it is perhaps because they touch on a universal predicament: the radical contingency (groundlessness) of human existence.

But there is more than one way to look at this condition, and it need not only be the occasion for melancholic brooding. In fact, it was only a matter of time before this downcast picture was turned on its head. What once appeared as a terrible loss—the subject deprived of substance, nostalgically oriented toward an unattainable past—was now heralded as a liberation: eviction from the old metaphysical home unleashed a terrific power, an undreamed of capacity for invention and transformation. This fresh spirit of adventure became known as postmodernism (to put a somewhat different spin on this familiar story), which opposed to modernist negativity the affirmative virtues of plasticity, mobility, and self-creation. Home was no longer something to mourn but to construct anew, and the alienation that stuck like a painful thorn in the subject's flesh became an opportunity to open oneself, fully and unreservedly, to the other. For it is because the self is split from within, a kind of foreigner in its own psychic milieu, that it is also able to recognize and welcome the foreigner on the outside. Internal otherness resonates with the otherness of the stranger, making possible a new kind of community based not on shared substance (blood, customs, land, etc.) but on a mutually shared "not belonging," a generous form of uprootedness. Such is the brave new cosmopolitan ideal.

With this brief sketch of a certain line of philosophical thought in mind, I'd like to offer some reflections on the problem of homelessness and migration as prevalent figures for understanding subjectivity.

🚶

"Philosophy is really homesickness..."

This not having a place in the world, or feeling out of place wherever one is, is the very starting point of philosophy. One could even say that philosophy is an exercise of misfits, which begins by positing a fundamental discordance between self and world: what is called "subject" is nothing other than a fissure, a gap, or a void in the great chain of being, the site of a failed or incomplete synthesis. How exactly to conceive this rupture is one of the key questions in the history of philosophy, and, of course, a matter of great contention. Without pretending to survey this enormous topic here, we can make one general observation. At the same time that philosophy takes as its task to reveal this gap and reflect upon it, it also typically attempts, in a therapeutic gesture, to heal the wound that it has brought to light, to "put Humpty-Dumpty back together again." This ambiguity was nicely captured in Novalis's phrase, "Philosophy is really homesickness, the wish to be at home everywhere."[1]

Take what may be considered the inaugural text of modern philosophy, Descartes's *Meditations*. There Descartes destroys the basis of customary knowledge and traditional authority with his method of radical doubt. Seeking to discover what he can know with absolute certainty through the use of his own reason, Descartes eventually posits, with the help of the hypothesis of the "evil god" who serves as the ultimate skeptical argument, the "I think" (cogito) as the new basis for philosophy. The strangeness and subversiveness of this operation should not be underestimated. What the autonomous power of reason produces is an oddly *unworldly* being, a self stripped of all qualities, a kind of punctual, vanishing identity that is the polar opposite of the "rich" or "thick" self embedded in society and immediately identified with a particular role. Yet soon after it appears, this autonomous cogito is quickly re-inserted into the familiar world that had

1 Novalis, *Philosophical Writings*, trans. and ed. Margaret Mahony Stoljar, Albany: SUNY Press, 1997, 135.

just previously vanished. In the chapters of the book that follow, Descartes endeavors to bring back tradition, authority, and their ultimate guarantee, the good, trustworthy God. But once this crack has been exposed, the game is, in a sense, already up: the return to the pre-modern universe where everything has its proper place is necessarily mediated, and hence fatally undermined, by the use of enlightened reason.

Such a double move is also already discernible in Plato. It is no coincidence that many of the dialogues are set outside the city walls, and one of the most striking descriptions made of Socrates is that he is *atopos*, unplaceable, a figure who is deeply disturbing, not because of his contrary views but because no one knows quite what to make of his eccentric behavior. "I know nothing," so the cleverest man of Athens repeats, "except the ways of Eros," which, as he defines it, is again only bottomless lack. How are we meant to take this irony? The disorienting effect of the philosopher's provocations, which aimed at revealing how muddle-headed people's beliefs typically are, was once colorfully compared to being stung by an electric ray. Philosophy is an uncomfortable shock that interrupts the soul's commerce with the world of appearances. But in order to do what? To bring this soul into contact with a truer world (of the pure intellect), or to instruct about the creation of an ideal, harmonious Republic in this one? Or are these dreamlands rather meant, as some commentators have argued, as ironic ploys on Plato's part, which only deepen the perplexity into which Socrates has plunged us? Which has the final word, the *atopia* of Socrates or the *utopia* of the philosopher-kings?

Let's look at how two key 20th-century thinkers have put homelessness at the center of their thought, from very different perspectives. There is a notorious passage in the work of Martin Heidegger that runs (to cite it in full):

> However hard and bitter, however hampering and threatening the lack of houses remains, the *real plight of dwelling* does not lie merely in a lack of houses. The real plight of dwelling is indeed older than the world wars with their destruction, older also than the increase of the earth's population and the condition of the industrial workers. The real dwelling plight lies in this, that mortals ever search anew for the nature of dwelling, that they *must ever learn to dwell.* What if man's homelessness consisted in this, that man still does not even think of the *real* plight of dwelling as *the* plight? Yet as soon as *man gives thought* to his homelessness, it is a misery no longer. Rightly considered and kept well in mind, it is the sole summons that *calls* mortals into their dwelling.[2]

2 Martin Heidegger, "Building Dwelling Thinking," in *Poetry, Language, Thought*, trans. Albert Hofstadter, New York: Harper & Row, 1971, 159.

This is typical Heideggerian rhetoric, and it is not hard to ridicule the philosopher's high "ontological" disdain for mere "ontic," empirical conditions, a continuing motif in his work. True homelessness, Heidegger tells us, has nothing to do with being deprived of shelter in the ordinary, vulgar sense, nor is it essentially tied to any social-historical conditions, like wartime devastation, forced expulsions, economic inequality, the alienation of mass society, and so on. The real "plight" of homelessness is rather first and foremost a problem of man's relation to Being, the out-of-joint character of human existence, and it is the failure to reflect on this condition that constitutes the true tragedy of our age. In my view, where Heidegger becomes interesting is the way that he characterizes this rupture. The difficulty, he argues, is not that man has abandoned his primordial home (through thoughtlessness, forgetfulness, bad metaphysics, immersion in anonymous social life, etc.), but that this "home" has abandoned him, thrown him out, as it were, made him a stranger. This reversal is crucial: it is not only we who leave home, but there is something in the nature of home as such that actively rejects us, that prevents us from "dwelling" there, that forces us to find our own way even as we cannot help remaining fundamentally attached to it. The paradoxical moral message of this philosophy is that we can never be "at home" at home, so that the problem of dwelling becomes that of finding a way to live this alienation without simply fleeing from it (see the contemporary return to nationalisms and chauvinisms that claim to give a proper meaning to identity), nor pretending to be able to fully embrace it (as preached by an overly optimistic philosophy of cosmopolitanism). Perhaps the trouble with Heidegger is not that his thought is too abstract, indifferent to factual conditions and real history, but that it is not abstract enough. Committed to the empirical ideal of the rustic countryside and quiet rural life, his ontological prognosis takes the form of an anti-modernist diatribe, promising to heal the ills caused by technological reason.

Inner migration

Contrary to Heidegger, Sigmund Freud aligned himself with scientific rationality, and claimed that psychoanalysis would revolutionize mankind's self-image in a similar manner as the great discoveries of Copernicus and Darwin. According to Freud, modernity is defined by a progressive de-centering of the subject, a debasement of its previously bloated self-estimation: heliocentrism, evolutionary theory, and—last but not least—the unconscious are the three great blows to human narcissism definitive of modern times.[3] Psychoanalysis announces that the ego is not master in its own house; the personalized self which considers itself the owner of mental life is in fact a secondary formation at the mercy of secret impersonal forces, the unconscious drives that constitute the real core of the psyche. The "it" thus dispossesses the "I": at the heart of the person is a kind of knot of wishes and desires that is both more intimate than any other thing, yet strangely anonymous, unrecognizable, inadmissible. In his later work, Freud insists on the dimension of guilt and masochism that marks a limit to therapy. There will always remain a part of the unconscious that is impervious to analysis and cannot be appropriated by the self; the ego can never fully inhabit its psychic space, never claim it as entirely its own. What psychoanalysis makes clear is that this thing that displaces the ego, the "unplaceable" unconscious, is a *menace* that must be protected against. Psychic life would not be possible without all kinds of defense mechanisms that keep the drives at a certain distance—and yet these same drives are the source of the psyche's dynamism, its creative energy. This is the basic idea of the *split subject:* the subject must defend itself from itself; the very forces that constitute its inner vitality also threaten to overwhelm it.

How does Freud conceive the nature of this threat? The Oedipus story was crucial in the way that it dramatically staged what for him are mankind's deepest desires: incest and parricide. Freud invented a painful neurotic home for the subject, complete with festering perverse secrets in the basement, a "family romance" that no one makes it through emotionally unscathed. It is remarkable that when Lacan re-interprets this theory, he shifts the main point of reference away from *Oedipus Rex,* with its tale of murder and sexual transgression, to *Oedipus at Colonus*, which recounts the aftermath of the great tragedy, the fate of the king who has become a miserable outcast wandering the earth in search of a final resting place. In Lacan's baroque vision, it is this play that best illustrates the "homeless" character of subjectivity, as a kind of *remainder* that cannot be assimilated by the order in which it is nevertheless situated. What is of particular interest in this more formal presentation of the structure of the subject is the twofold movement that Lacan highlights, an oscillation between a lack and a surplus. To an empty, unoccupied space (a no-place, *atopia*) is juxtaposed a kind of itinerant object that disrupts whatever context it appears in, an

3. Sigmund Freud, "A Difficulty in the Path of Psycho-Analysis," in The Standard Edition of the *Complete Psychological Works of Sigmund Freud*, trans. James Strachey, London: Hogarth 1955, vol. XVI, 140-41.

excessive presence that cannot be settled or "domesticated." The aim of a unifying, harmonious synthesis (a well-ordered "Republic") thus fails from two different, yet closely linked, perspectives: the subject is both irremediable lack, missing its proper place, searching in vain for something that would complete it, *and* an excessive object, an unmanageable, unruly surplus which manifests itself in diverse forms of disturbance. Something is absent; something sticks out.

One of the crucial definitions of home is a place of withdrawal, of privacy, of separation. If hell is other people, home is where one can be alone. And the ultimate space of withdrawal is no doubt the inner space of the psyche, one's own private *Heimat*. Yet even (and, following Freud, *especially*) here, it is not possible to comfortably settle—though we, at least neurotics, cannot avoid visiting from time to time. Again we can cite Novalis: "The inner world is as it were more mine than the *external*. It is so intimate, so secret. One would like to live wholly in it—it is like one's homeland. A shame that it is so dreamlike, so uncertain. Must then the best, the truest thing look so feigned—and what is feigned look so true? What is outside me is in me, is mine—and conversely."[4] Freud would concur about this hazinesss of the border between inner and outer, psychic reality and external reality: the interior world, which is more "mine" than anything else, can easily become something nightmarish and uncertain, full of phantoms and flickering, half-formed thoughts. Just as the inhospitality of the outside world can sometimes force us into an inner migration—escaping from painful or difficult external circumstances into a private fantasy space—so can the inhospitality our own interior universe cause us to turn to the outside world, for the assurance of solidity and reality that we cannot provide ourselves.

Aaron Schuster is a writer based in Berlin, where he is a fellow at the Institute for Cultural Inquiry. He received his Ph.D. in philosophy from the Katholieke Universiteit Leuven.

4 Novalis, 130.

Acknowledgments

First of all, I would like to thank all the artists for the inspiring exchange of ideas that gave rise to *Where Do We Migrate To?* The title of the project is borrowed from Julika Rudelius's eponymous 2005 video. A very special thanks goes out to Svetlana Boym, Amitava Kumar, and Aaron Schuster for their thought-provoking and insightful essays, Kelley Bell and Antonia Gardner for their indispensable work on the catalogue, and the crew at the Center for Art, Design and Visual Culture, especially Symmes Gardner, without whose enthusiasm and support the exhibition could not have been realized. Also a thank you to Frank Verpoorten from Flanders House for providing essential support. I am indebted to many friends and colleagues from whom I received inspiring intellectual feedback throughout the project's many stages, specifically Lieven De Cauter and Debashree Mukherjee, as well as Donald Russell from Provisions Learning Project. Lastly, I would like to thank Sonja Simonyi, who curated an accompanying film series which forms an essential part of *Where Do We Migrate To?* Her intelligent contribution and numerous humorous interventions were substantial in the formation of the project, as they are in my life.

This exhibition is dedicated to the memory of Philippe Vandenberg, 1952 – 2009.

Niels Van Tomme

About the Center for Art, Design and Visual Culture

The Center for Art and Visual Culture at the University of Maryland Baltimore County is a nonprofit organization dedicated to the study of contemporary art and visual culture, critical theory, art and cultural history, criticism, and the relationship between society and the arts. The Center is committed to a rethinking of the relationship between arts institutions and the public, placing special emphasis on well-written, viewer-friendly catalogue and wall texts, rigorously documented and researched catalogues, the lucid application of critical social theory to build connections between visual culture and the society at large, and creative exhibition and catalogue design. Disciplines represented include painting, sculpture, drawing, printmaking, photography, digital art, video, film, television, design, architecture, advertising, and installation and performance art. The Center sponsors art exhibitions, community outreach and public art projects, and publications. Its exhibitions and accompanying travelogues—one-person and retrospective shows as well as thematic and experimental projects—give voice to the artists, subjects, and curatorial approaches that are often ignored or underrepresented in mainstream museums.

The Center for Art, Design and Visual Culture serves as a forum for students, faculty, and the general public for the discussion of important aesthetic and social issues of the day. Through its traveling exhibitions and publications series, Issues in Cultural Theory, the Center is building a broad national and international audience. The Center places special emphasis on the role of education in the arts. Symposia, lecture series, conferences, film series, workshops, and visiting artist residencies create an ongoing dialogue about contemporary art and culture—from K-12 school-based initiatives to adult education and community outreach in Baltimore City. In 2000, the Center's Community Outreach/Public Part Initiative launched its inaugural project in Baltimore, the Joseph Beuys Tree Partnership.

Issues in Cultural Theory

A series published by the Center for Art, Design and Visual Culture

1 **Minimal Politics: Performativity and Minimalism in Recent American Art**
Maurice Berger

2 **Bruno Monguzzi: A Designer's Perspective**
Franc Nunoo-Quarcoo

3 **Adrian Piper: A Retrospective**
Maurice Berger

4 **Fred Wilson: Objects and Installations, 1979-2000**
Maurice Berger

5 **Postmodernism: A Virtual Discussion**
Edited by Maurice Berger

6 **Paul Rand: Modernist Design**
Franc Nunoo-Quarcoo

7 **White: Whiteness and Race in Contemporary Art**
Maurice Berger

8 **Museums of Tomorrow: A Virtual Discussion**
Edited by Maurice Berger

9 **Blur of the Otherworldly: Contemporary Art, Technology, and the Paranormal**
Mark Alice Durant and Jane Marshing

10 **The 1980s: A Virtual Discussion**
Edited by Maurice Berger

11 **Andrea Robbins and Max Becher: Portraits**
Maurice Berger

12 **Dana Hoey: Experiments in Primitive Living**
Maurice Berger

13 **Visual Culture and Bioscience: An Online Symposium**
Edited by Suzanne Anker and J. D. Talasek

Emmanuel Guibert

ARiOL

Le CHEVALiER CHEVAL

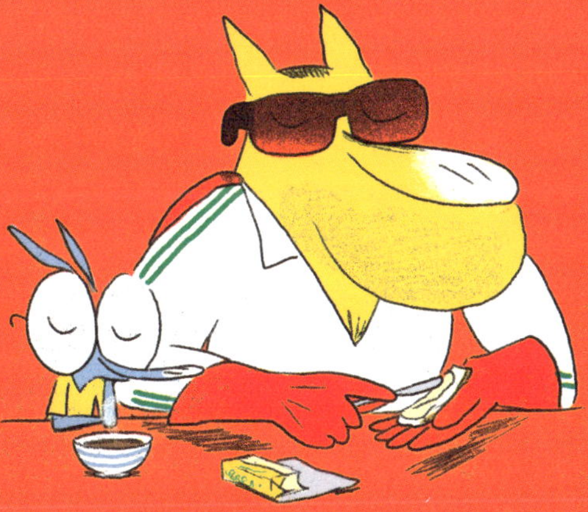

BD
BAYARD

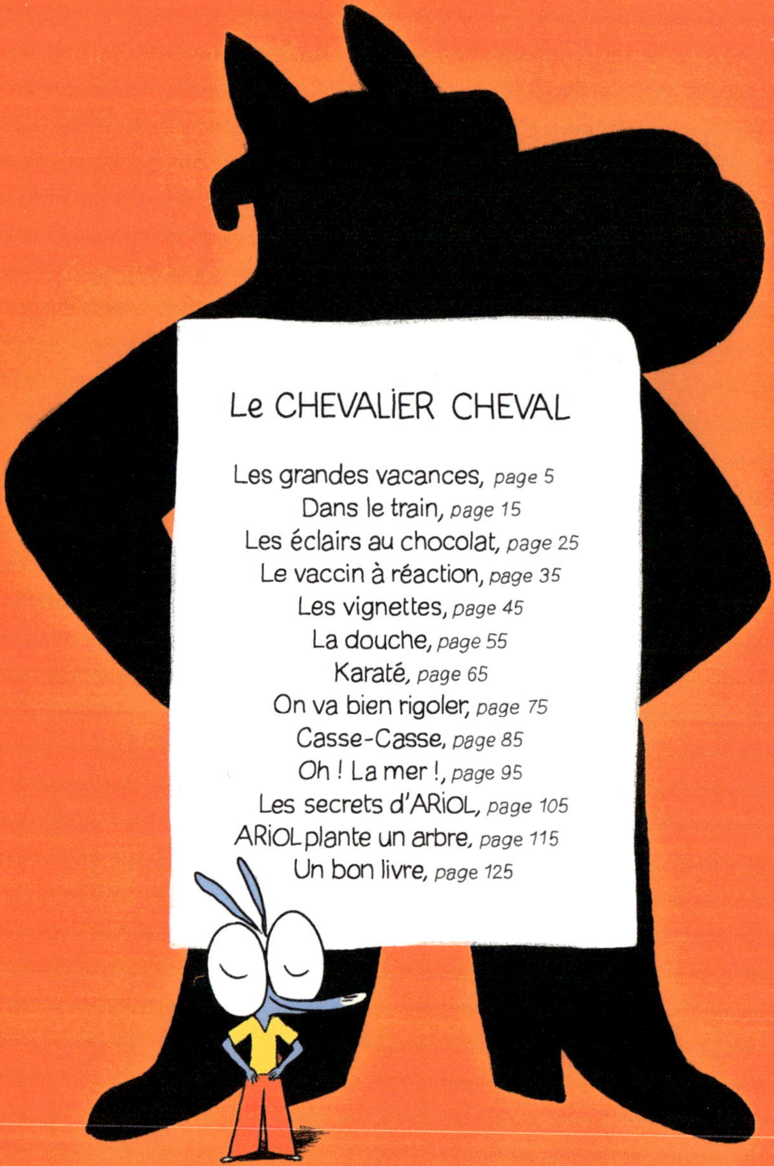

Le CHEVALIER CHEVAL

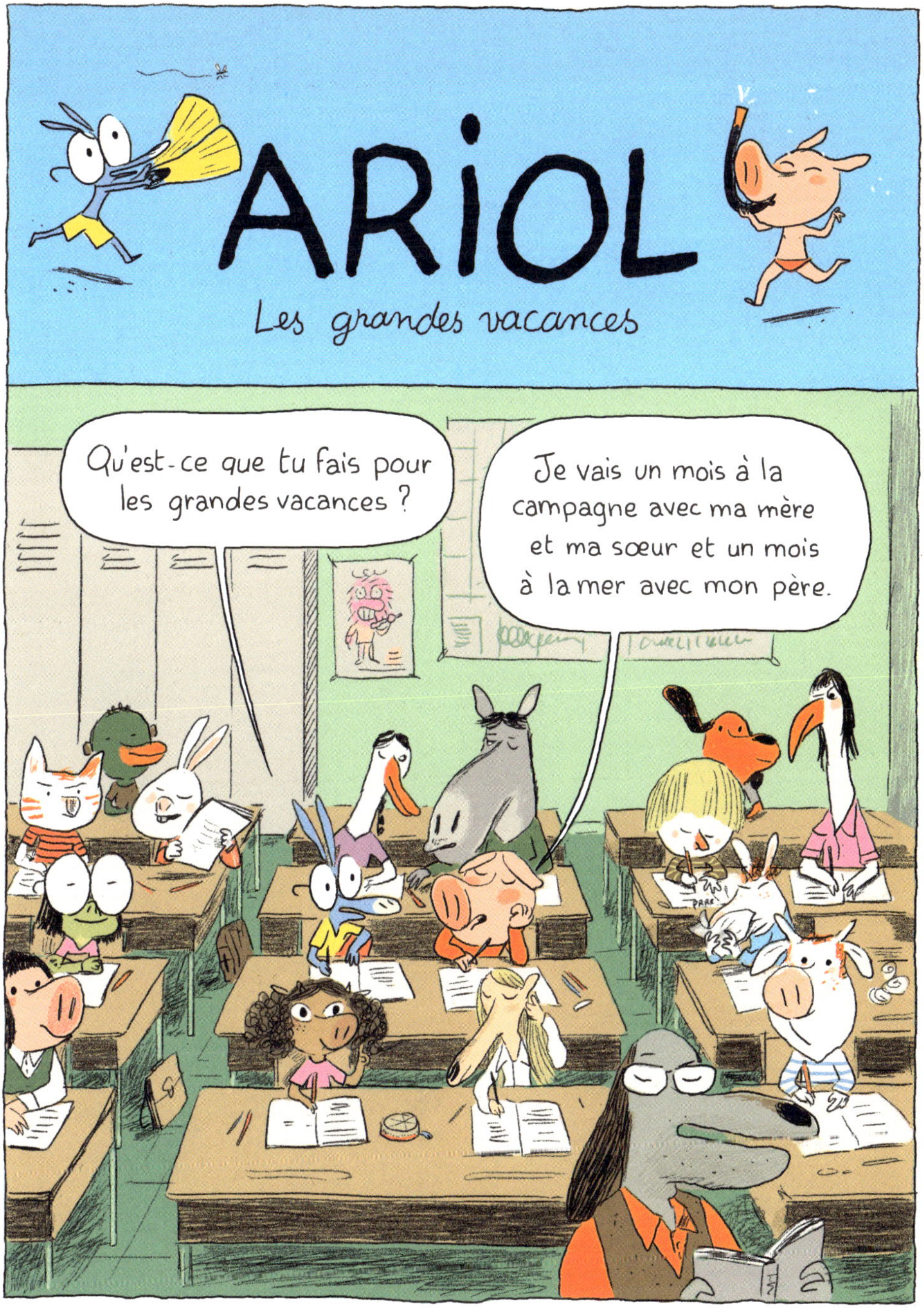
ARiOL
Les grandes vacances
Qu'est-ce que tu fais pour les grandes vacances ?
Je vais un mois à la campagne avec ma mère et ma sœur et un mois à la mer avec mon père.

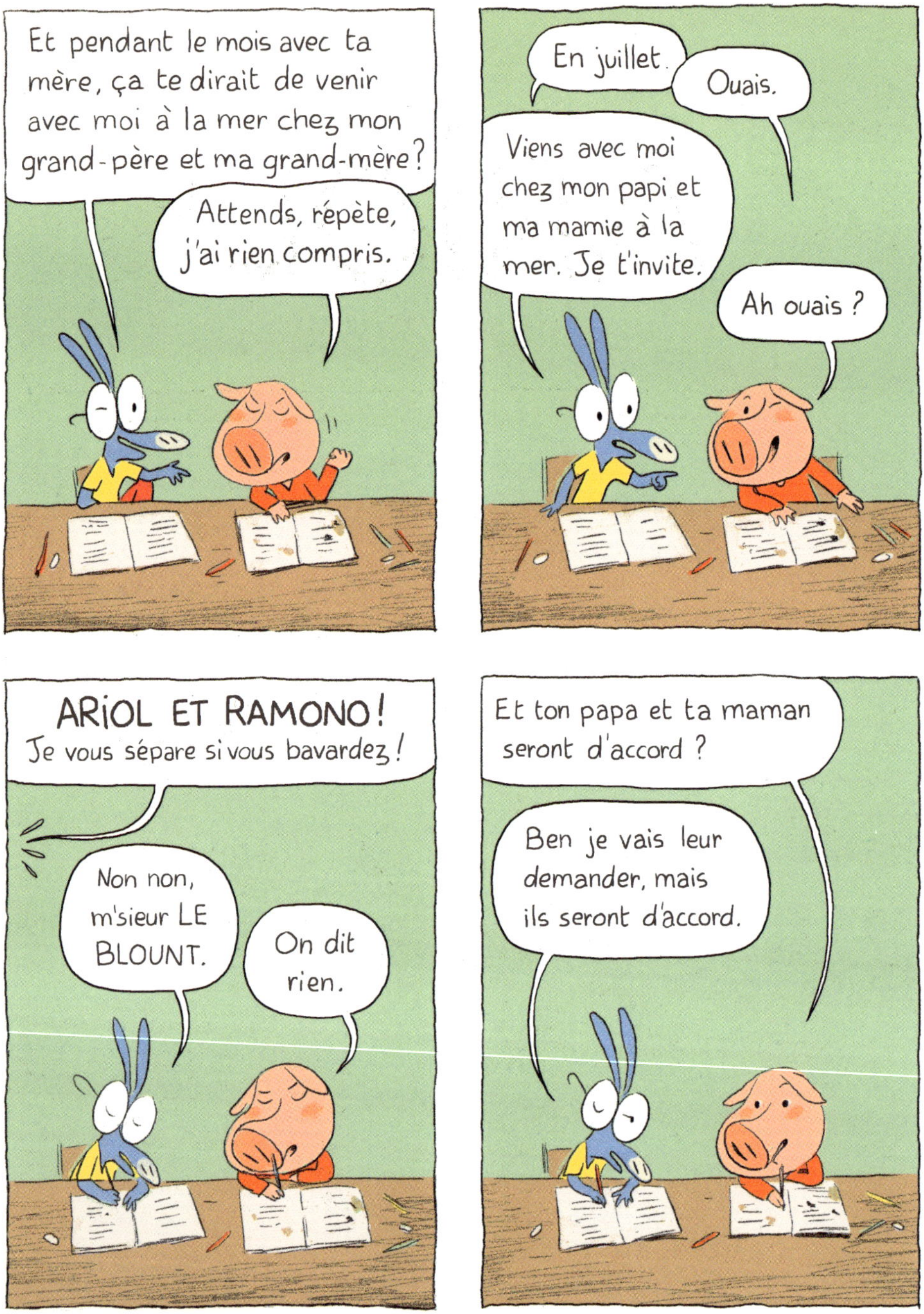
Et pendant le mois avec ta mère, ça te dirait de venir avec moi à la mer chez mon grand-père et ma grand-mère ?
Attends, répète, j'ai rien compris.
En juillet.
Ouais.
Viens avec moi chez mon papi et ma mamie à la mer. Je t'invite.
Ah ouais ?
ARiOL ET RAMONO ! Je vous sépare si vous bavardez !
Non non, m'sieur LE BLOUNT.
On dit rien.
Et ton papa et ta maman seront d'accord ?
Ben je vais leur demander, mais ils seront d'accord.

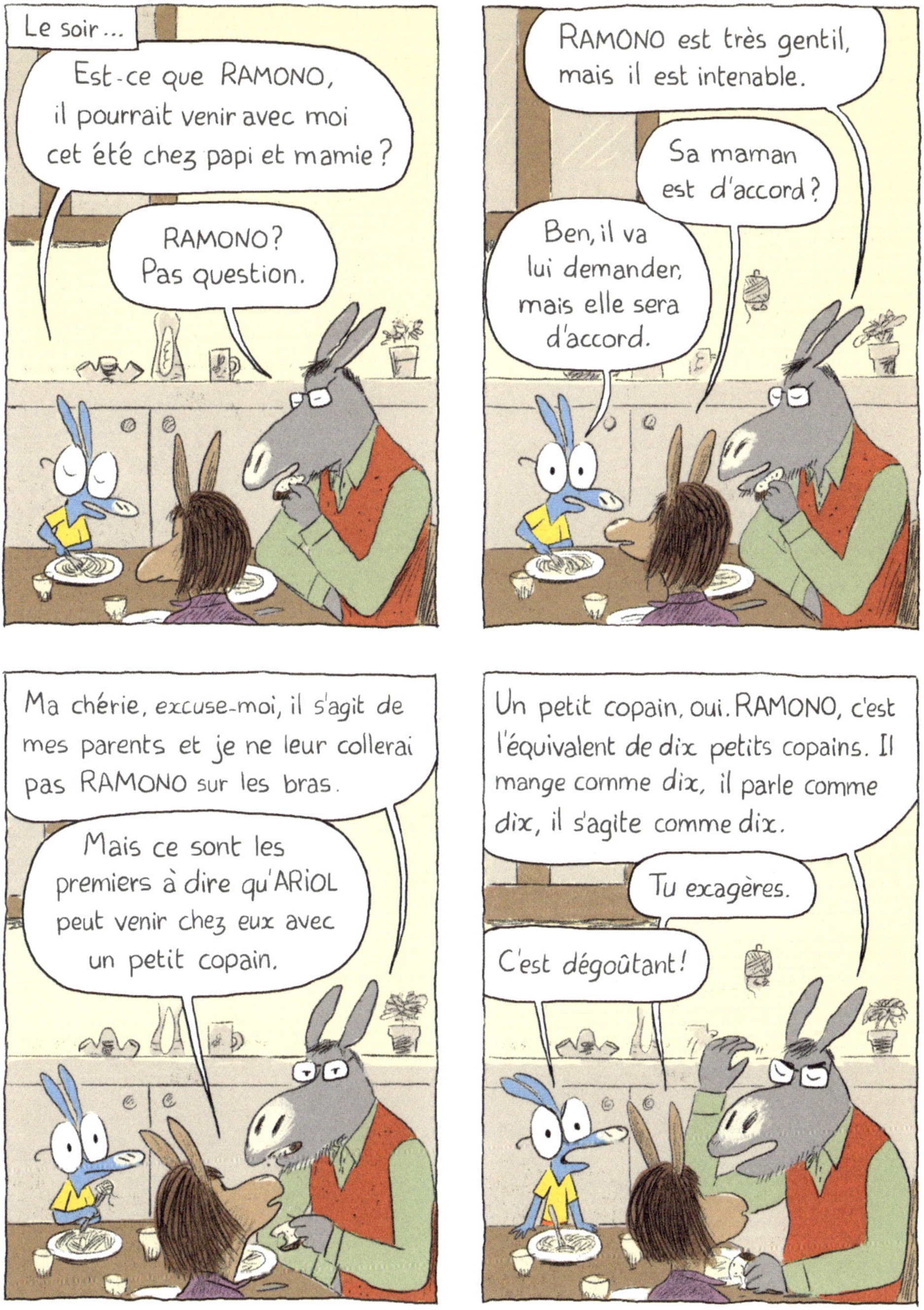
Le soir...
Est-ce que RAMONO, il pourrait venir avec moi cet été chez papi et mamie ?
RAMONO? Pas question.
RAMONO est très gentil, mais il est intenable.
Sa maman est d'accord?
Ben, il va lui demander, mais elle sera d'accord.
Ma chérie, excuse-moi, il s'agit de mes parents et je ne leur collerai pas RAMONO sur les bras.
Mais ce sont les premiers à dire qu'ARIOL peut venir chez eux avec un petit copain.
Un petit copain, oui. RAMONO, c'est l'équivalent de dix petits copains. Il mange comme dix, il parle comme dix, il s'agite comme dix.
Tu exagères.
C'est dégoûtant!

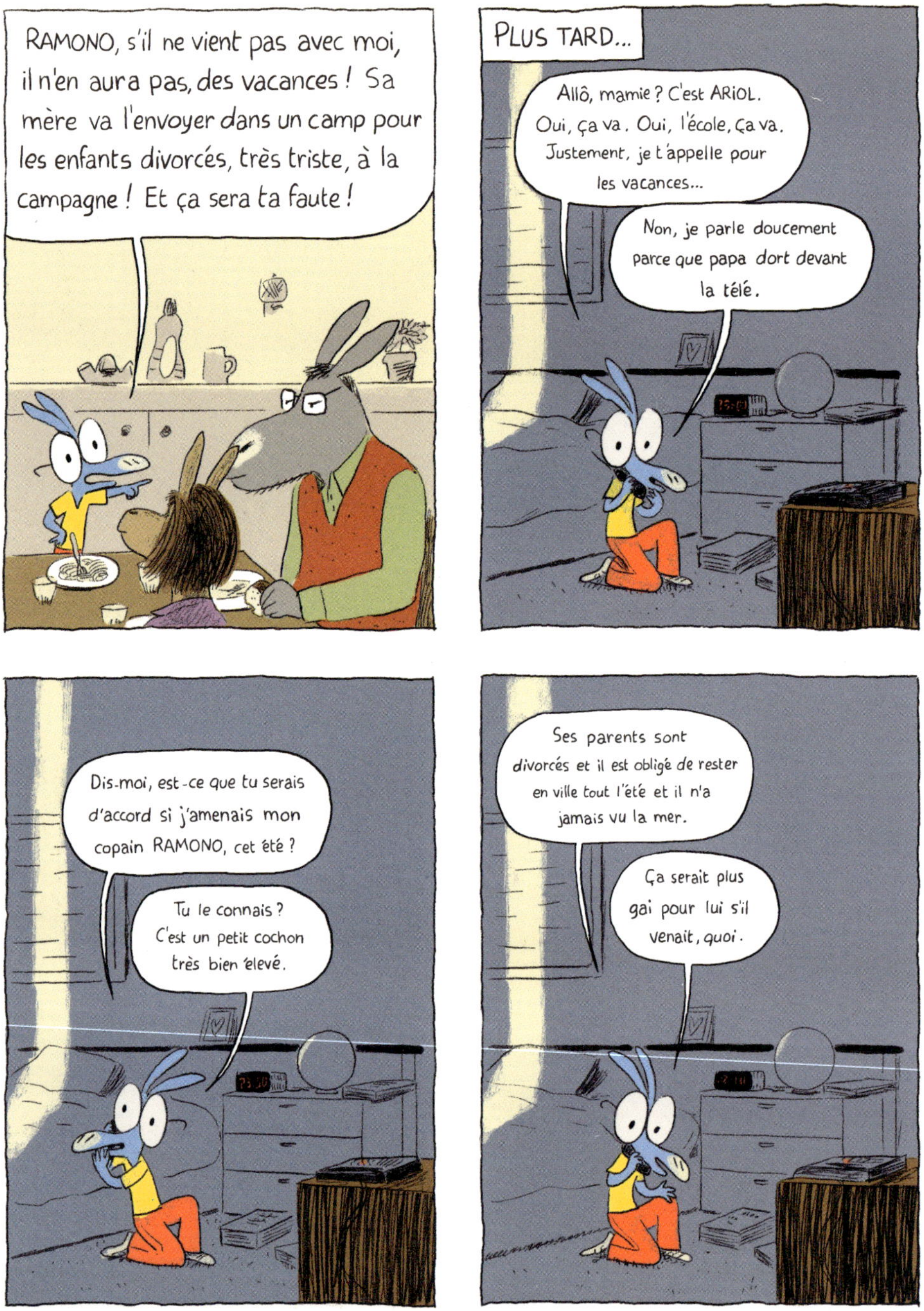
RAMONO, s'il ne vient pas avec moi, il n'en aura pas, des vacances ! Sa mère va l'envoyer dans un camp pour les enfants divorcés, très triste, à la campagne ! Et ça sera ta faute !
PLUS TARD...
Allô, mamie ? C'est ARIOL. Oui, ça va. Oui, l'école, ça va. Justement, je t'appelle pour les vacances...
Non, je parle doucement parce que papa dort devant la télé.
Dis-moi, est-ce que tu serais d'accord si j'amenais mon copain RAMONO, cet été ?
Tu le connais ? C'est un petit cochon très bien élevé.
Ses parents sont divorcés et il est obligé de rester en ville tout l'été et il n'a jamais vu la mer.
Ça serait plus gai pour lui s'il venait, quoi.

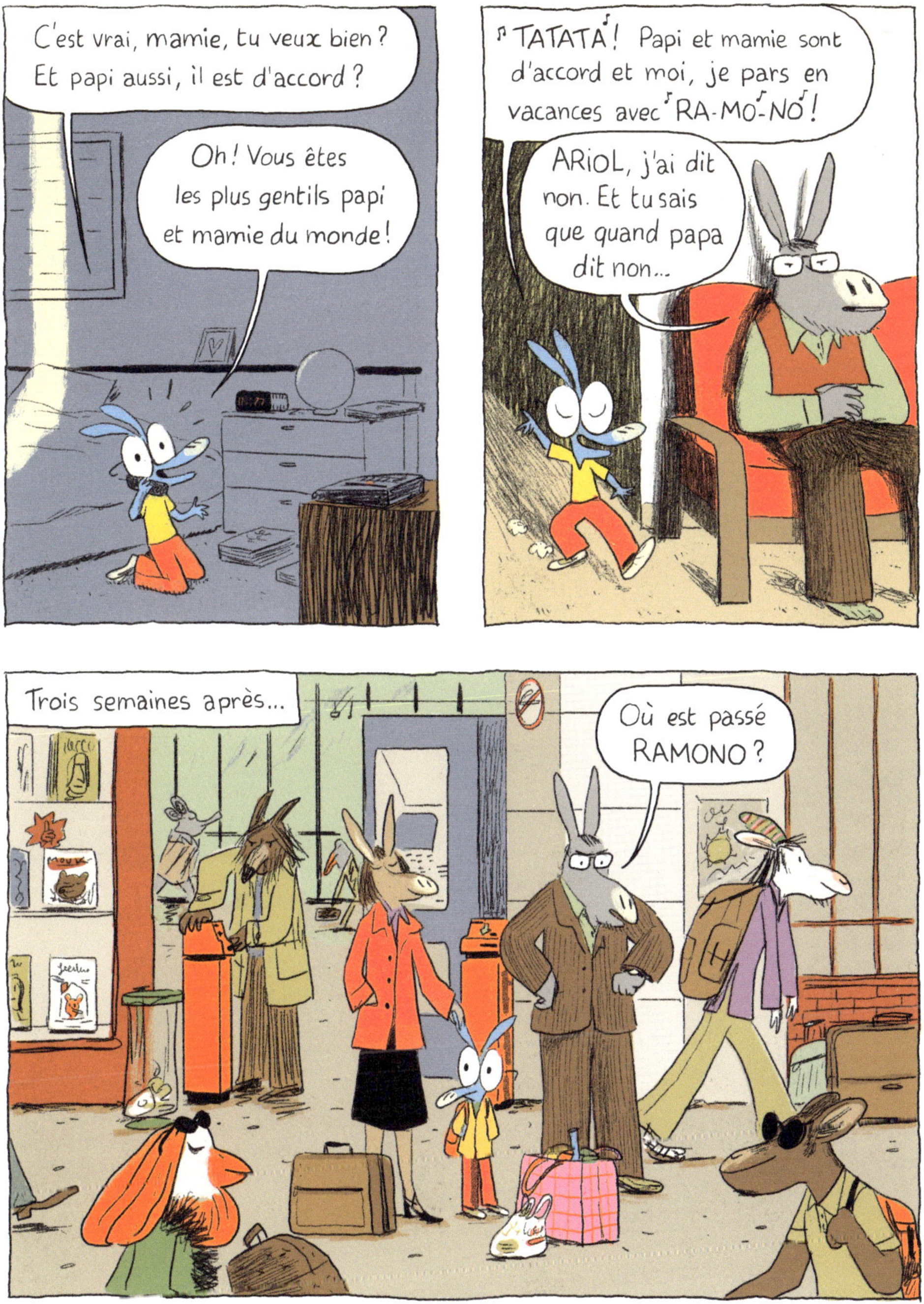

C'est vrai, mamie, tu veux bien ? Et papi aussi, il est d'accord ?
Oh ! Vous êtes les plus gentils papi et mamie du monde !
TATATA ! Papi et mamie sont d'accord et moi, je pars en vacances avec RA-MO-NO !
ARIOL, j'ai dit non. Et tu sais que quand papa dit non...
Trois semaines après...
Où est passé RAMONO ?

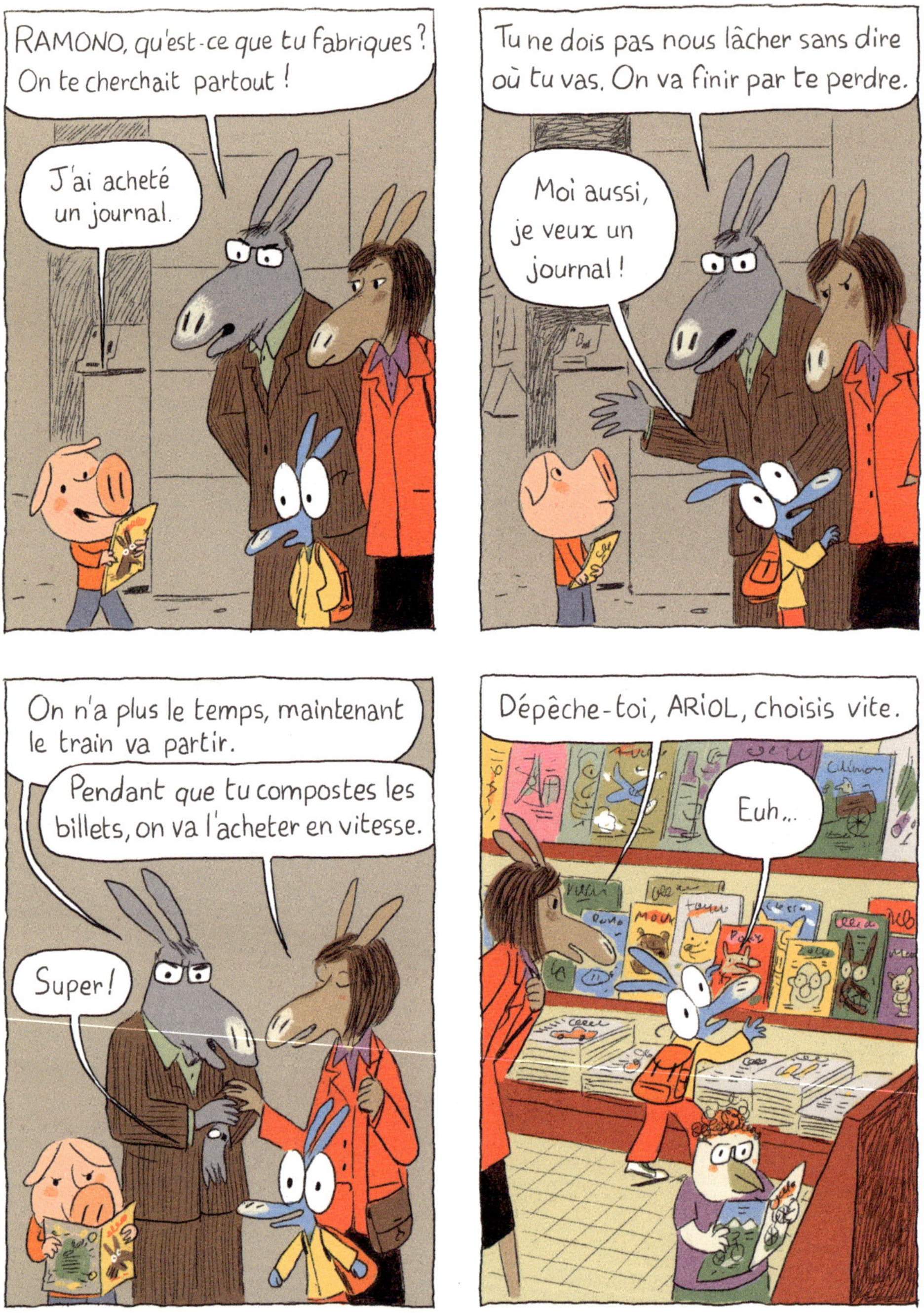
RAMONO, qu'est-ce que tu fabriques? On te cherchait partout!
J'ai acheté un journal.
Tu ne dois pas nous lâcher sans dire où tu vas. On va finir par te perdre.
Moi aussi, je veux un journal!
On n'a plus le temps, maintenant le train va partir.
Pendant que tu compostes les billets, on va l'acheter en vitesse.
Super!
Dépêche-toi, ARIOL, choisis vite.
Euh...

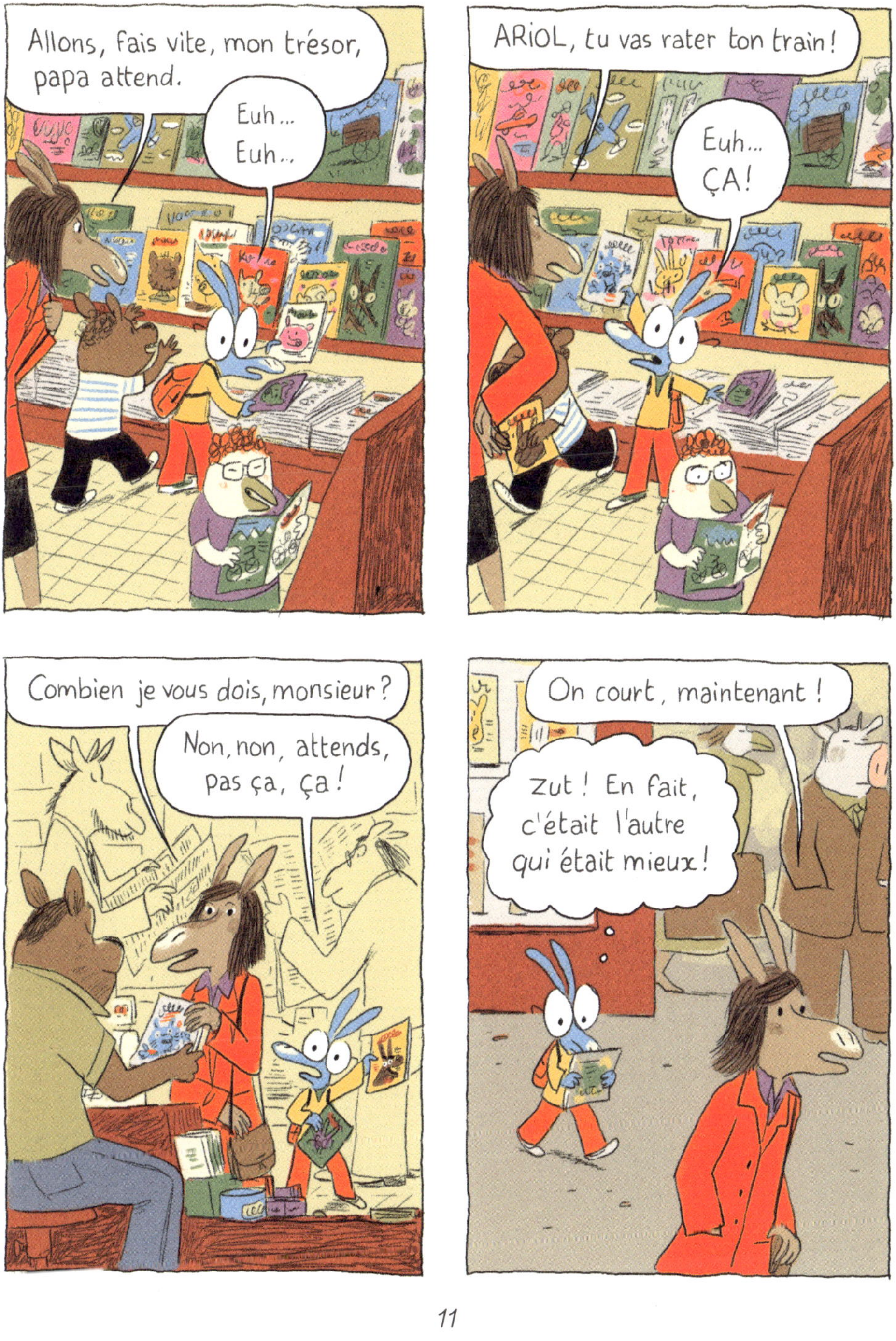
Allons, fais vite, mon trésor, papa attend.
Euh... Euh...
ARiOL, tu vas rater ton train!
Euh... ÇA!
Combien je vous dois, monsieur?
Non, non, attends, pas ça, ça!
On court, maintenant!
Zut! En fait, c'était l'autre qui était mieux!

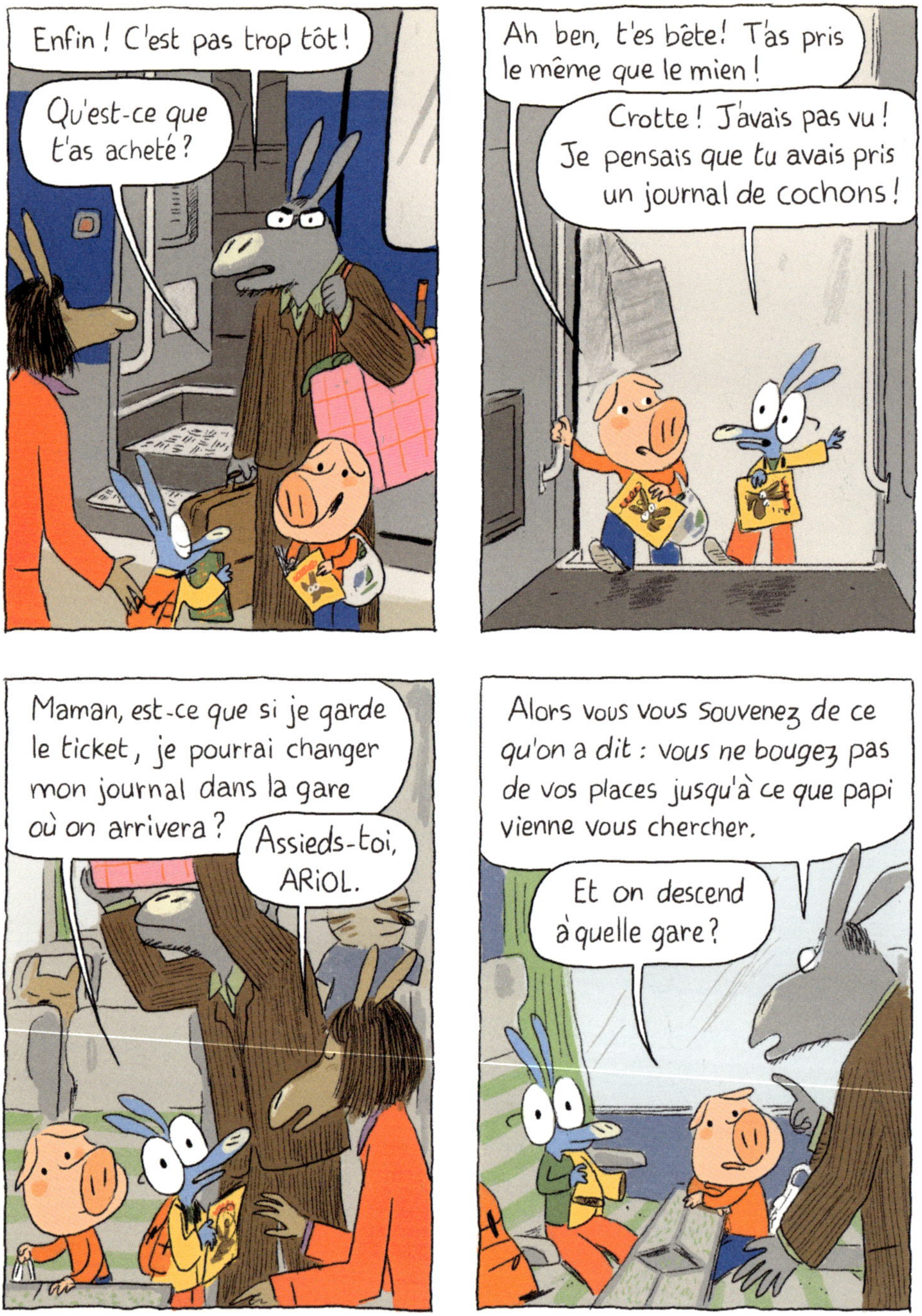
Enfin ! C'est pas trop tôt !
Qu'est-ce que t'as acheté ?
Ah ben, t'es bête ! T'as pris le même que le mien !
Crotte ! J'avais pas vu ! Je pensais que tu avais pris un journal de cochons !
Maman, est-ce que si je garde le ticket, je pourrai changer mon journal dans la gare où on arrivera ?
Assieds-toi, ARIOL.
Alors vous vous souvenez de ce qu'on a dit : vous ne bougez pas de vos places jusqu'à ce que papi vienne vous chercher.
Et on descend à quelle gare ?

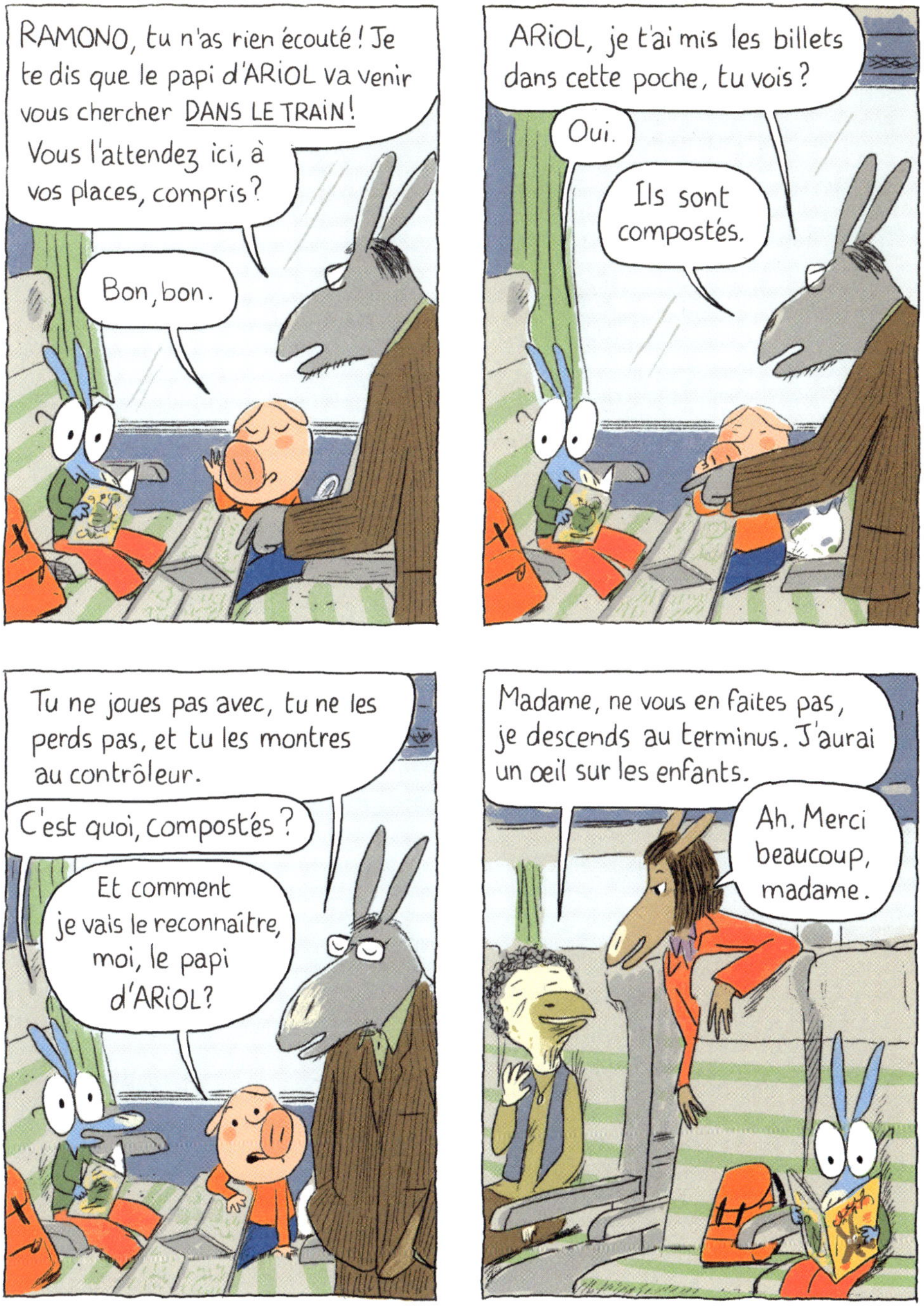
RAMONO, tu n'as rien écouté ! Je te dis que le papi d'ARIOL va venir vous chercher DANS LE TRAIN !
Vous l'attendez ici, à vos places, compris ?
Bon, bon.
ARIOL, je t'ai mis les billets dans cette poche, tu vois ?
Oui.
Ils sont compostés.
Tu ne joues pas avec, tu ne les perds pas, et tu les montres au contrôleur.
C'est quoi, compostés ?
Et comment je vais le reconnaître, moi, le papi d'ARIOL ?
Madame, ne vous en faites pas, je descends au terminus. J'aurai un oeil sur les enfants.
Ah. Merci beaucoup, madame.

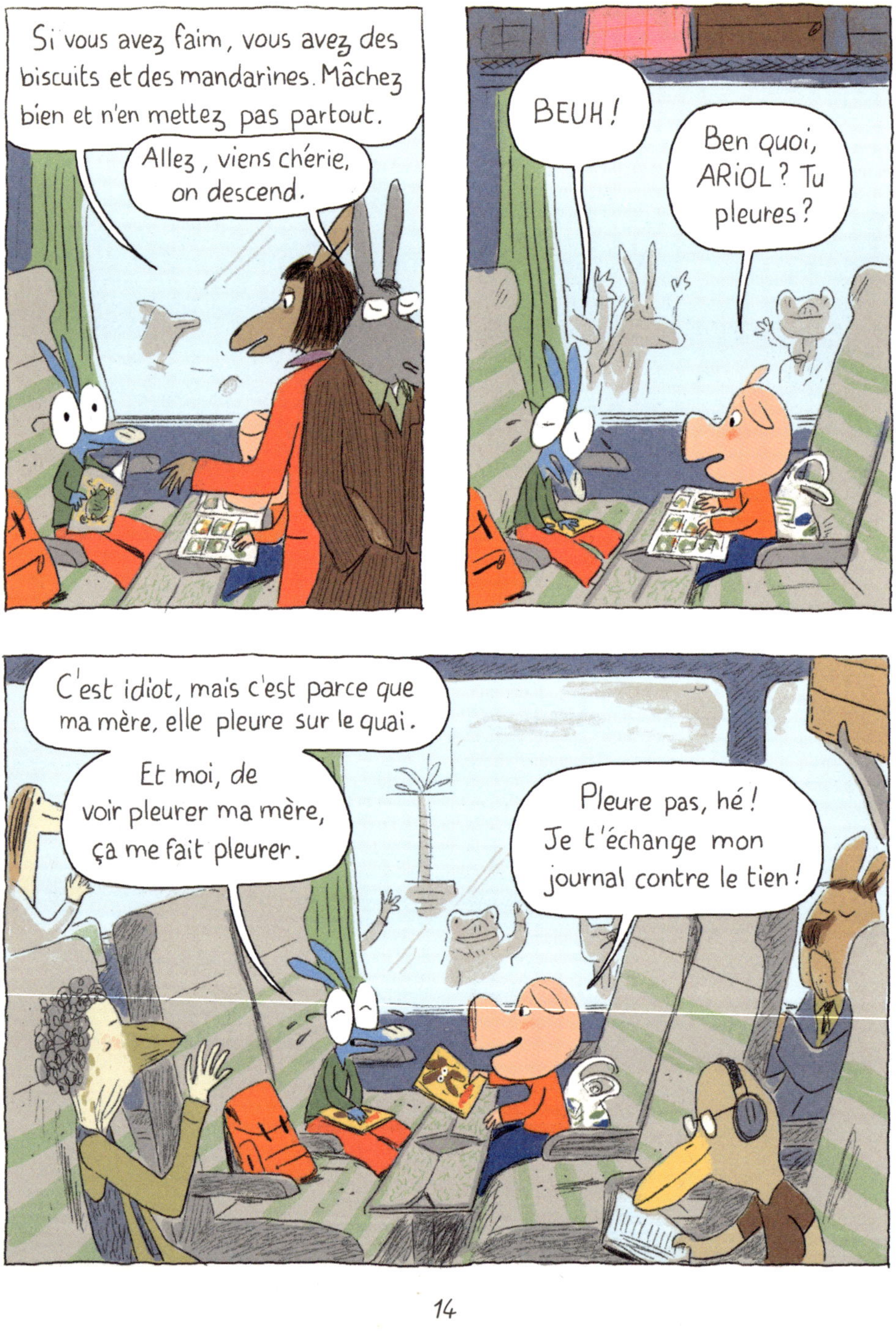
Si vous avez faim, vous avez des biscuits et des mandarines. Mâchez bien et n'en mettez pas partout.
Allez, viens chérie, on descend.
BEUH!
Ben quoi, ARIOL? Tu pleures?
C'est idiot, mais c'est parce que ma mère, elle pleure sur le quai.
Et moi, de voir pleurer ma mère, ça me fait pleurer.
Pleure pas, hé! Je t'échange mon journal contre le tien!

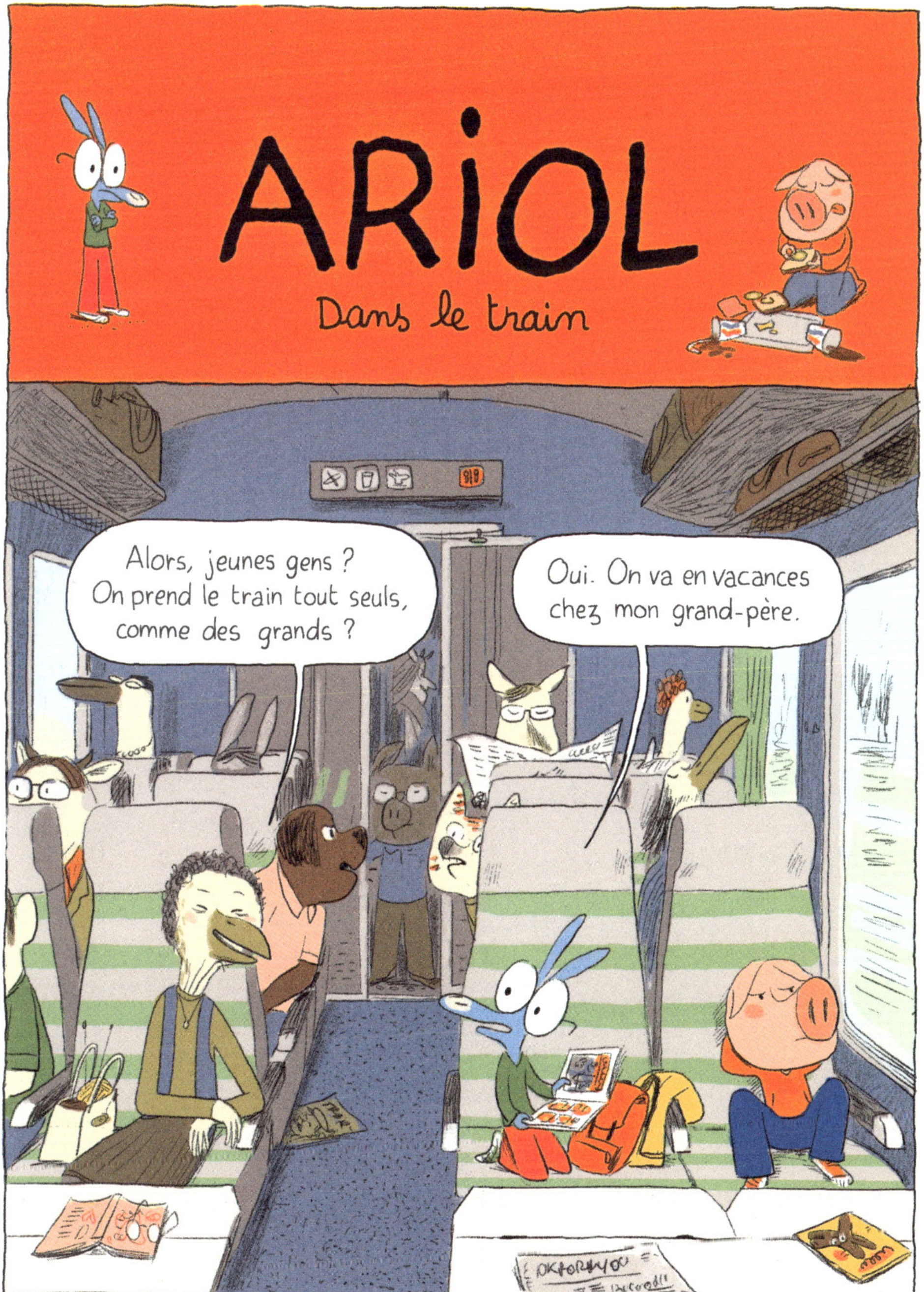
ARIOL
Dans le train
Alors, jeunes gens ? On prend le train tout seuls, comme des grands ?
Oui. On va en vacances chez mon grand-père.

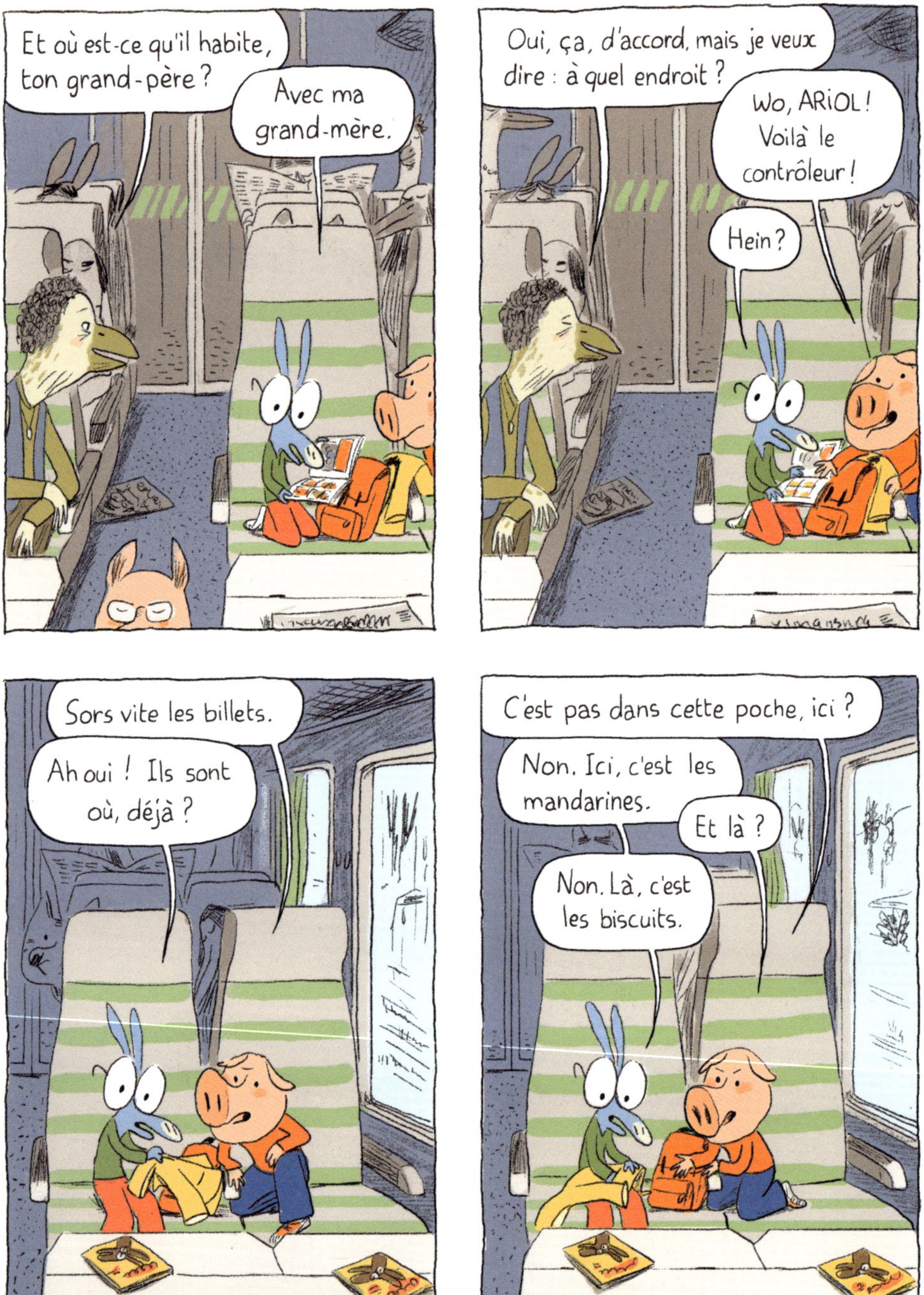
Et où est-ce qu'il habite, ton grand-père ?
Avec ma grand-mère.
Oui, ça, d'accord, mais je veux dire : à quel endroit ?
Wo, ARIOL ! Voilà le contrôleur !
Hein ?
Sors vite les billets.
Ah oui ! Ils sont où, déjà ?
C'est pas dans cette poche, ici ?
Non. Ici, c'est les mandarines.
Et là ?
Non. Là, c'est les biscuits.

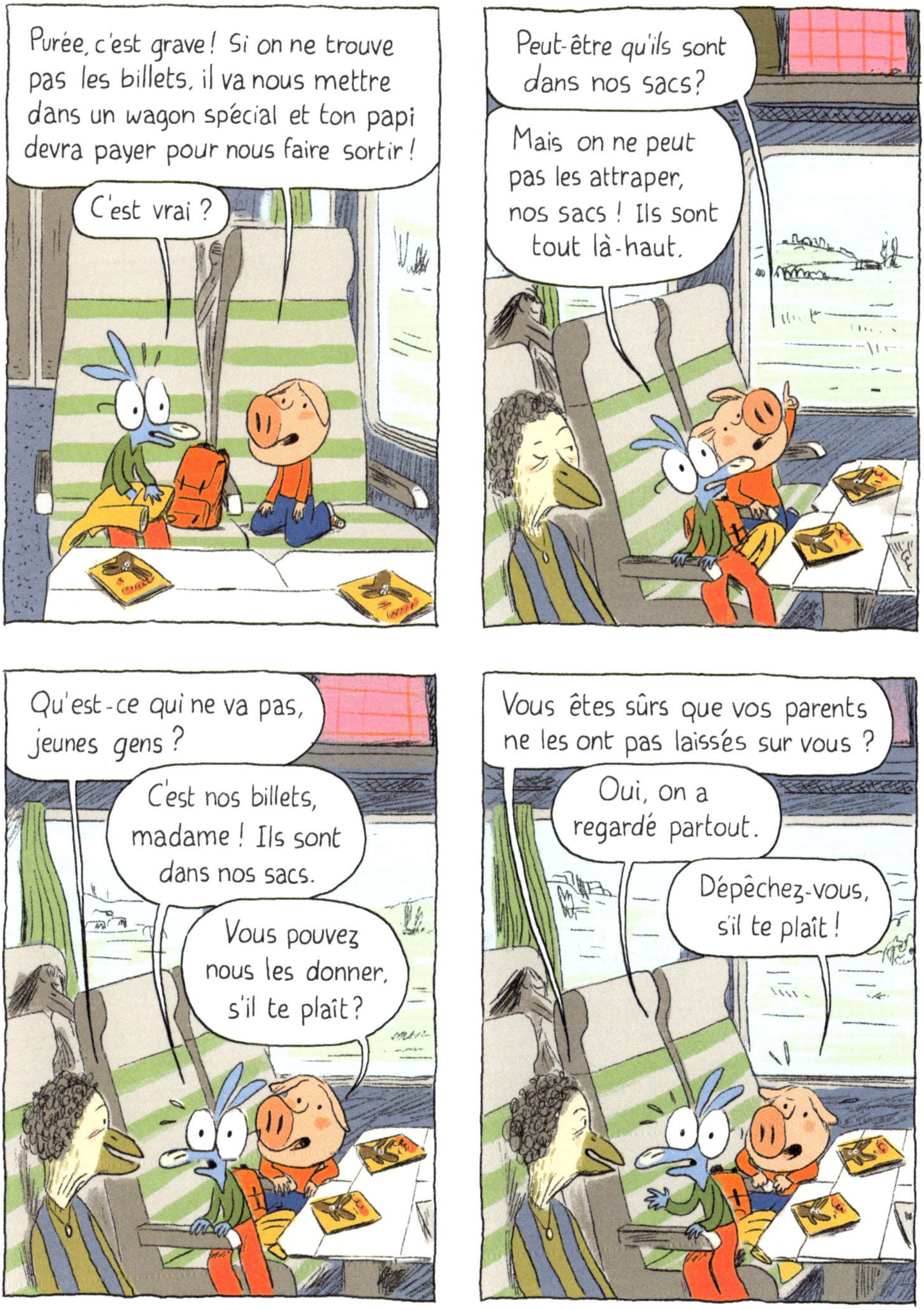

Purée, c'est grave ! Si on ne trouve pas les billets, il va nous mettre dans un wagon spécial et ton papi devra payer pour nous faire sortir !
C'est vrai ?
Peut-être qu'ils sont dans nos sacs ?
Mais on ne peut pas les attraper, nos sacs ! Ils sont tout là-haut.
Qu'est-ce qui ne va pas, jeunes gens ?
C'est nos billets, madame ! Ils sont dans nos sacs.
Vous pouvez nous les donner, s'il te plaît ?
Vous êtes sûrs que vos parents ne les ont pas laissés sur vous ?
Oui, on a regardé partout.
Dépêchez-vous, s'il te plaît !

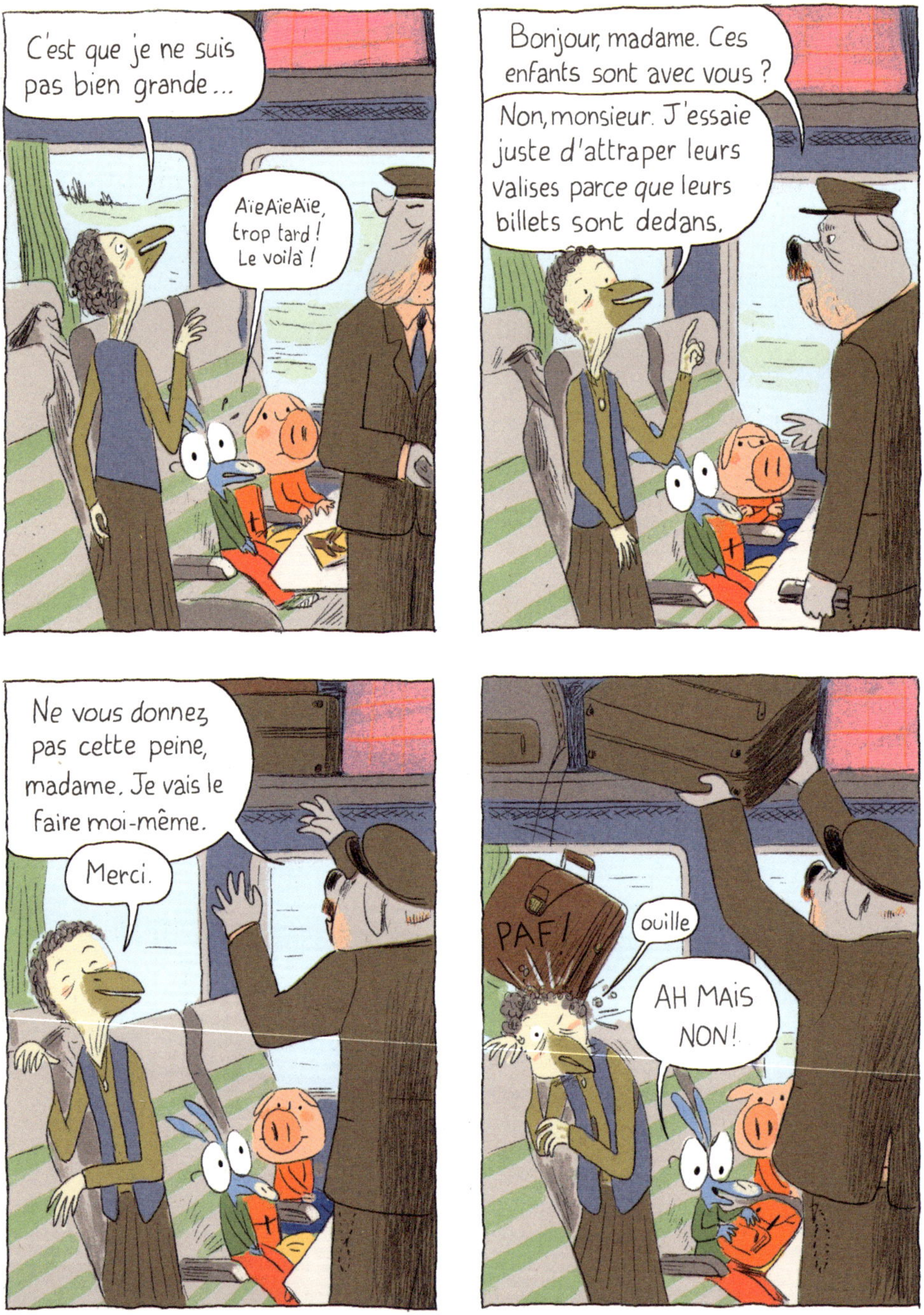
C'est que je ne suis pas bien grande...
AïeAïeAïe, trop tard ! Le voilà !
Bonjour, madame. Ces enfants sont avec vous ?
Non, monsieur. J'essaie juste d'attraper leurs valises parce que leurs billets sont dedans.
Ne vous donnez pas cette peine, madame. Je vais le faire moi-même.
Merci.
PAF !
ouille
AH MAIS NON !

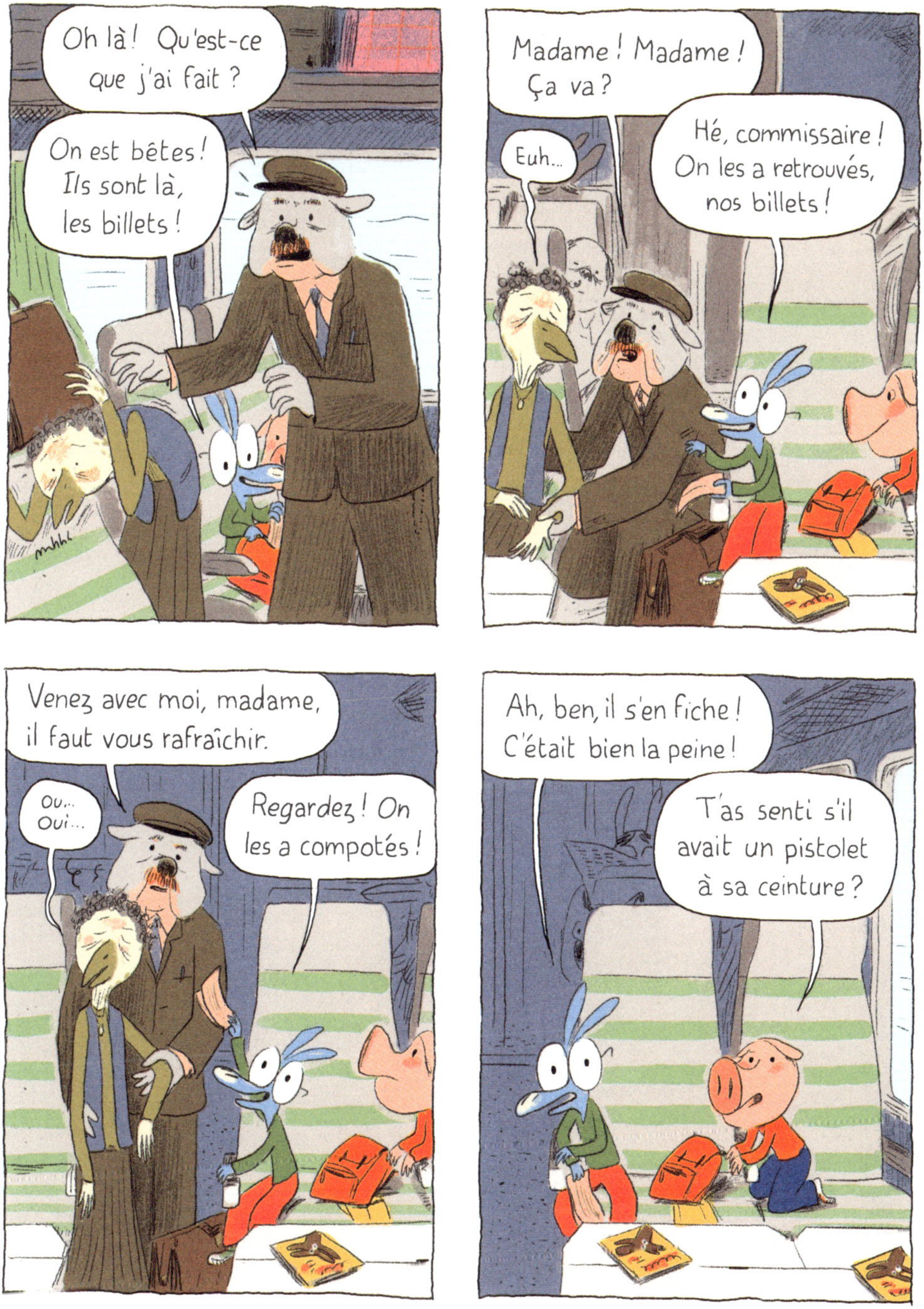
Oh là ! Qu'est-ce que j'ai fait ?
On est bêtes ! Ils sont là, les billets !
Madame ! Madame ! Ça va ?
Euh...
Hé, commissaire ! On les a retrouvés, nos billets !
Venez avec moi, madame, il faut vous rafraîchir.
Ou... Oui...
Regardez ! On les a compotés !
Ah, ben, il s'en fiche ! C'était bien la peine !
T'as senti s'il avait un pistolet à sa ceinture ?

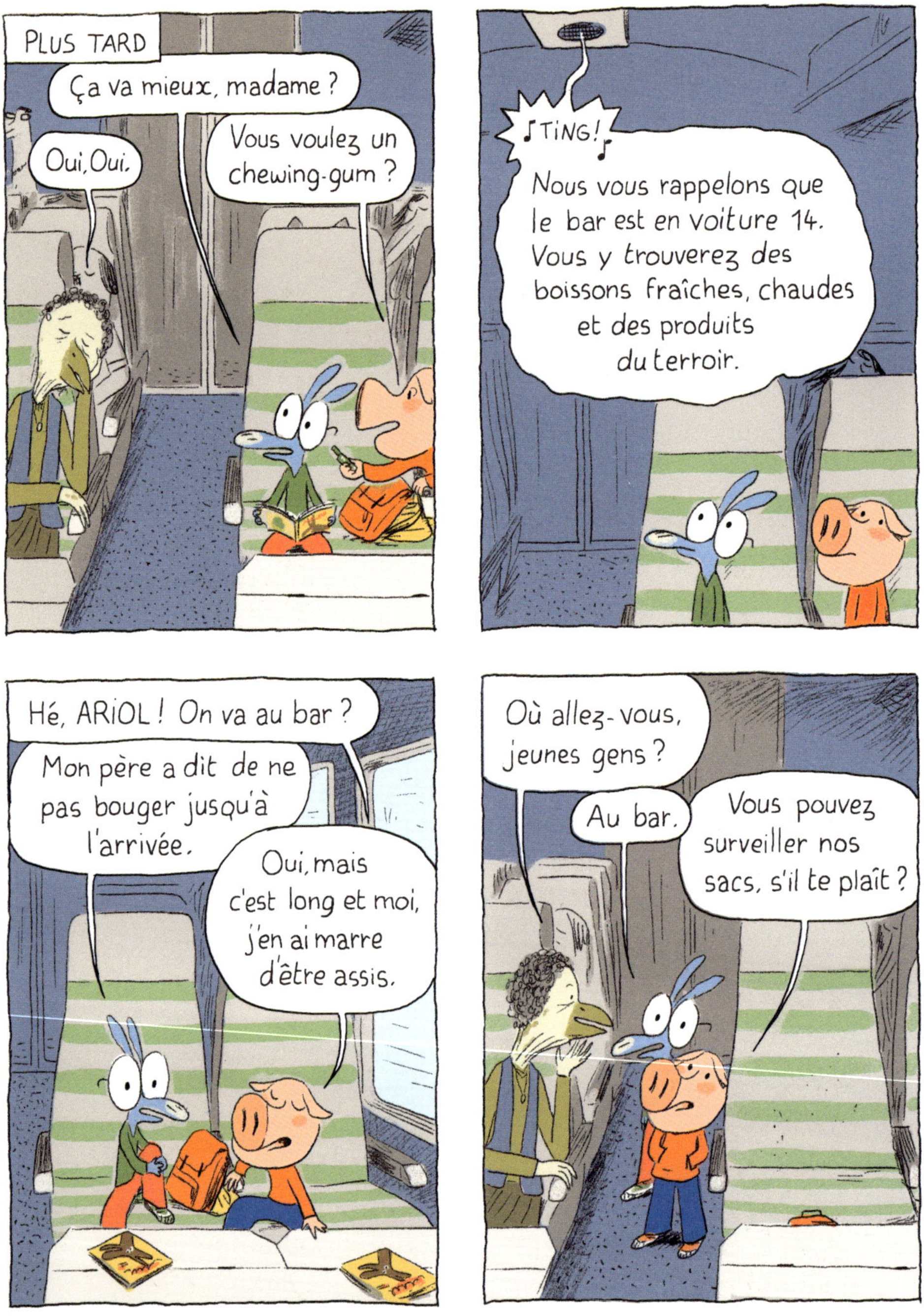
PLUS TARD
Ça va mieux, madame ?
Oui, Oui.
Vous voulez un chewing-gum ?
♪TING!♪
Nous vous rappelons que le bar est en voiture 14. Vous y trouverez des boissons fraîches, chaudes et des produits du terroir.
Hé, ARIOL ! On va au bar ?
Mon père a dit de ne pas bouger jusqu'à l'arrivée.
Oui, mais c'est long et moi, j'en ai marre d'être assis.
Où allez-vous, jeunes gens ?
Au bar.
Vous pouvez surveiller nos sacs, s'il te plaît ?

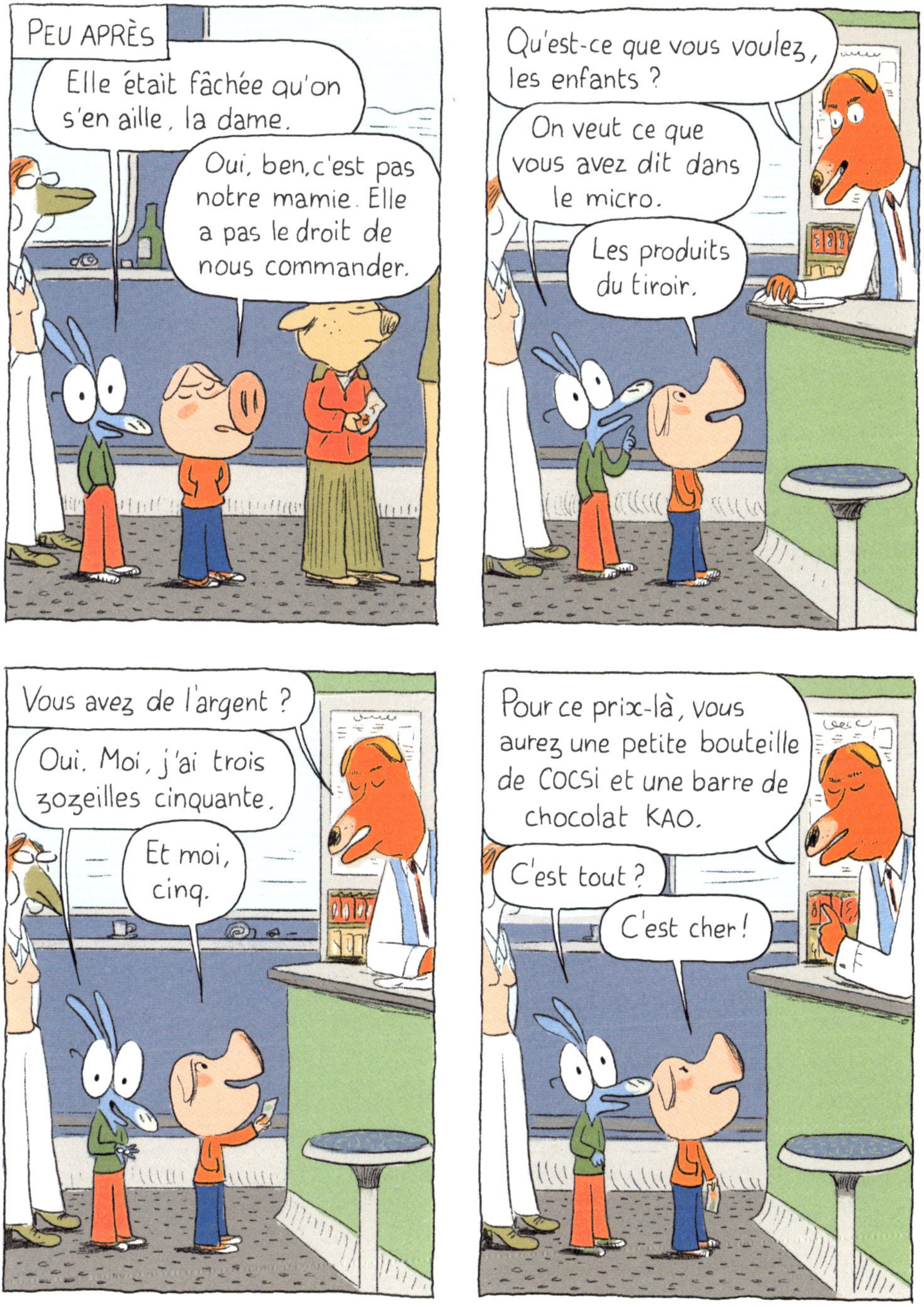
PEU APRÈS
Elle était fâchée qu'on s'en aille, la dame.
Oui, ben, c'est pas notre mamie. Elle a pas le droit de nous commander.
Qu'est-ce que vous voulez, les enfants ?
On veut ce que vous avez dit dans le micro.
Les produits du tiroir.
Vous avez de l'argent ?
Oui. Moi, j'ai trois zozeilles cinquante.
Et moi, cinq.
Pour ce prix-là, vous aurez une petite bouteille de COCSI et une barre de chocolat KAO.
C'est tout ?
C'est cher !

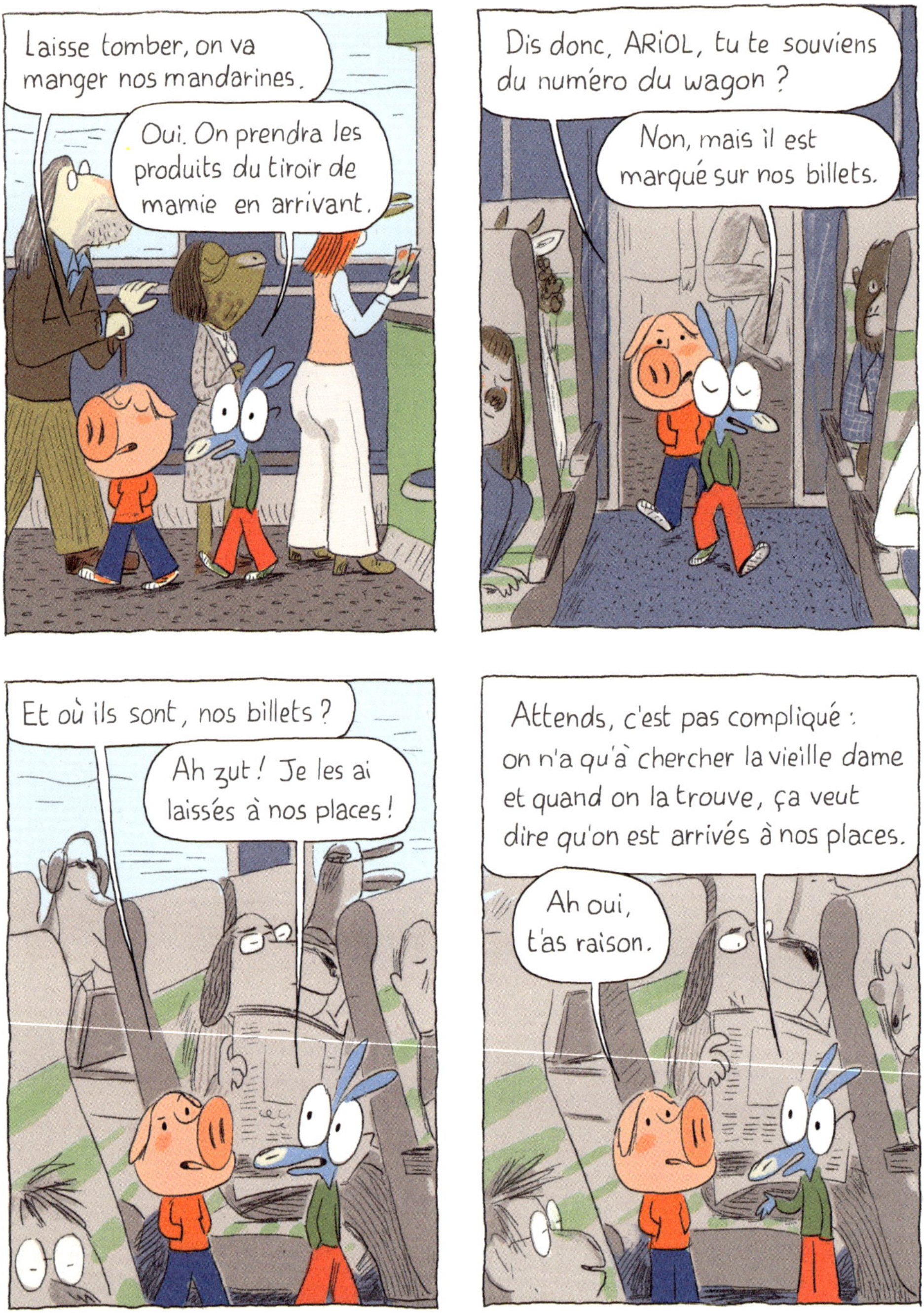
Laisse tomber, on va manger nos mandarines.
Oui. On prendra les produits du tiroir de mamie en arrivant.
Dis donc, ARIOL, tu te souviens du numéro du wagon ?
Non, mais il est marqué sur nos billets.
Et où ils sont, nos billets ?
Ah zut ! Je les ai laissés à nos places !
Attends, c'est pas compliqué : on n'a qu'à chercher la vieille dame et quand on la trouve, ça veut dire qu'on est arrivés à nos places.
Ah oui, t'as raison.

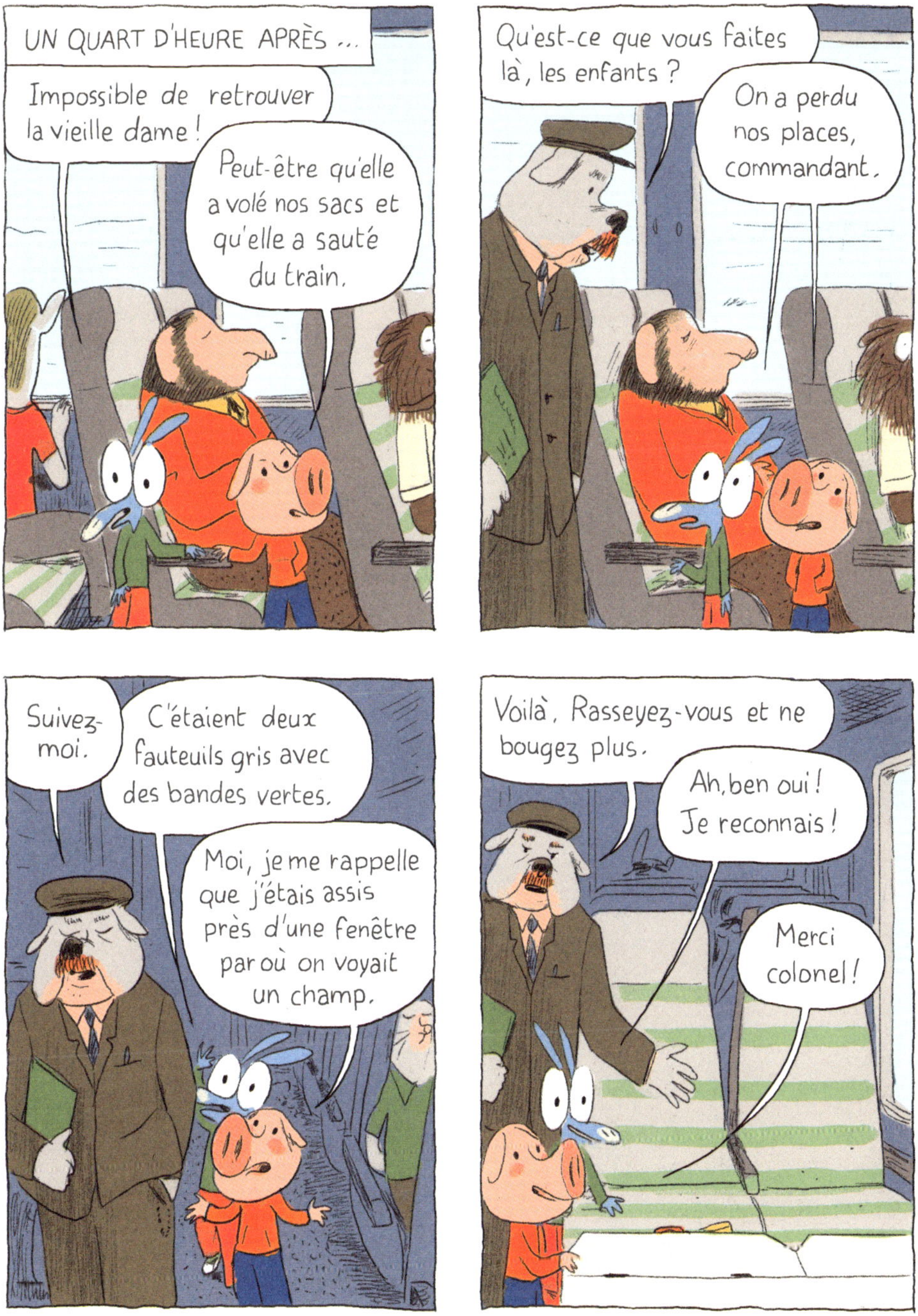
UN QUART D'HEURE APRÈS ...
Impossible de retrouver la vieille dame !
Peut-être qu'elle a volé nos sacs et qu'elle a sauté du train.
Qu'est-ce que vous faites là, les enfants ?
On a perdu nos places, commandant.
Suivez-moi.
C'étaient deux fauteuils gris avec des bandes vertes.
Moi, je me rappelle que j'étais assis près d'une fenêtre par où on voyait un champ.
Voilà. Rasseyez-vous et ne bougez plus.
Ah, ben oui ! Je reconnais !
Merci colonel !

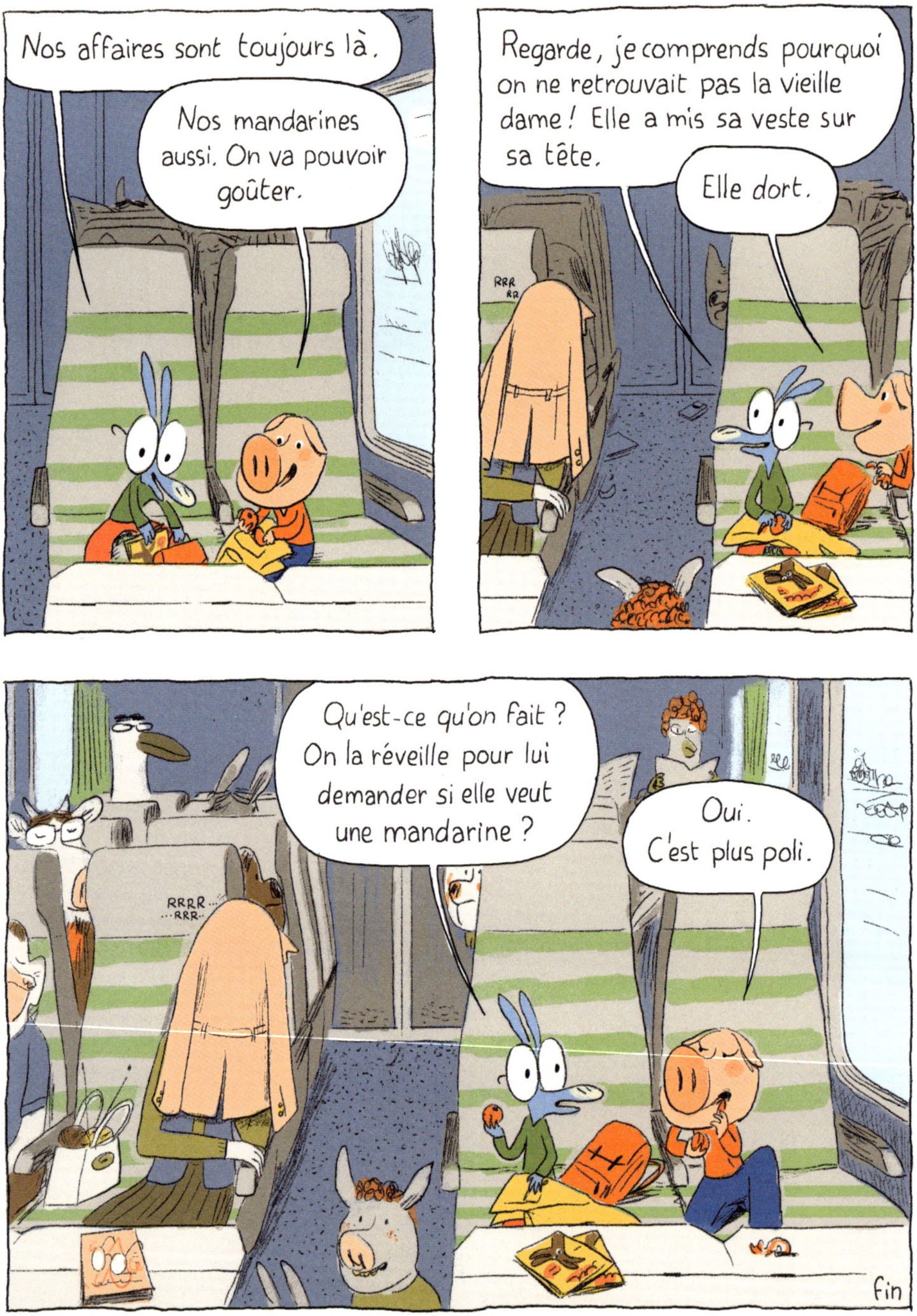

Nos affaires sont toujours là.
Nos mandarines aussi. On va pouvoir goûter.
Regarde, je comprends pourquoi on ne retrouvait pas la vieille dame ! Elle a mis sa veste sur sa tête.
Elle dort.
RRR RR
Qu'est-ce qu'on fait ? On la réveille pour lui demander si elle veut une mandarine ?
Oui. C'est plus poli.
RRRR... ...RRR..
Fin

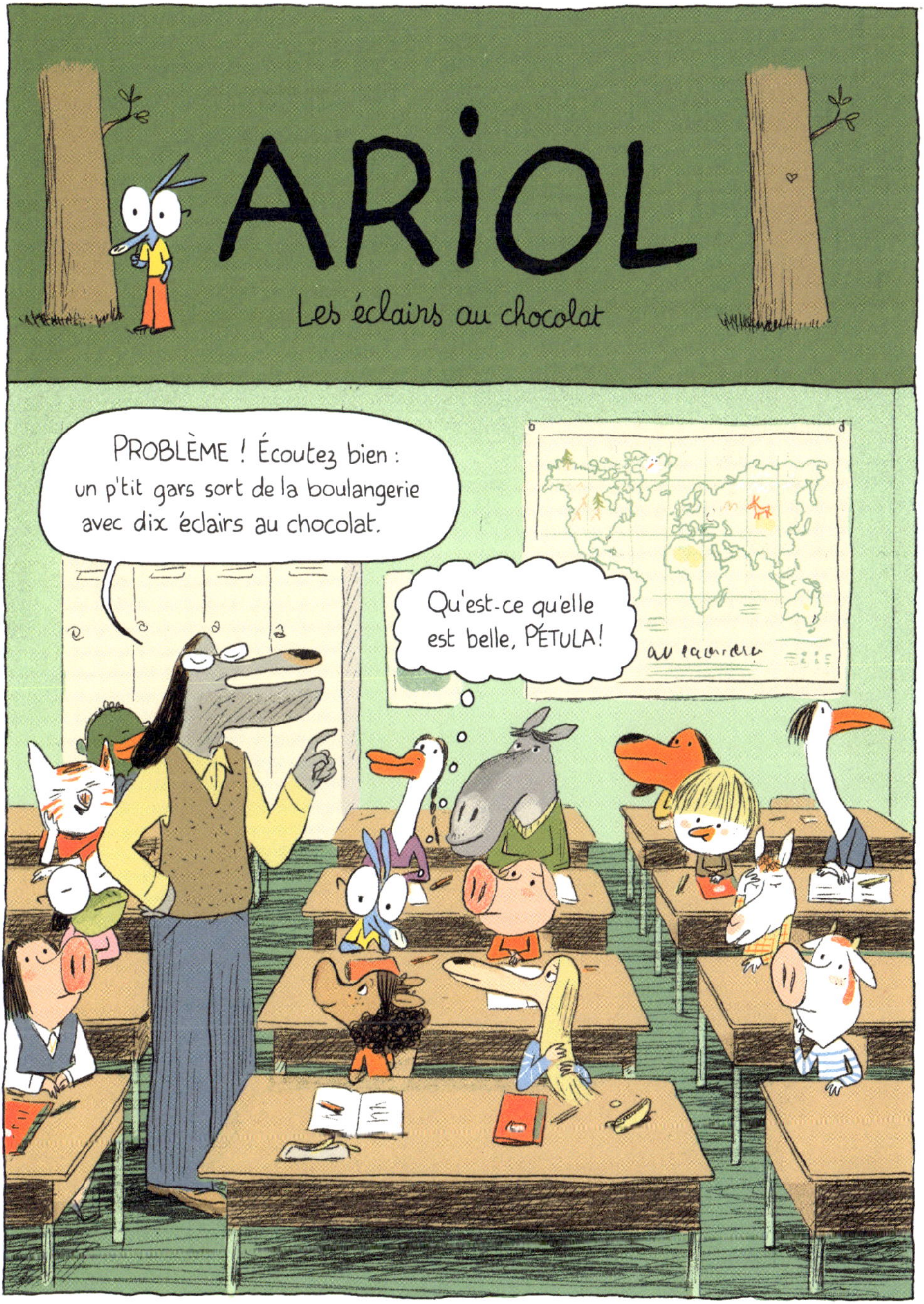
ARIOL
Les éclairs au chocolat
PROBLÈME ! Écoutez bien : un p'tit gars sort de la boulangerie avec dix éclairs au chocolat.
Qu'est-ce qu'elle est belle, PÉTULA !

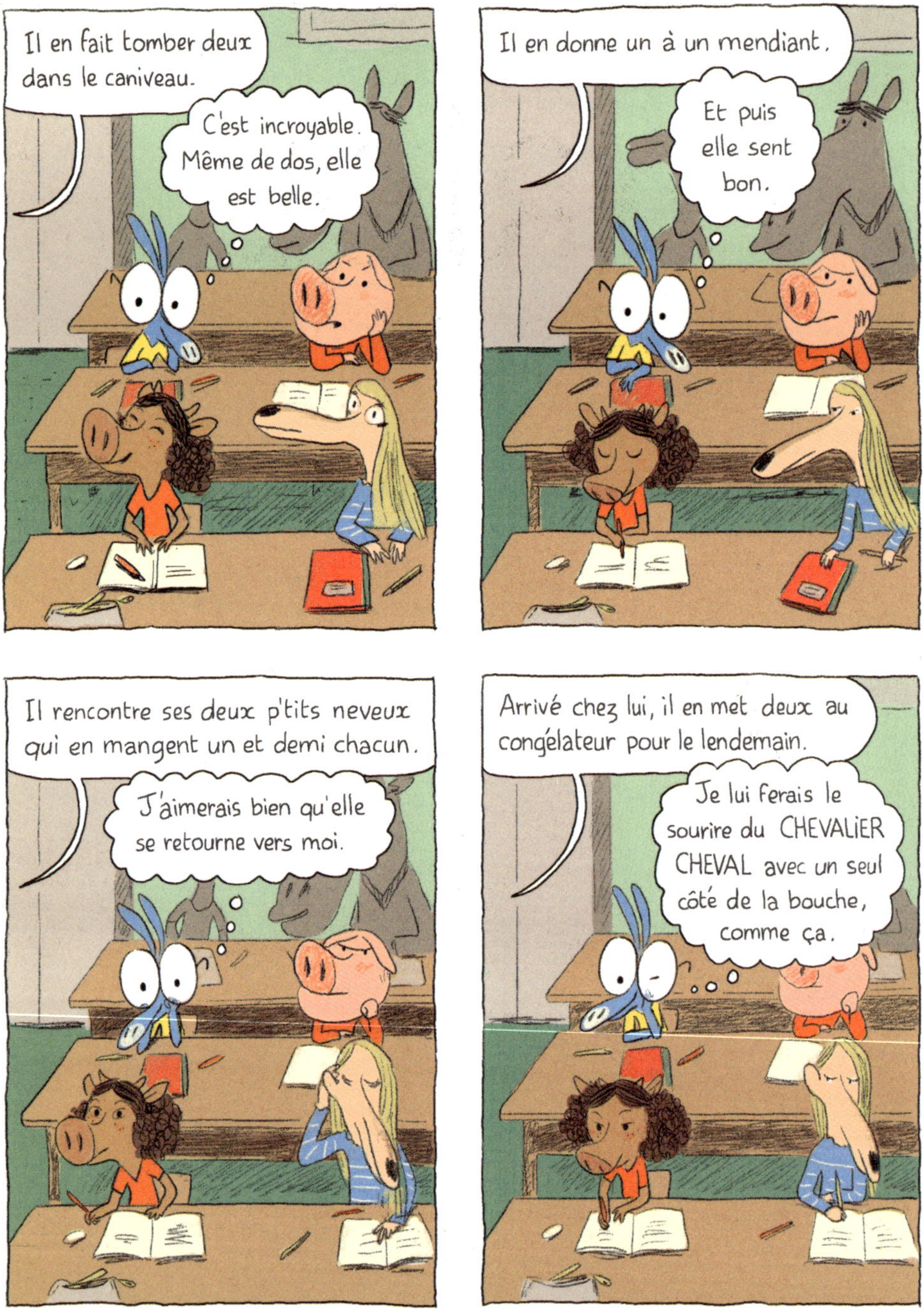
Il en fait tomber deux dans le caniveau.
C'est incroyable. Même de dos, elle est belle.
Il en donne un à un mendiant.
Et puis elle sent bon.
Il rencontre ses deux p'tits neveux qui en mangent un et demi chacun.
J'aimerais bien qu'elle se retourne vers moi.
Arrivé chez lui, il en met deux au congélateur pour le lendemain.
Je lui ferais le sourire du CHEVALIER CHEVAL avec un seul côté de la bouche, comme ça.

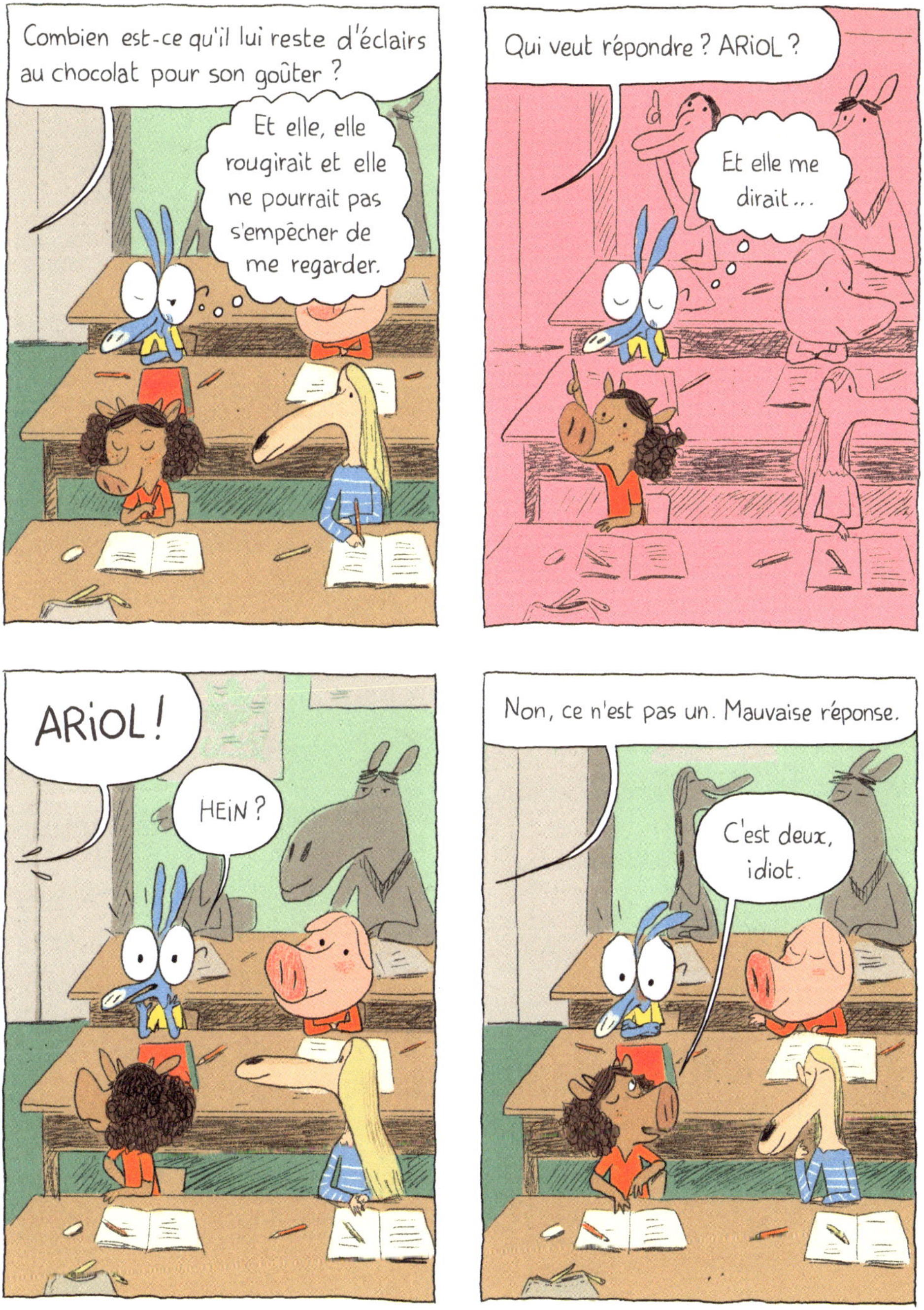
Combien est-ce qu'il lui reste d'éclairs au chocolat pour son goûter ?
Et elle, elle rougirait et elle ne pourrait pas s'empêcher de me regarder.
Qui veut répondre ? ARIOL ?
Et elle me dirait...
ARIOL !
HEIN ?
Non, ce n'est pas un. Mauvaise réponse.
C'est deux, idiot.

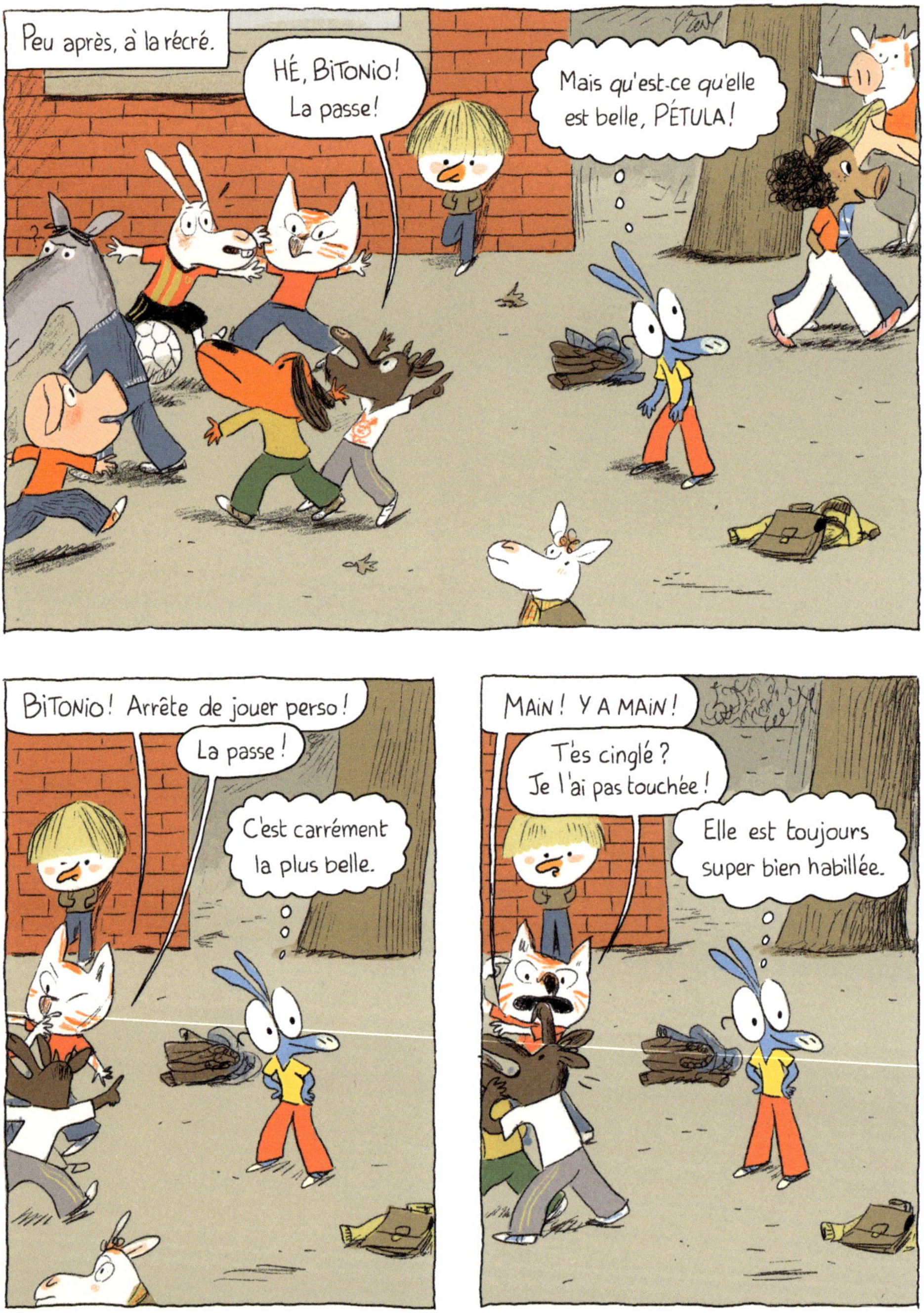
Peu après, à la récré.
HÉ, BITONIO ! La passe !
Mais qu'est-ce qu'elle est belle, PÉTULA !
BITONIO ! Arrête de jouer perso !
La passe !
C'est carrément la plus belle.
MAIN ! Y A MAIN !
T'es cinglé ? Je l'ai pas touchée !
Elle est toujours super bien habillée.

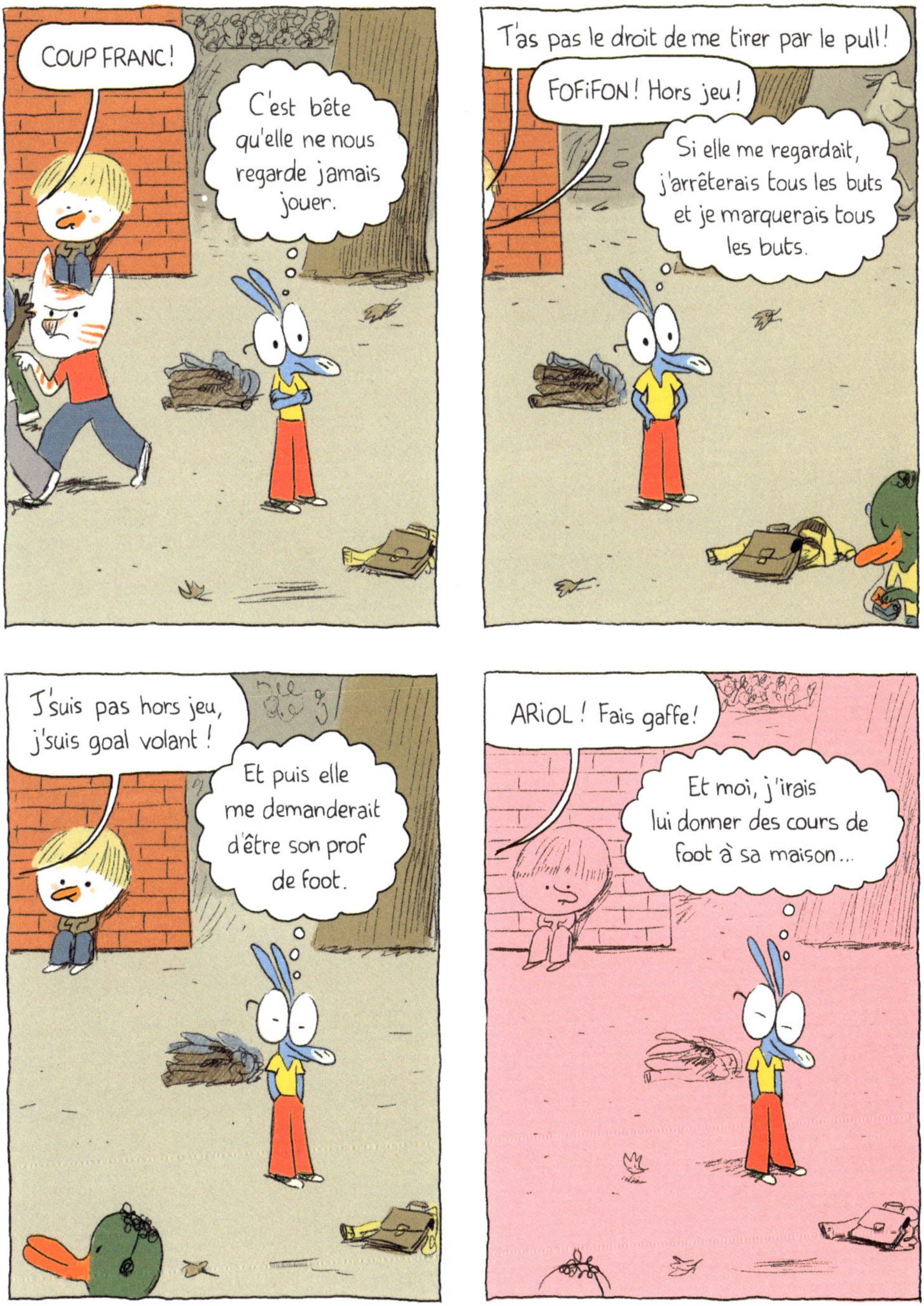
COUP FRANC !
C'est bête qu'elle ne nous regarde jamais jouer.
T'as pas le droit de me tirer par le pull !
FOFIFON ! Hors jeu !
Si elle me regardait, j'arrêterais tous les buts et je marquerais tous les buts.
J'suis pas hors jeu, j'suis goal volant !
Et puis elle me demanderait d'être son prof de foot.
ARIOL ! Fais gaffe !
Et moi, j'irais lui donner des cours de foot à sa maison...

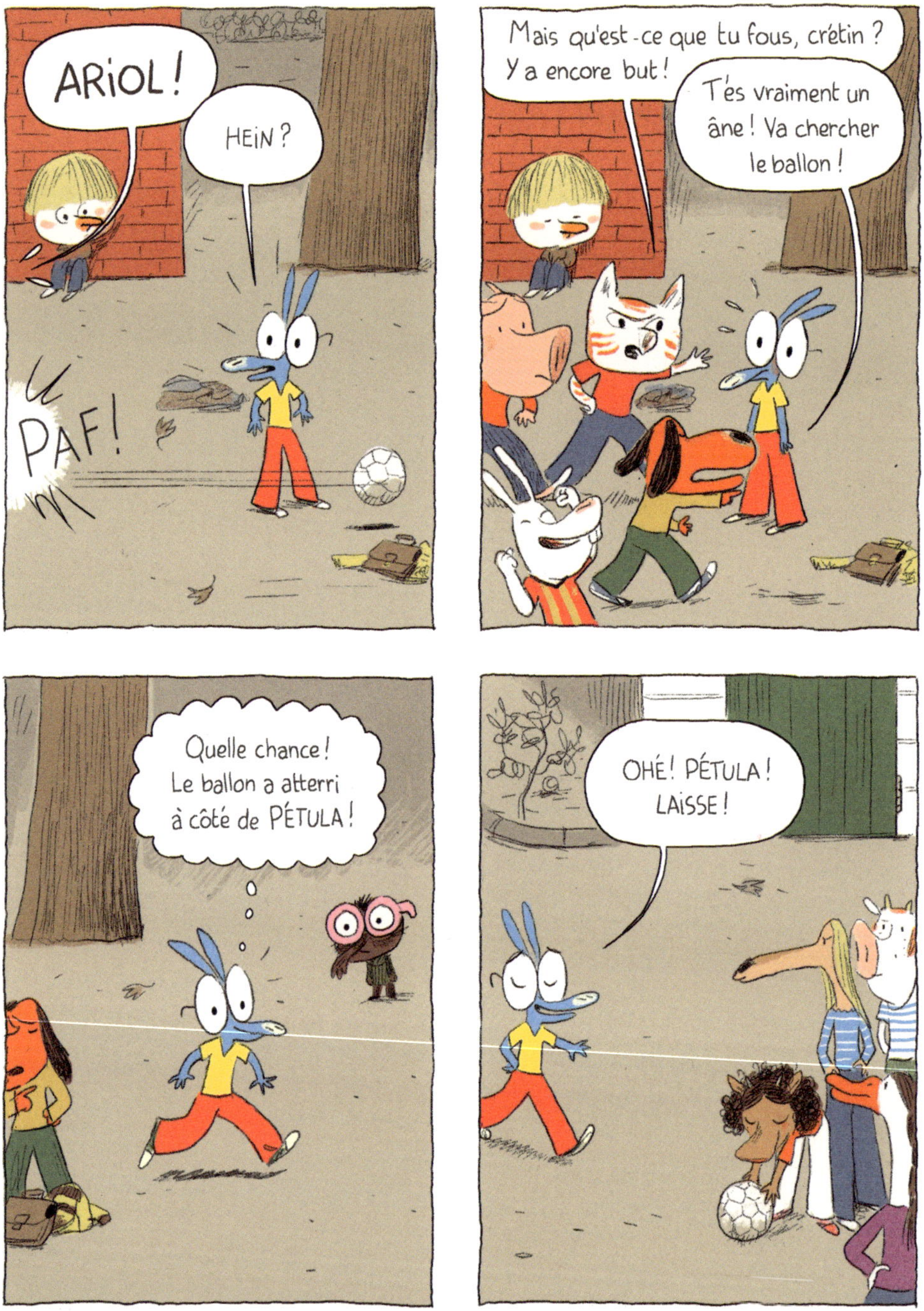
ARiOL !
HEiN ?
PAF !
Mais qu'est-ce que tu fous, crétin ? Y a encore but !
T'es vraiment un âne ! Va chercher le ballon !
Quelle chance ! Le ballon a atterri à côté de PÉTULA !
OHÉ ! PÉTULA ! LAISSE !

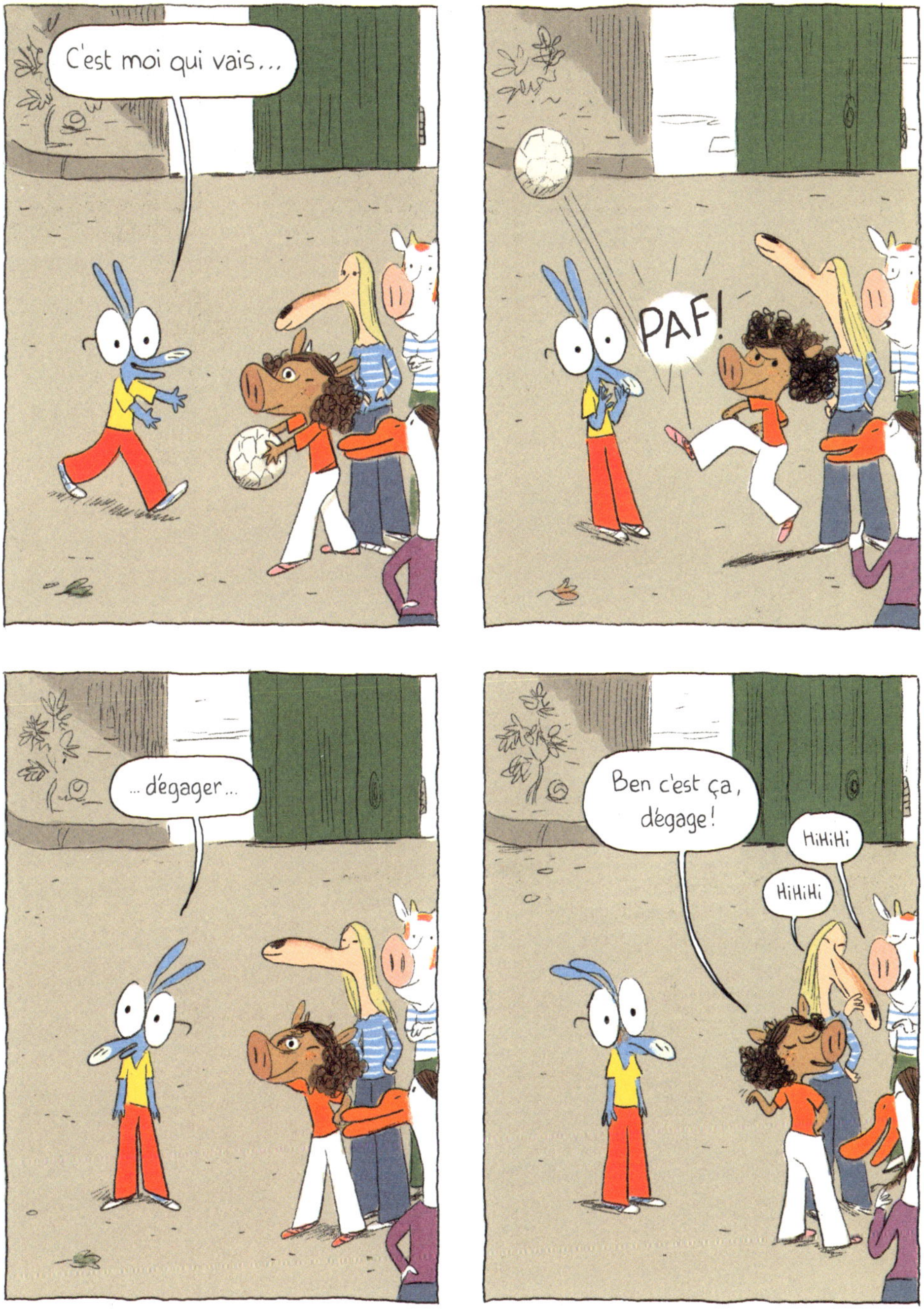
C'est moi qui vais...
PAF!
... dégager...
Ben c'est ça, dégage!
HiHiHi
HiHiHi

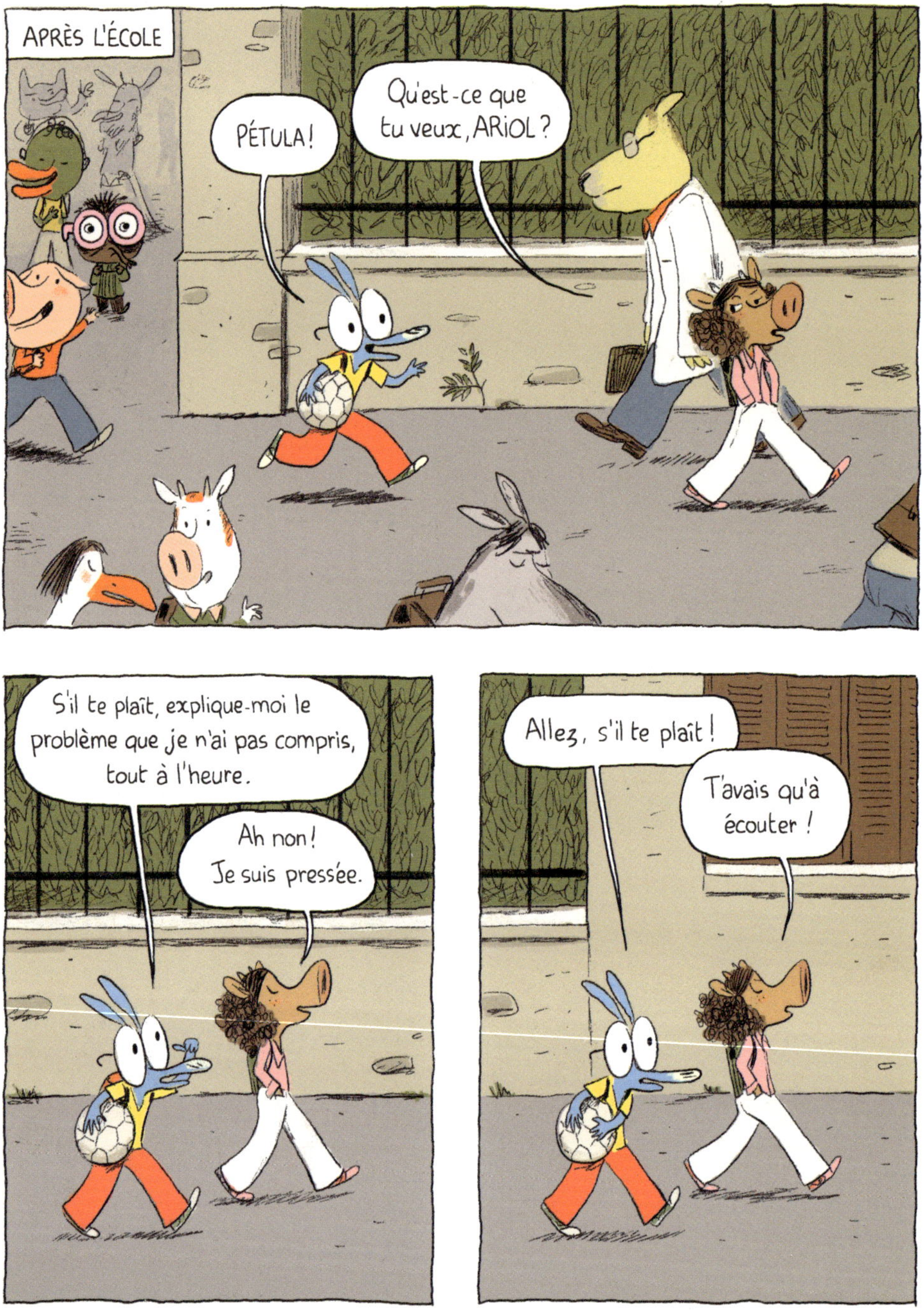
APRÈS L'ÉCOLE
PÉTULA !
Qu'est-ce que tu veux, ARIOL ?
S'il te plaît, explique-moi le problème que je n'ai pas compris, tout à l'heure.
Ah non ! Je suis pressée.
Allez, s'il te plaît !
T'avais qu'à écouter !

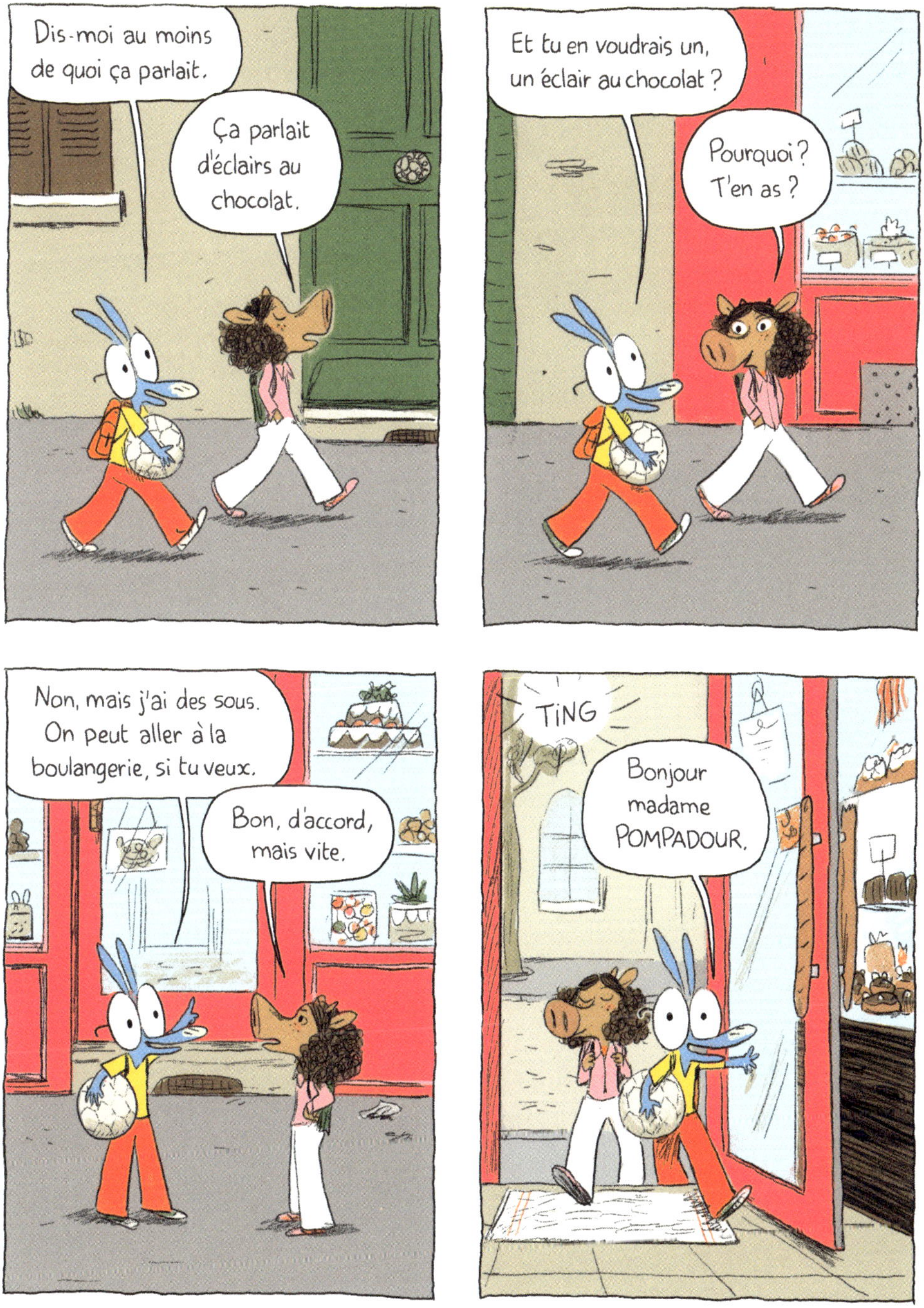
Dis-moi au moins de quoi ça parlait.
Ça parlait d'éclairs au chocolat.
Et tu en voudrais un, un éclair au chocolat ?
Pourquoi ? T'en as ?
Non, mais j'ai des sous. On peut aller à la boulangerie, si tu veux.
Bon, d'accord, mais vite.
TING
Bonjour madame POMPADOUR.

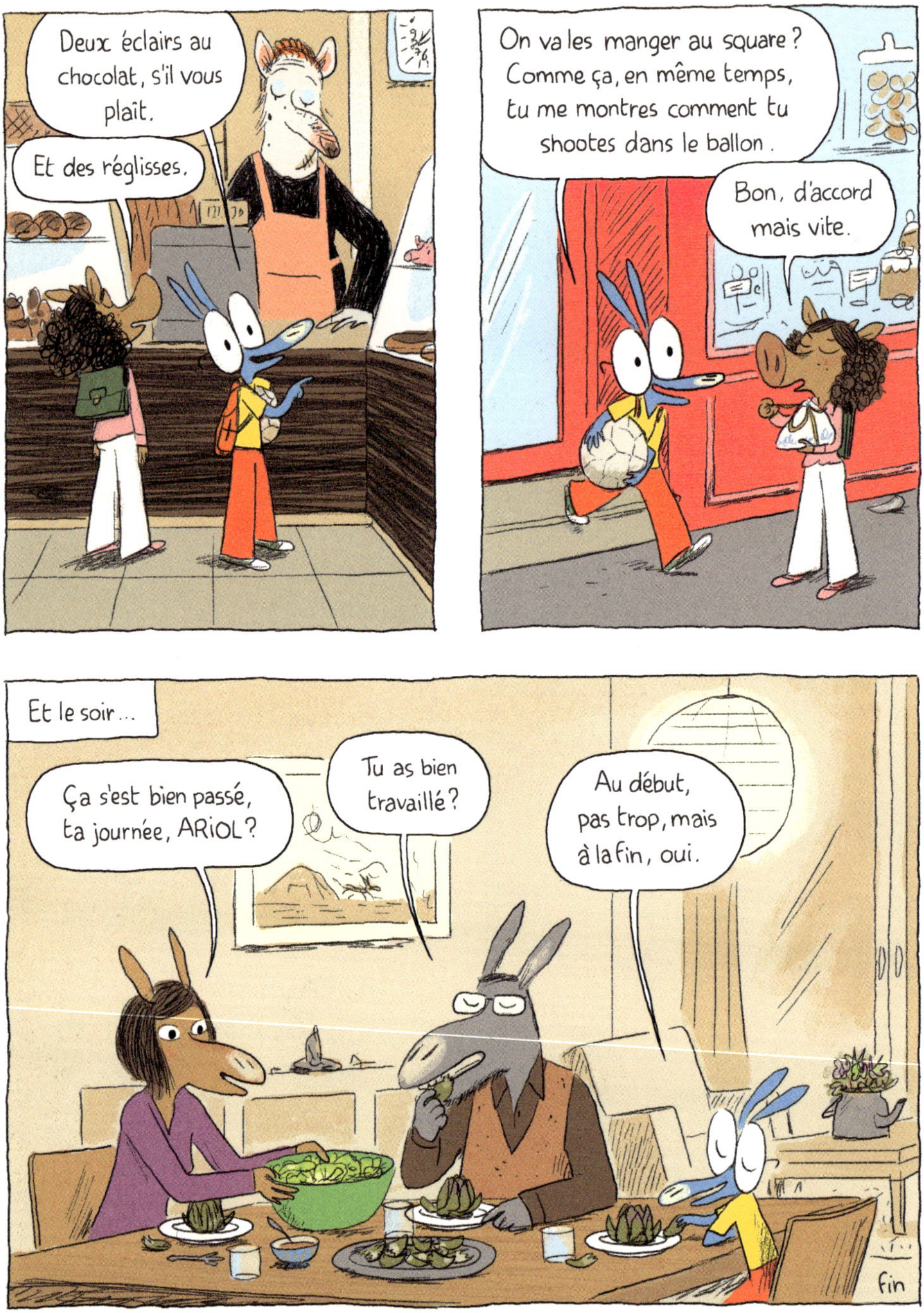
Deux éclairs au chocolat, s'il vous plaît.
Et des réglisses.
On va les manger au square ? Comme ça, en même temps, tu me montres comment tu shootes dans le ballon.
Bon, d'accord mais vite.
Et le soir...
Ça s'est bien passé, ta journée, ARIOL ?
Tu as bien travaillé ?
Au début, pas trop, mais à la fin, oui.
Fin

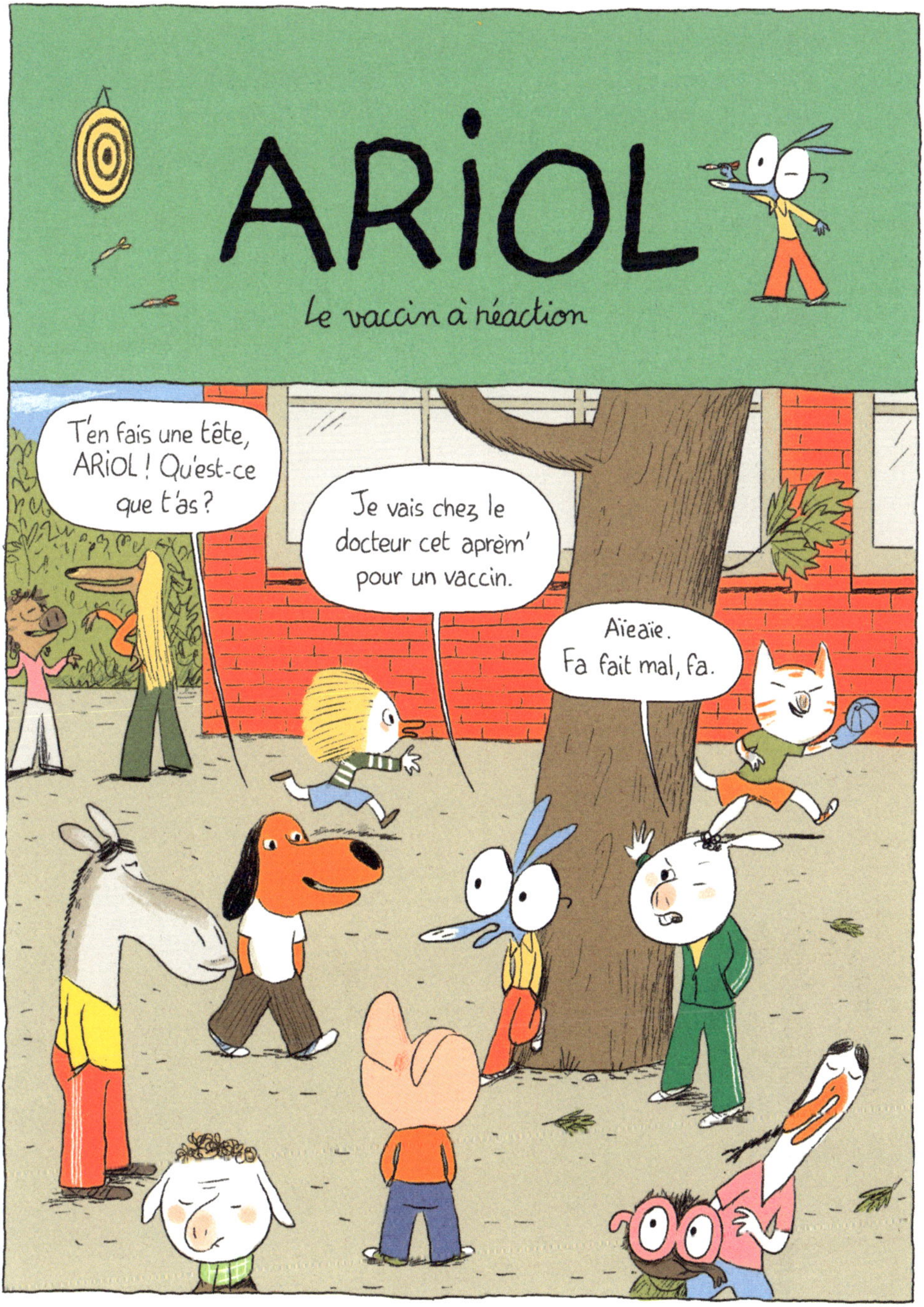
ARiOL
Le vaccin à réaction
T'en fais une tête, ARiOL ! Qu'est-ce que t'as ?
Je vais chez le docteur cet aprèm' pour un vaccin.
Aïeaïe. Fa fait mal, fa.

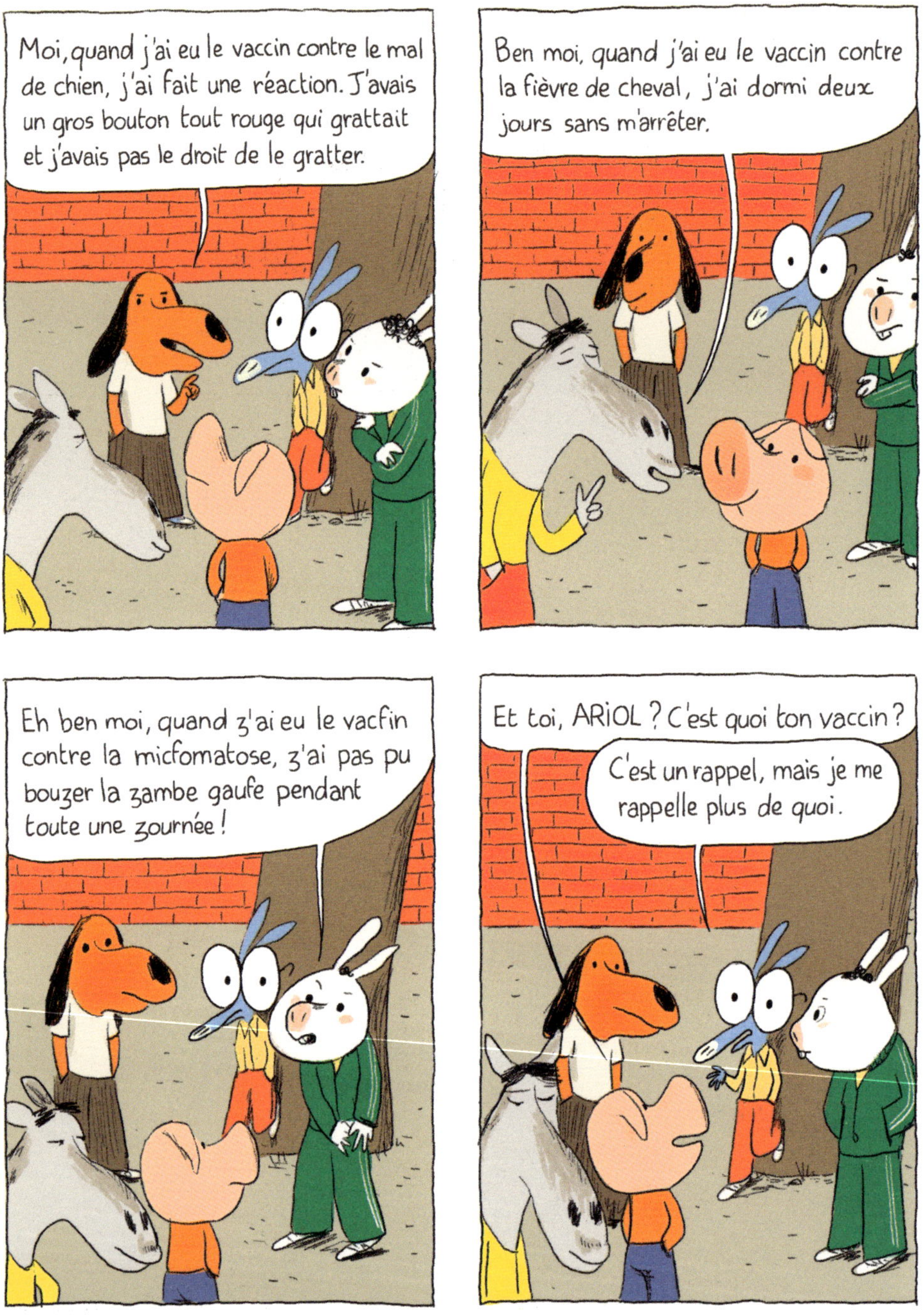

Moi, quand j'ai eu le vaccin contre le mal de chien, j'ai fait une réaction. J'avais un gros bouton tout rouge qui grattait et j'avais pas le droit de le gratter.
Ben moi, quand j'ai eu le vaccin contre la fièvre de cheval, j'ai dormi deux jours sans m'arrêter.
Eh ben moi, quand z'ai eu le vacfin contre la micfomatose, z'ai pas pu bouzer la zambe gaufe pendant toute une zournée !
Et toi, ARIOL ? C'est quoi ton vaccin ?
C'est un rappel, mais je me rappelle plus de quoi.

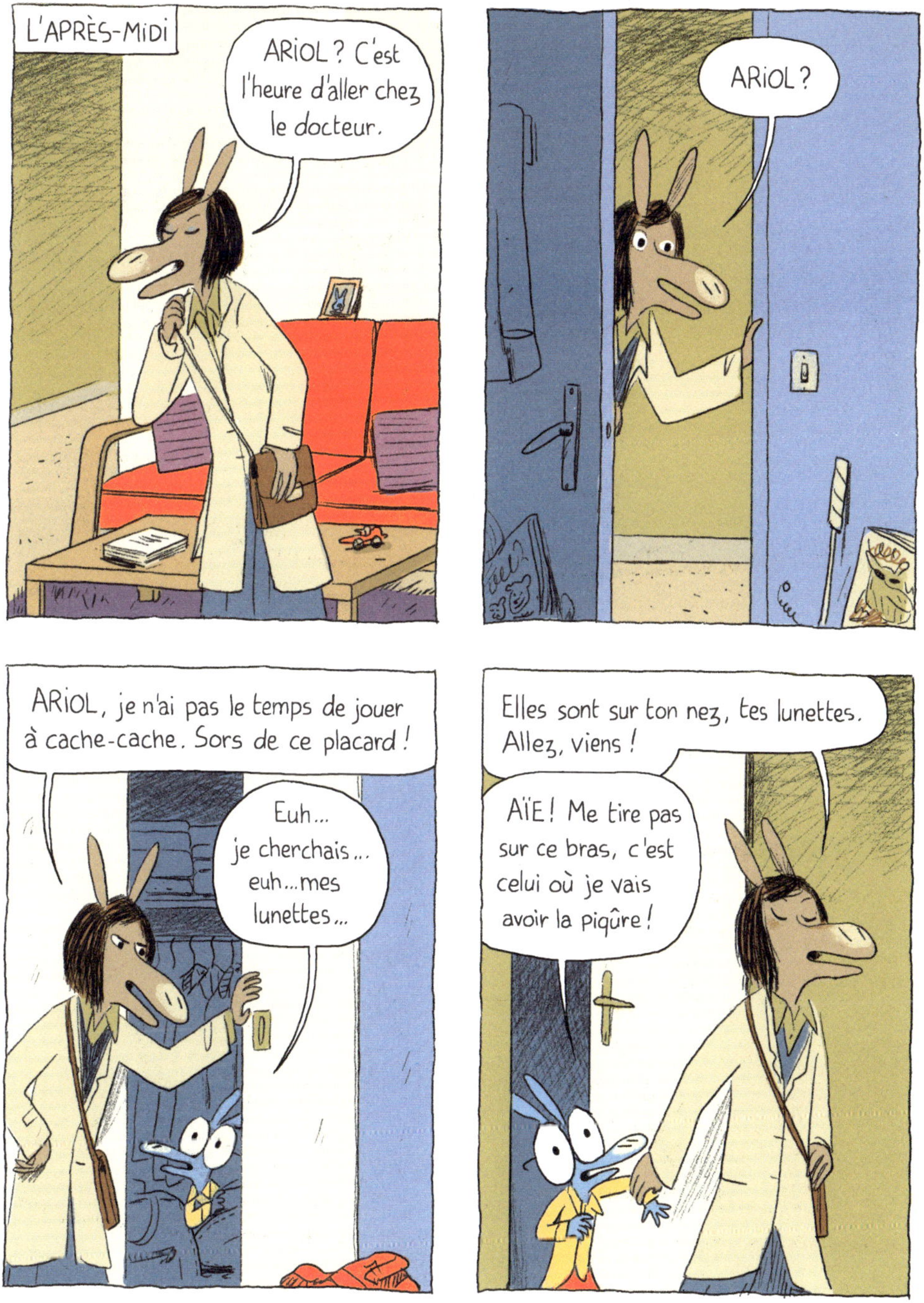
L'APRÈS-MIDI
ARIOL ? C'est l'heure d'aller chez le docteur.
ARIOL ?
ARIOL, je n'ai pas le temps de jouer à cache-cache. Sors de ce placard !
Euh... je cherchais... euh... mes lunettes...
Elles sont sur ton nez, tes lunettes. Allez, viens !
AÏE ! Me tire pas sur ce bras, c'est celui où je vais avoir la piqûre !

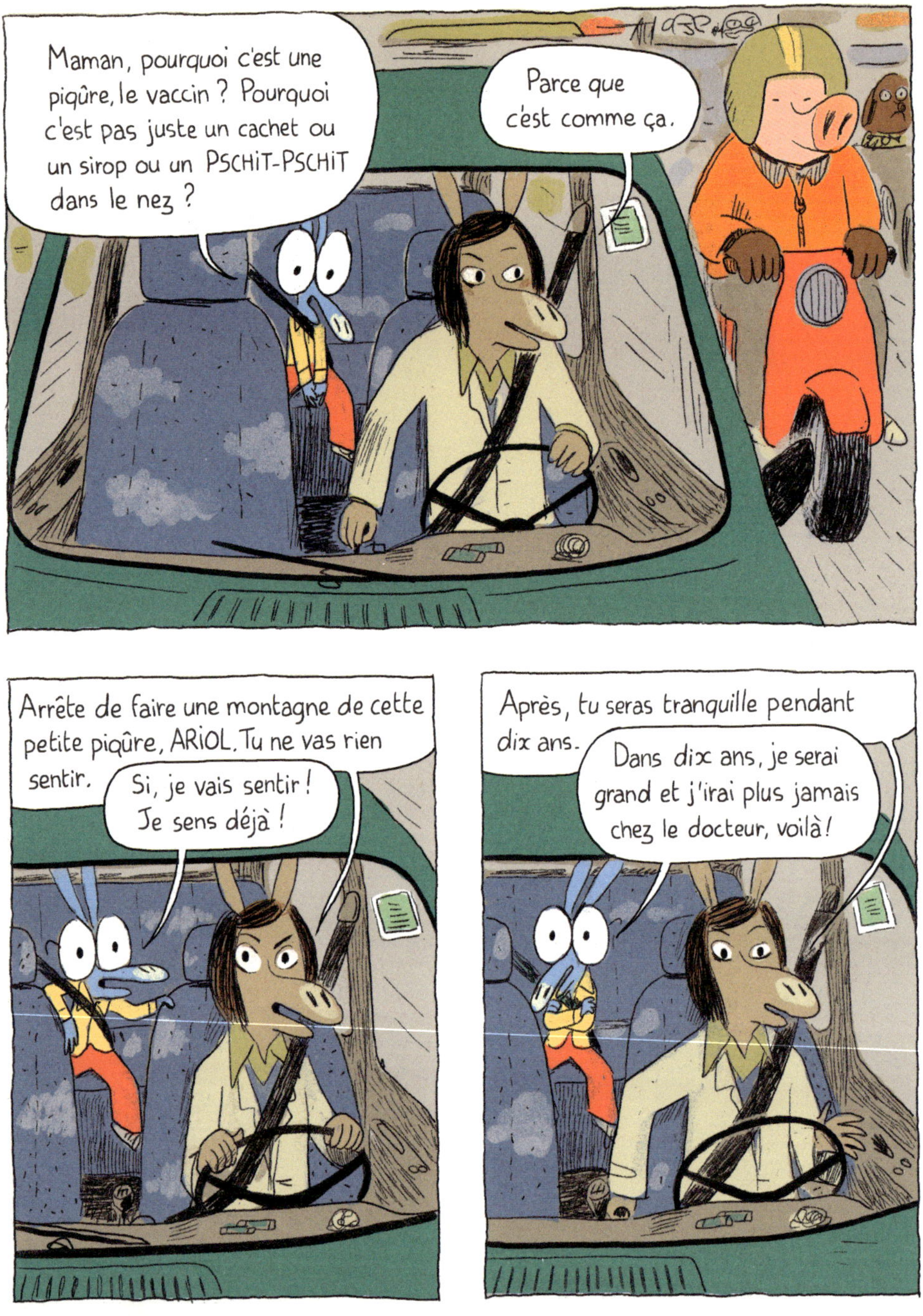
Maman, pourquoi c'est une piqûre, le vaccin ? Pourquoi c'est pas juste un cachet ou un sirop ou un PSCHIT-PSCHIT dans le nez ?
Parce que c'est comme ça.
Arrête de faire une montagne de cette petite piqûre, ARIOL. Tu ne vas rien sentir.
Si, je vais sentir ! Je sens déjà !
Après, tu seras tranquille pendant dix ans.
Dans dix ans, je serai grand et j'irai plus jamais chez le docteur, voilà !

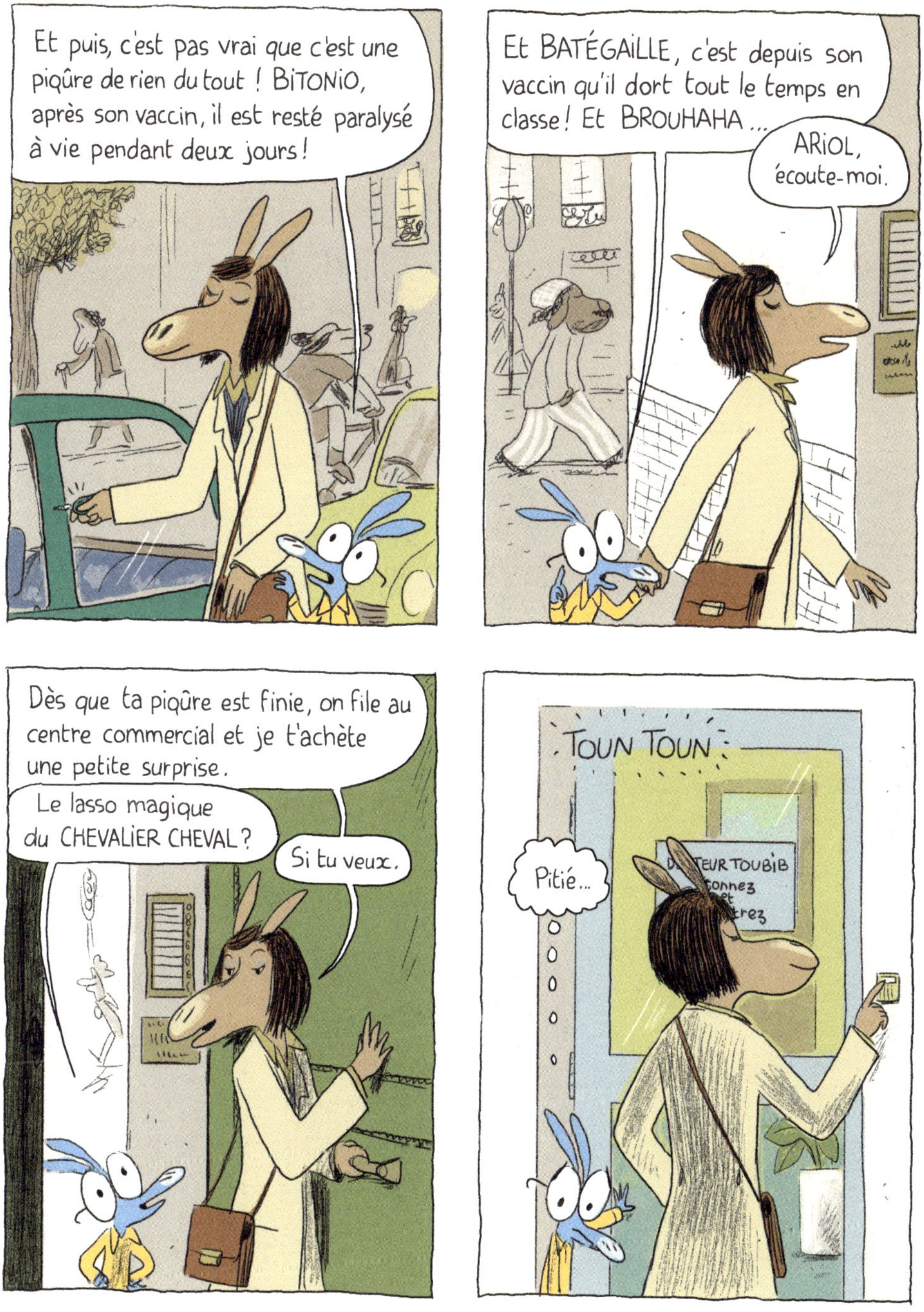
Et puis, c'est pas vrai que c'est une piqûre de rien du tout ! BITONIO, après son vaccin, il est resté paralysé à vie pendant deux jours !
Et BATÉGAILLE, c'est depuis son vaccin qu'il dort tout le temps en classe ! Et BROUHAHA ...
ARIOL, écoute-moi.
Dès que ta piqûre est finie, on file au centre commercial et je t'achète une petite surprise.
Le lasso magique du CHEVALIER CHEVAL ?
Si tu veux.
TOUN TOUN
Pitié...

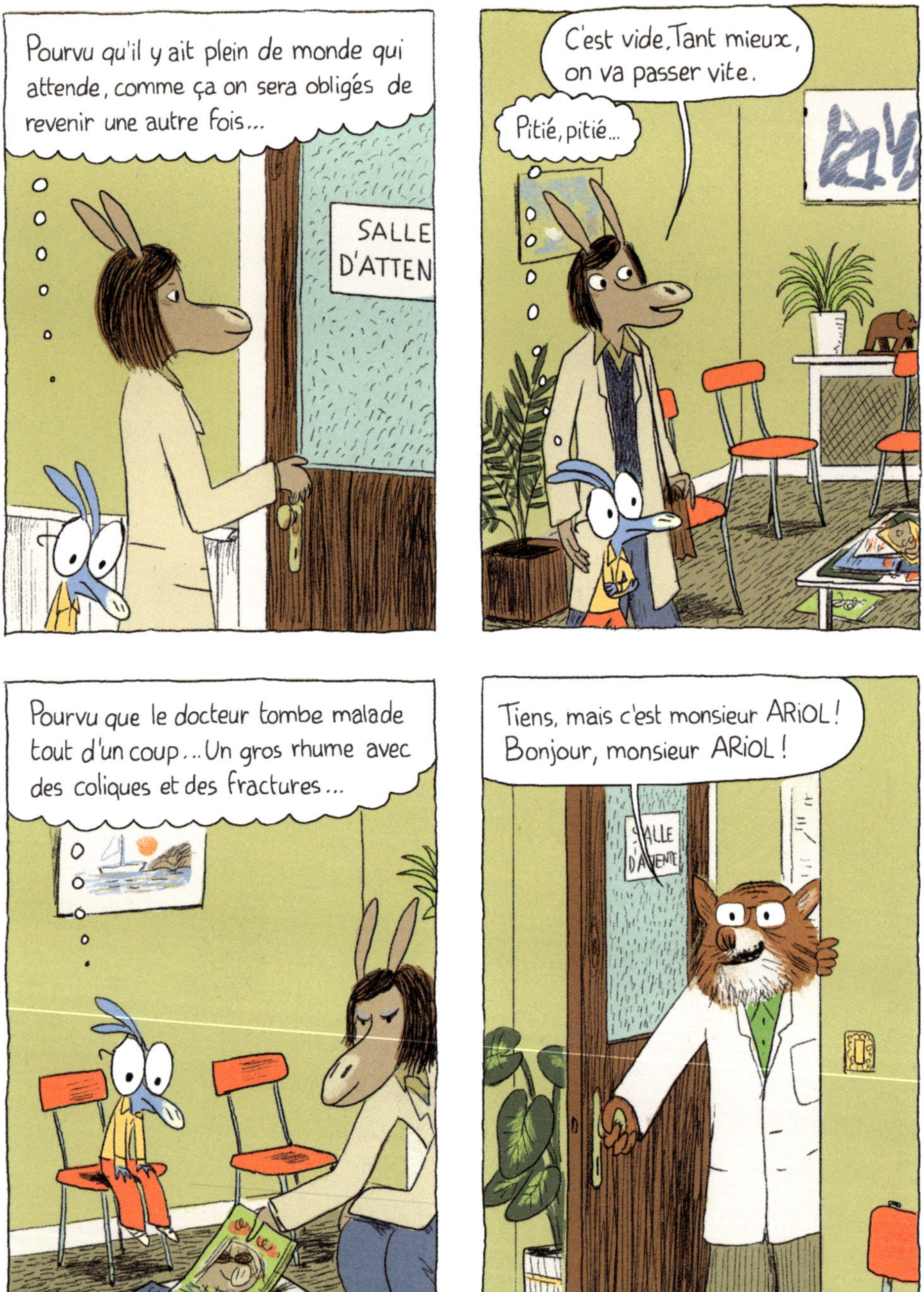
Pourvu qu'il y ait plein de monde qui attende, comme ça on sera obligés de revenir une autre fois...
SALLE D'ATTEN
C'est vide. Tant mieux, on va passer vite.
Pitié, pitié...
Pourvu que le docteur tombe malade tout d'un coup... Un gros rhume avec des coliques et des fractures...
Tiens, mais c'est monsieur ARIOL ! Bonjour, monsieur ARIOL !

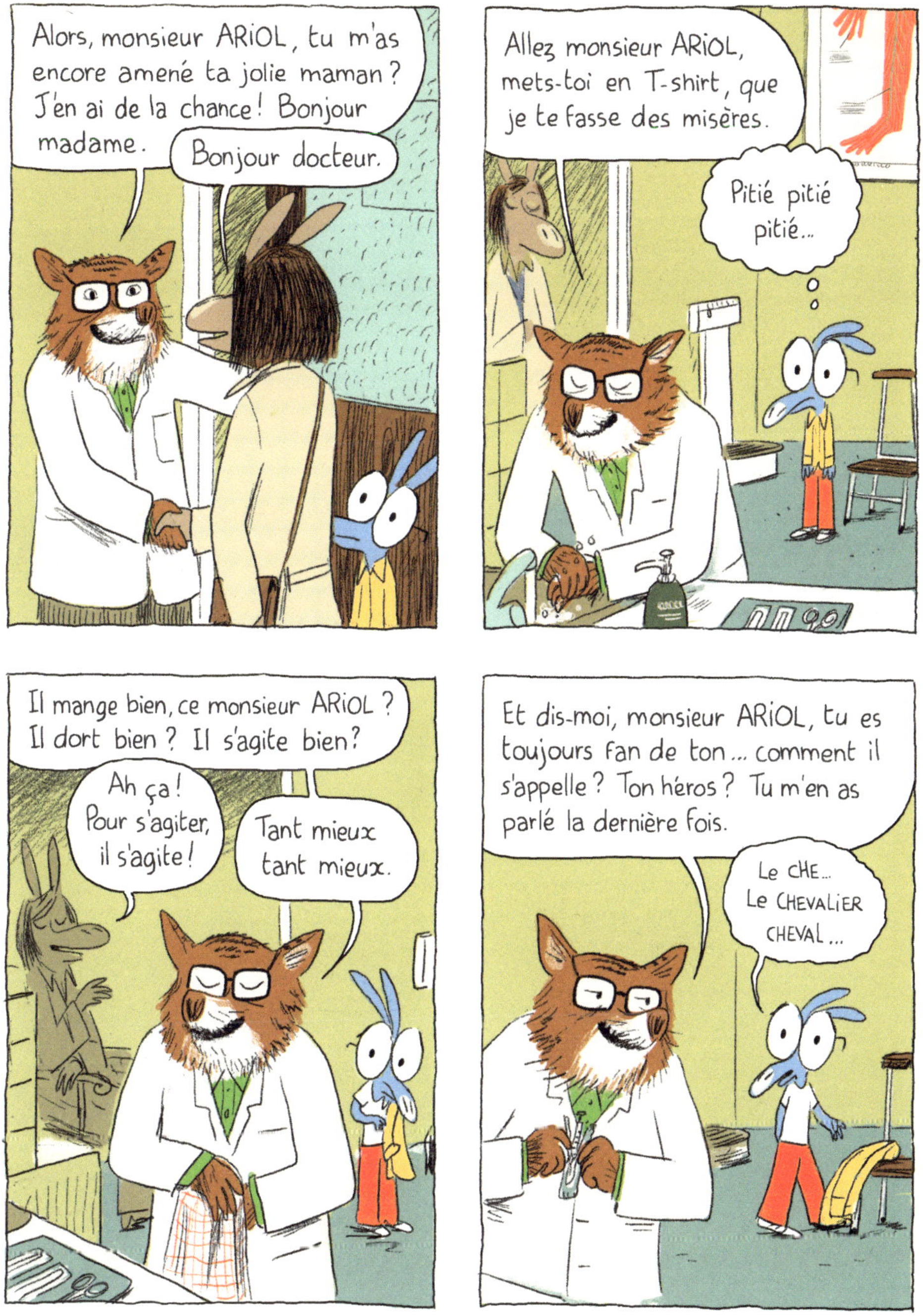
Alors, monsieur ARiOL, tu m'as encore amené ta jolie maman ? J'en ai de la chance ! Bonjour madame.
Bonjour docteur.
Allez monsieur ARiOL, mets-toi en T-shirt, que je te fasse des misères.
Pitié pitié pitié...
Il mange bien, ce monsieur ARiOL ? Il dort bien ? Il s'agite bien?
Ah ça ! Pour s'agiter, il s'agite !
Tant mieux tant mieux.
Et dis-moi, monsieur ARiOL, tu es toujours fan de ton... comment il s'appelle ? Ton héros ? Tu m'en as parlé la dernière fois.
Le CHE... Le CHEVALIER CHEVAL...

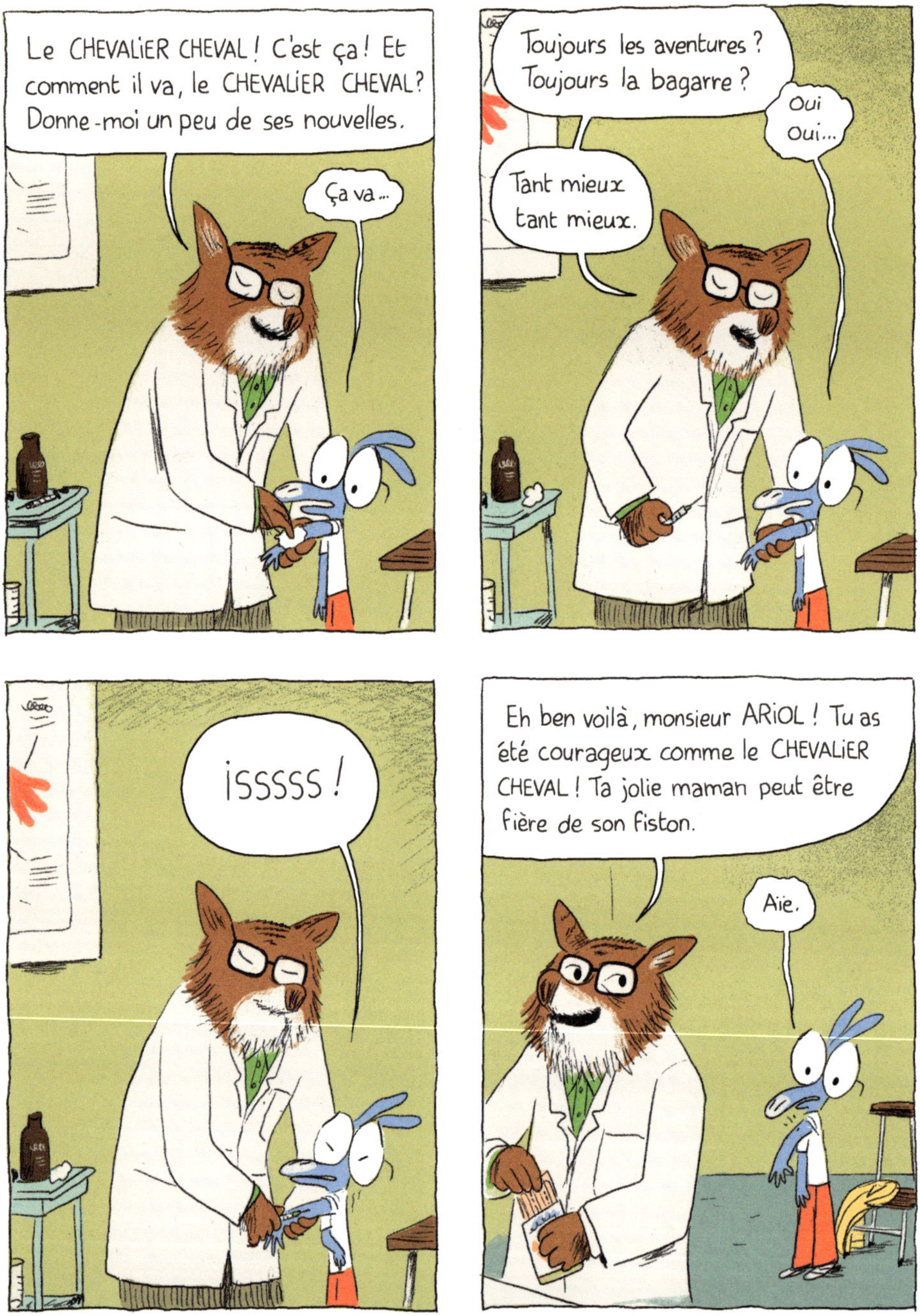
Le CHEVALIER CHEVAL ! C'est ça ! Et comment il va, le CHEVALIER CHEVAL ? Donne-moi un peu de ses nouvelles.
Ça va...
Toujours les aventures ? Toujours la bagarre ?
Oui oui...
Tant mieux tant mieux.
¡SSSSS !
Eh ben voilà, monsieur ARIOL ! Tu as été courageux comme le CHEVALIER CHEVAL ! Ta jolie maman peut être fière de son fiston.
Aïe.

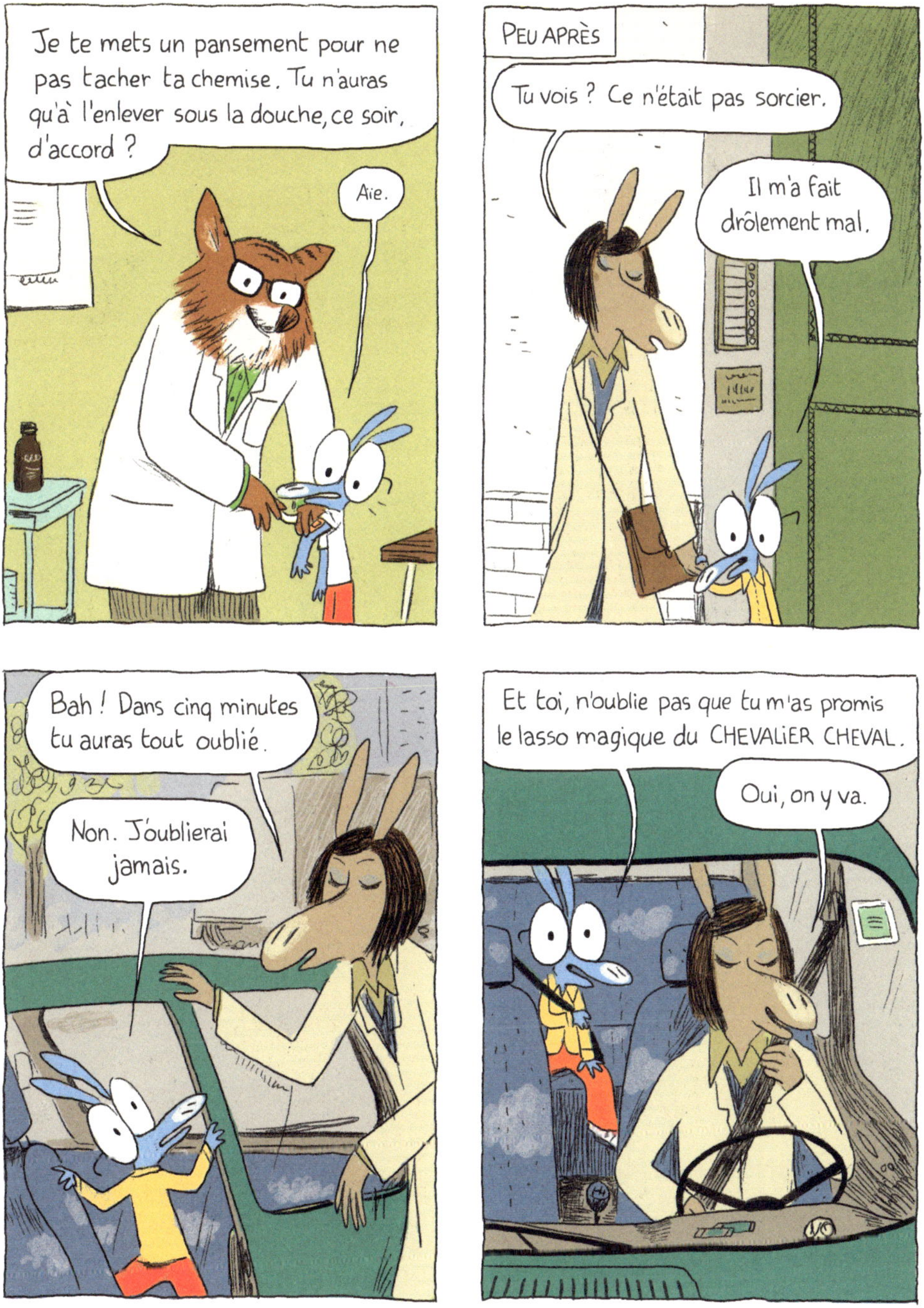
Je te mets un pansement pour ne pas tacher ta chemise. Tu n'auras qu'à l'enlever sous la douche, ce soir, d'accord ?
Aïe.
PEU APRÈS
Tu vois ? Ce n'était pas sorcier.
Il m'a fait drôlement mal.
Bah ! Dans cinq minutes tu auras tout oublié.
Non. J'oublierai jamais.
Et toi, n'oublie pas que tu m'as promis le lasso magique du CHEVALIER CHEVAL.
Oui, on y va.

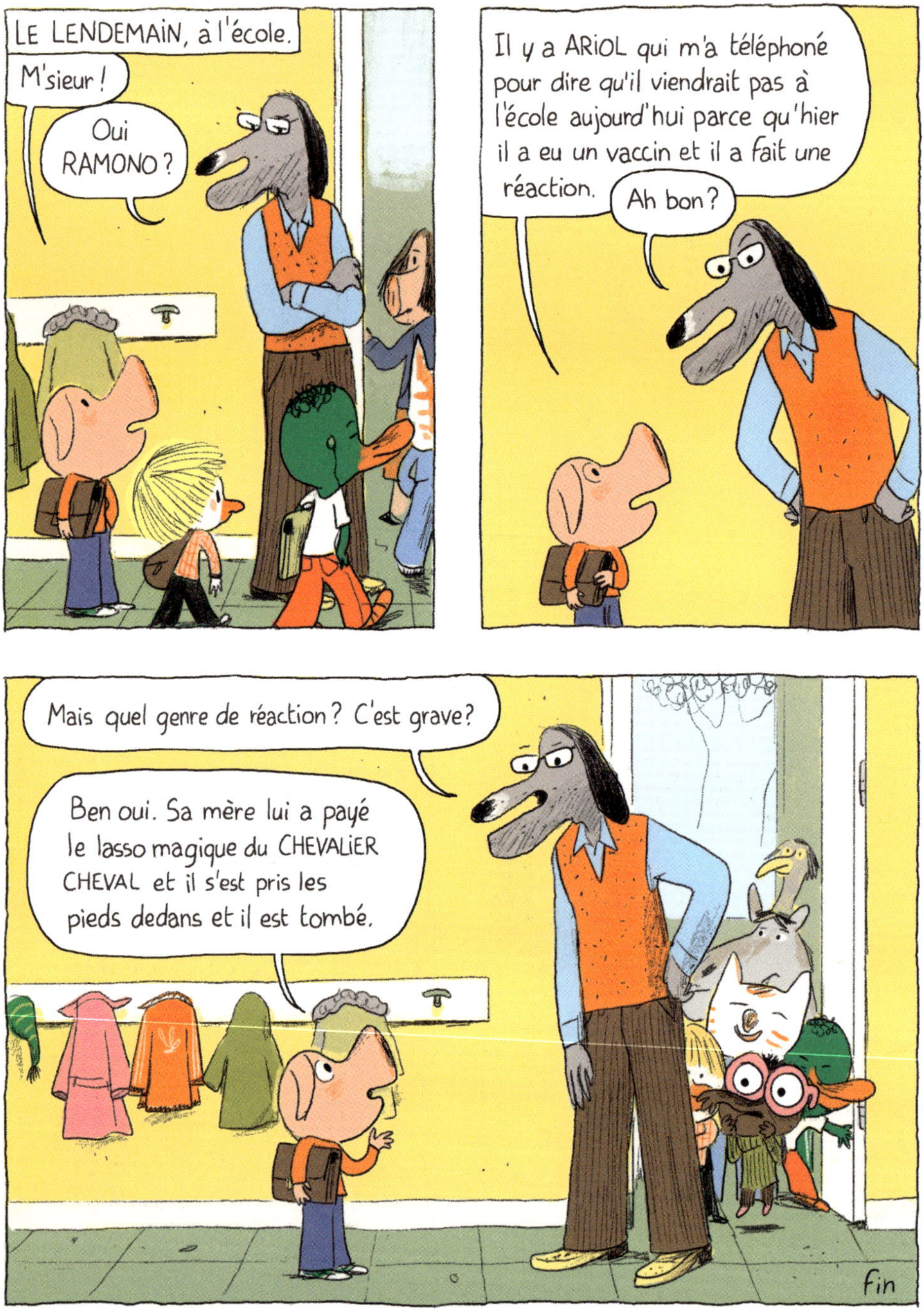
LE LENDEMAIN, à l'école.
M'sieur !
Oui RAMONO ?
Il y a ARIOL qui m'a téléphoné pour dire qu'il viendrait pas à l'école aujourd'hui parce qu'hier il a eu un vaccin et il a fait une réaction.
Ah bon ?
Mais quel genre de réaction ? C'est grave ?
Ben oui. Sa mère lui a payé le lasso magique du CHEVALIER CHEVAL et il s'est pris les pieds dedans et il est tombé.
fin

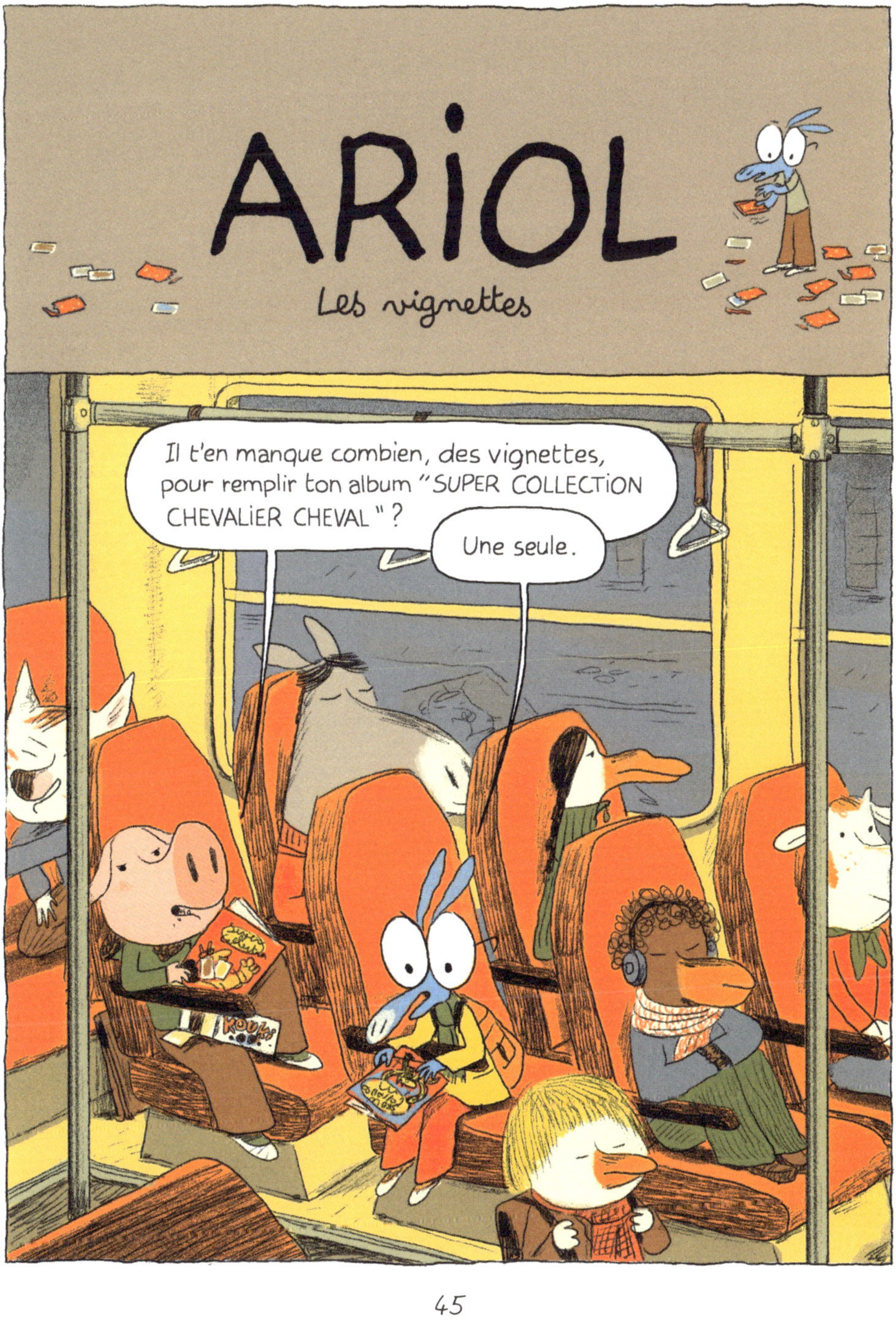
ARiOL
Les vignettes
Il t'en manque combien, des vignettes, pour remplir ton album "SUPER COLLECTiON CHEVALiER CHEVAL" ?
Une seule.

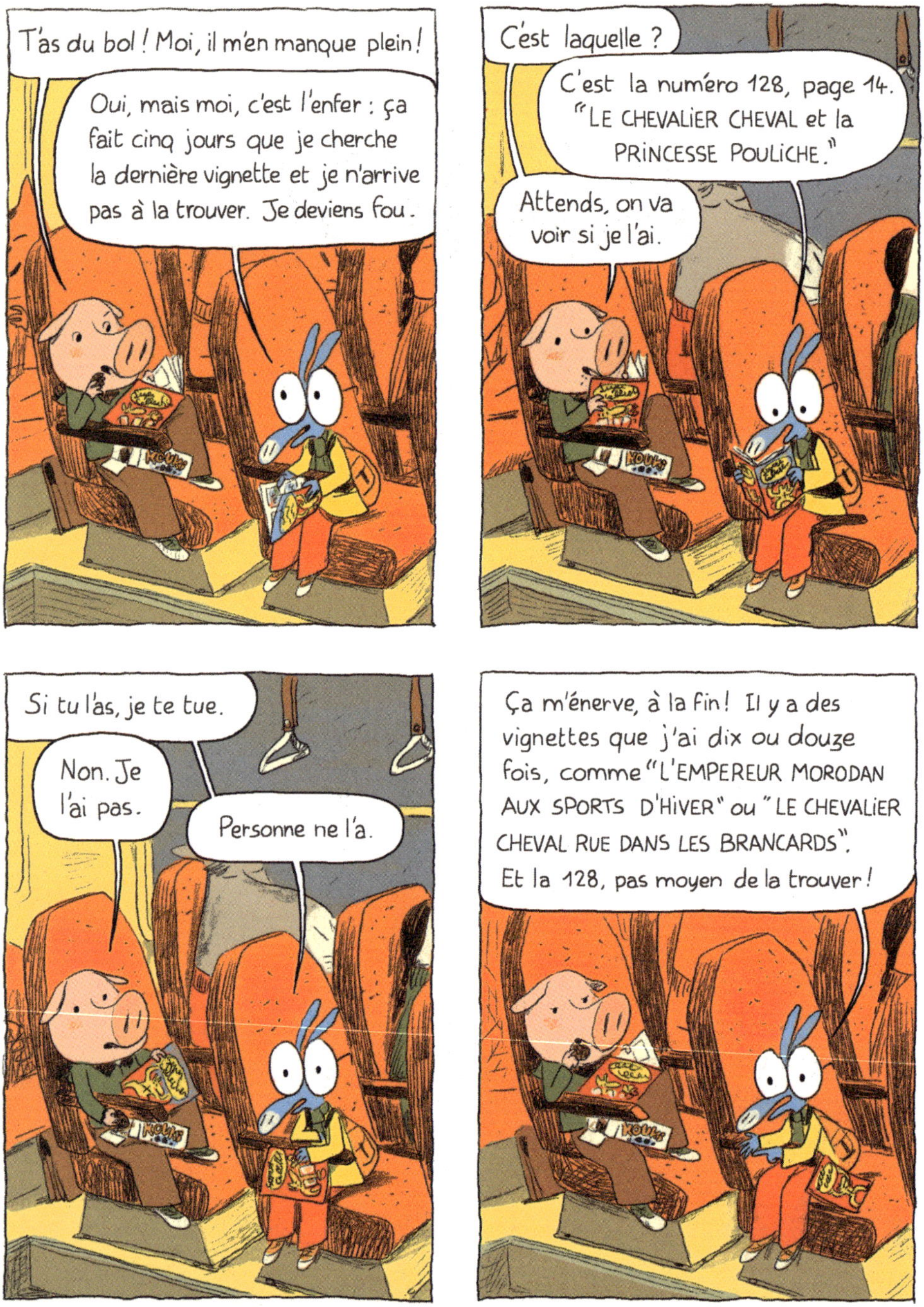
T'as du bol ! Moi, il m'en manque plein !
Oui, mais moi, c'est l'enfer : ça fait cinq jours que je cherche la dernière vignette et je n'arrive pas à la trouver. Je deviens fou.
C'est laquelle ?
C'est la numéro 128, page 14. "LE CHEVALIER CHEVAL et la PRINCESSE POULICHE."
Attends, on va voir si je l'ai.
Si tu l'as, je te tue.
Non. Je l'ai pas.
Personne ne l'a.
Ça m'énerve, à la fin ! Il y a des vignettes que j'ai dix ou douze fois, comme "L'EMPEREUR MORODAN AUX SPORTS D'HIVER" ou "LE CHEVALIER CHEVAL RUE DANS LES BRANCARDS". Et la 128, pas moyen de la trouver !

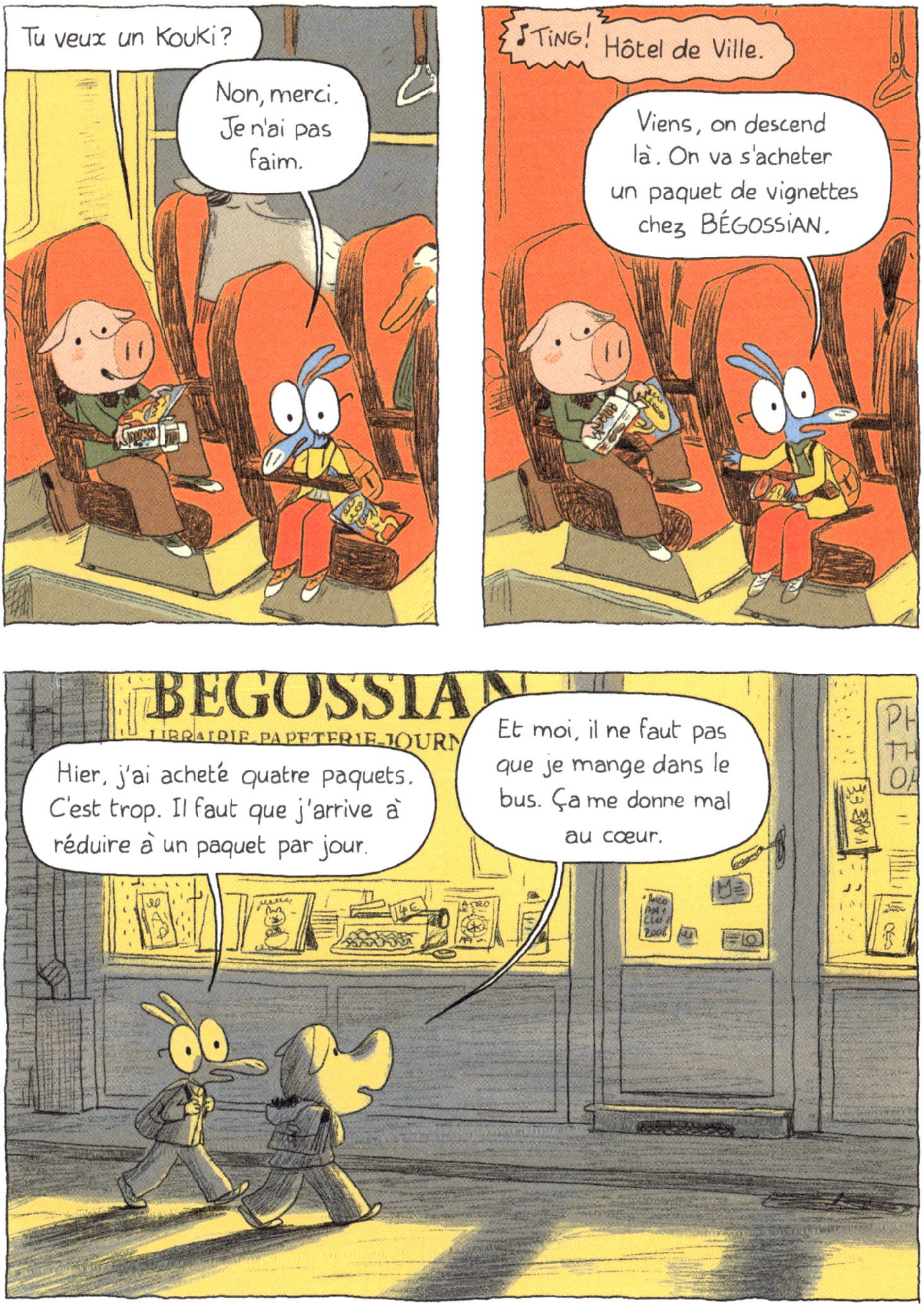
Tu veux un Kouki?
Non, merci. Je n'ai pas faim.
TING!
Hôtel de Ville.
Viens, on descend là. On va s'acheter un paquet de vignettes chez BÉGOSSIAN.
BEGOSSIAN
LIBRAIRIE-PAPETERIE-JOURN
Hier, j'ai acheté quatre paquets. C'est trop. Il faut que j'arrive à réduire à un paquet par jour.
Et moi, il ne faut pas que je mange dans le bus. Ça me donne mal au cœur.

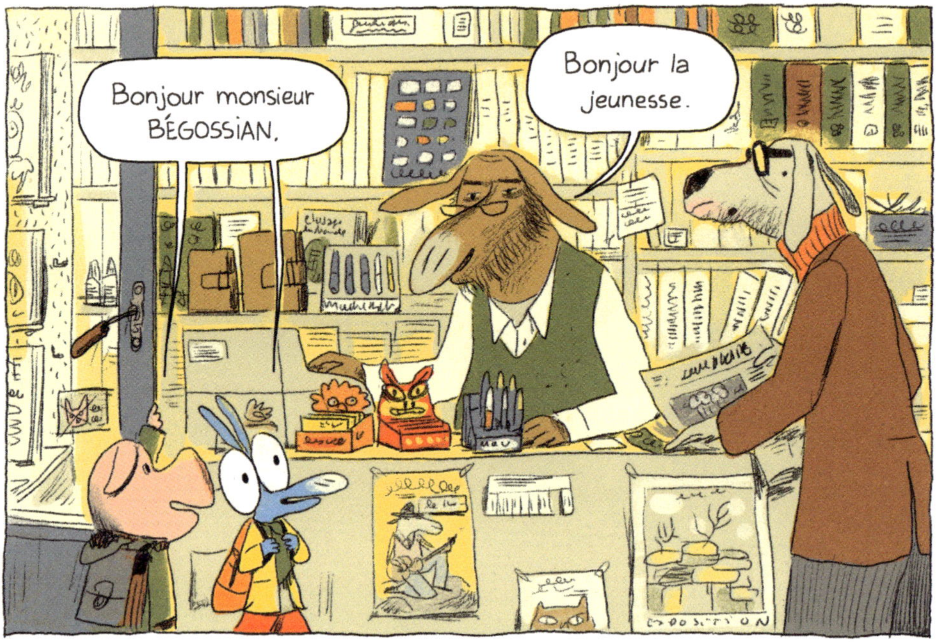
Bonjour monsieur BÉGOSSIAN.
Bonjour la jeunesse.

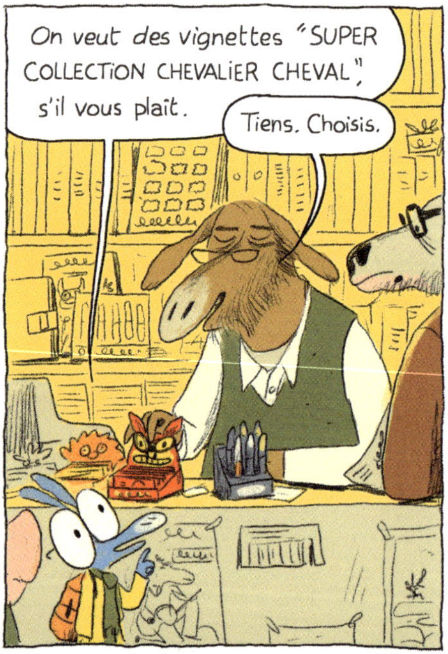
On veut des vignettes "SUPER COLLECTION CHEVALIER CHEVAL", s'il vous plaît.
Tiens. Choisis.

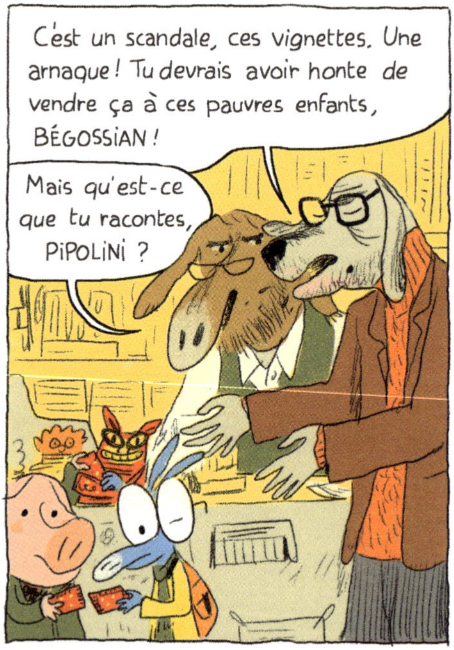
C'est un scandale, ces vignettes. Une arnaque ! Tu devrais avoir honte de vendre ça à ces pauvres enfants, BÉGOSSIAN !
Mais qu'est-ce que tu racontes, PIPOLINI ?

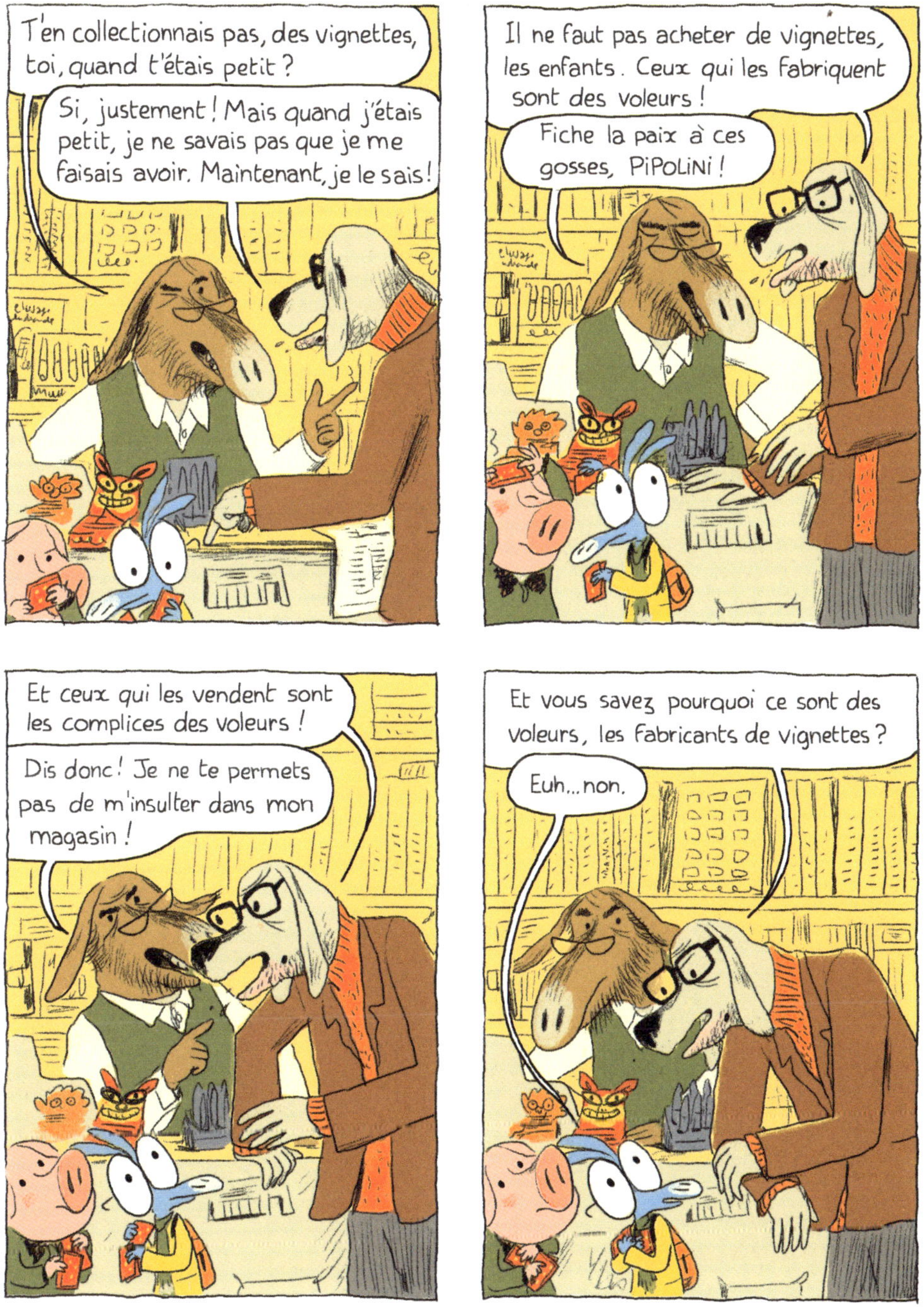

T'en collectionnais pas, des vignettes, toi, quand t'étais petit ?
Si, justement ! Mais quand j'étais petit, je ne savais pas que je me faisais avoir. Maintenant, je le sais !
Il ne faut pas acheter de vignettes, les enfants. Ceux qui les fabriquent sont des voleurs !
Fiche la paix à ces gosses, PIPOLINI !
Et ceux qui les vendent sont les complices des voleurs !
Dis donc ! Je ne te permets pas de m'insulter dans mon magasin !
Et vous savez pourquoi ce sont des voleurs, les fabricants de vignettes ?
Euh... non.

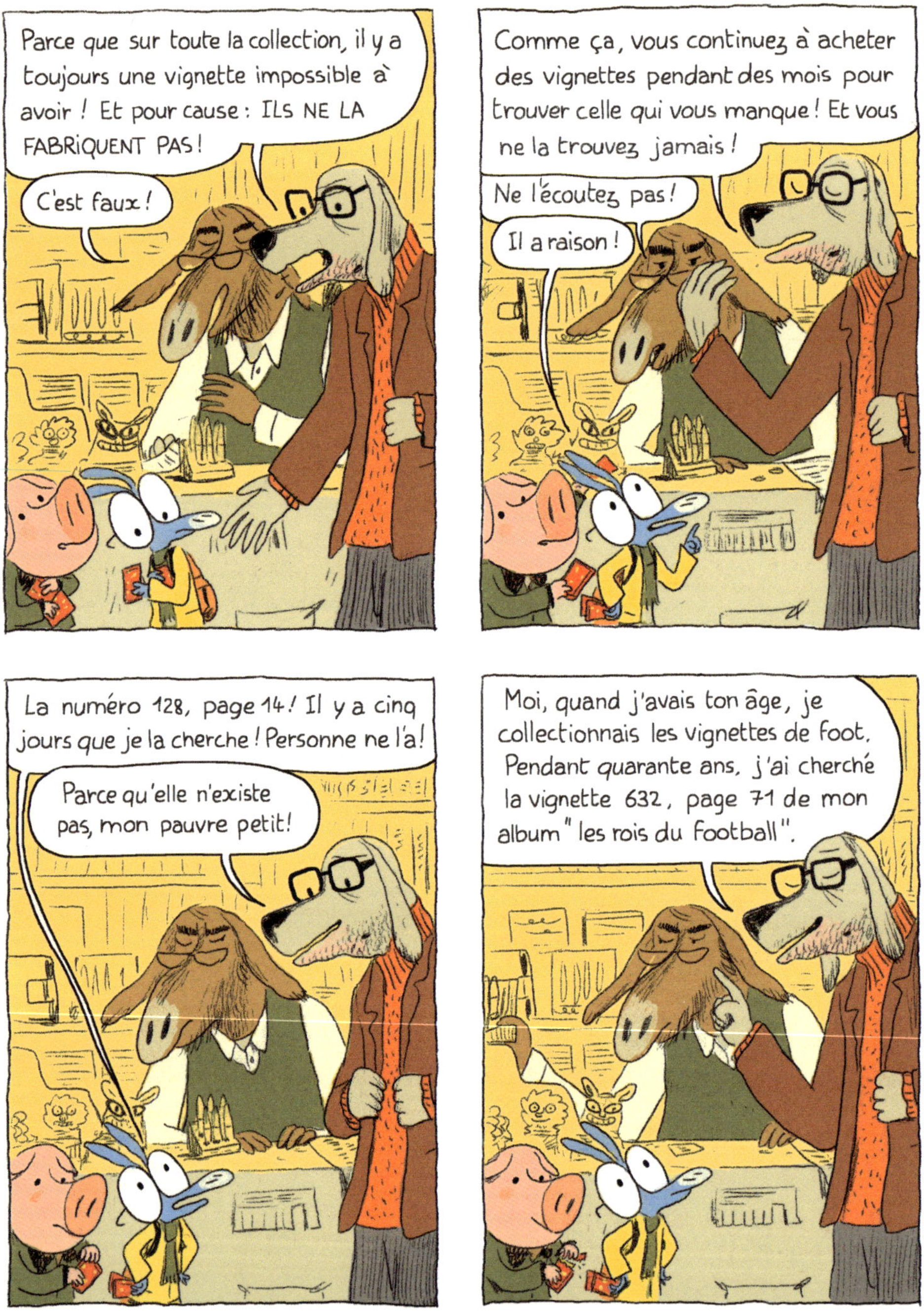
Parce que sur toute la collection, il y a toujours une vignette impossible à avoir ! Et pour cause : ILS NE LA FABRIQUENT PAS !
C'est faux !
Comme ça, vous continuez à acheter des vignettes pendant des mois pour trouver celle qui vous manque ! Et vous ne la trouvez jamais !
Ne l'écoutez pas !
Il a raison !
La numéro 128, page 14 ! Il y a cinq jours que je la cherche ! Personne ne l'a !
Parce qu'elle n'existe pas, mon pauvre petit !
Moi, quand j'avais ton âge, je collectionnais les vignettes de foot. Pendant quarante ans, j'ai cherché la vignette 632, page 71 de mon album "les rois du football".

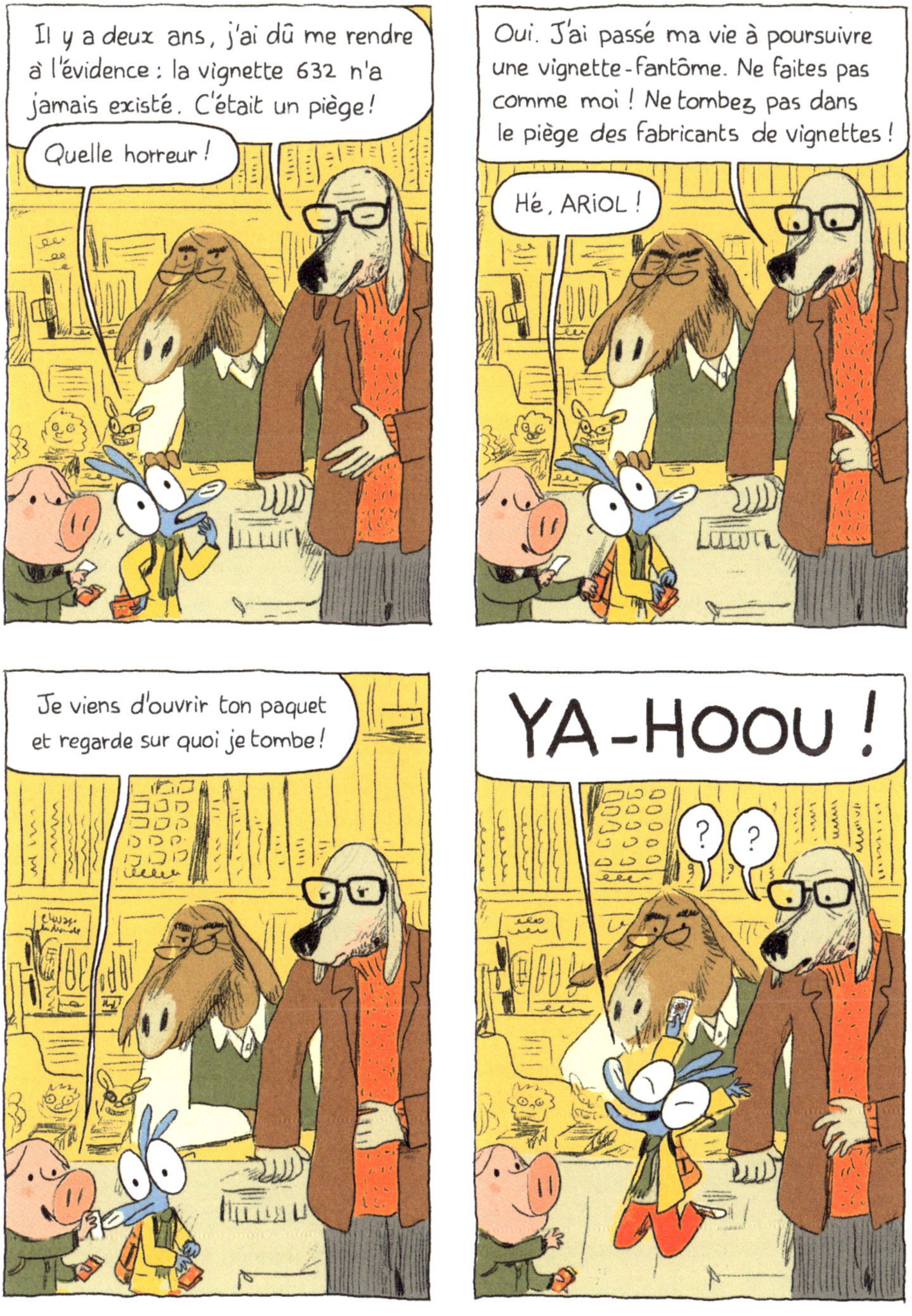
Il y a deux ans, j'ai dû me rendre à l'évidence : la vignette 632 n'a jamais existé. C'était un piège !
Quelle horreur !
Oui. J'ai passé ma vie à poursuivre une vignette-fantôme. Ne faites pas comme moi ! Ne tombez pas dans le piège des fabricants de vignettes !
Hé, ARIOL !
Je viens d'ouvrir ton paquet et regarde sur quoi je tombe !
YA-HOOU !
?
?

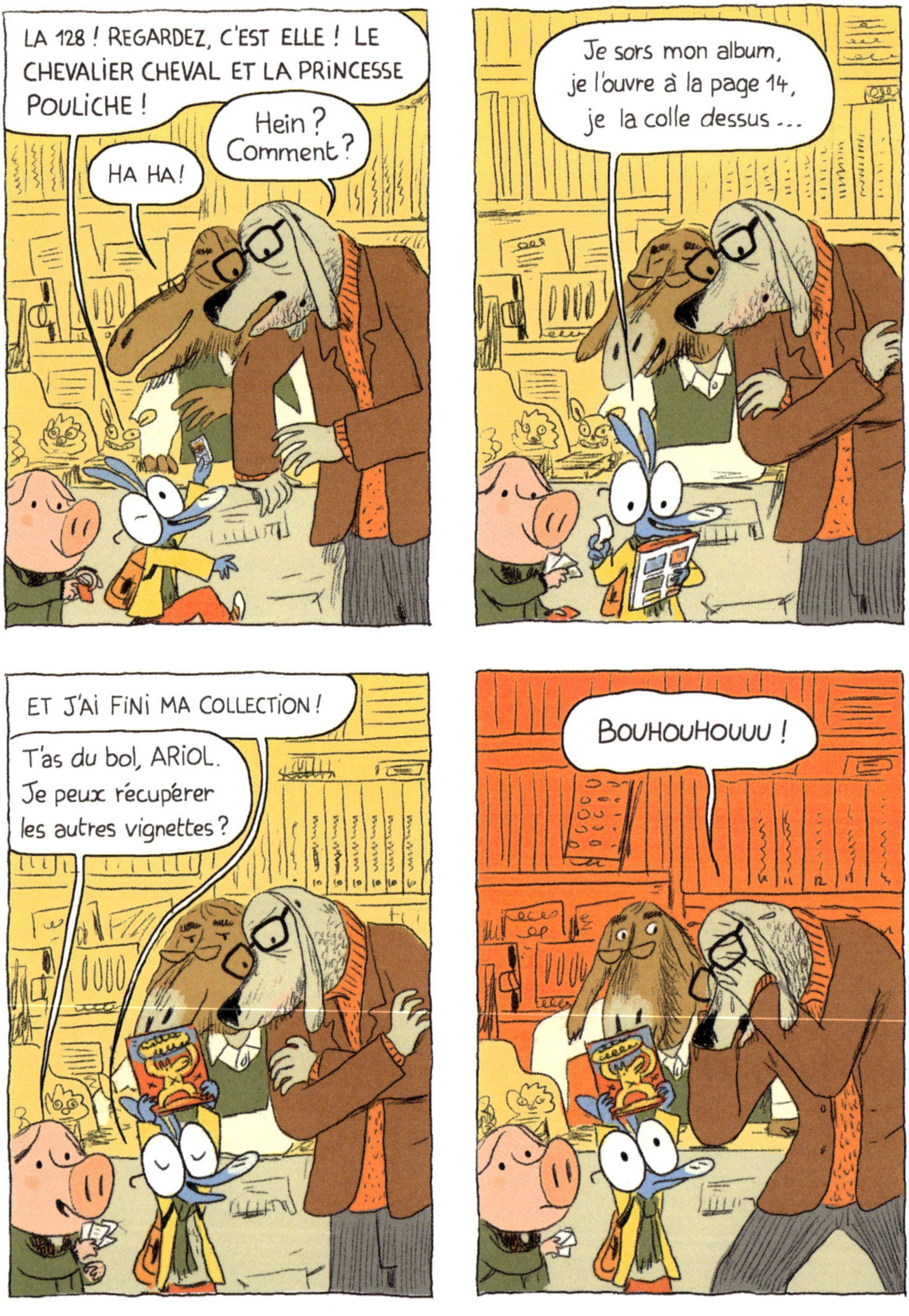
LA 128 ! REGARDEZ, C'EST ELLE ! LE CHEVALIER CHEVAL ET LA PRINCESSE POULICHE !
HA HA !
Hein ? Comment ?
Je sors mon album, je l'ouvre à la page 14, je la colle dessus ...
ET J'AI FINI MA COLLECTION !
T'as du bol, ARIOL. Je peux récupérer les autres vignettes ?
BOUHOUHOUUU !

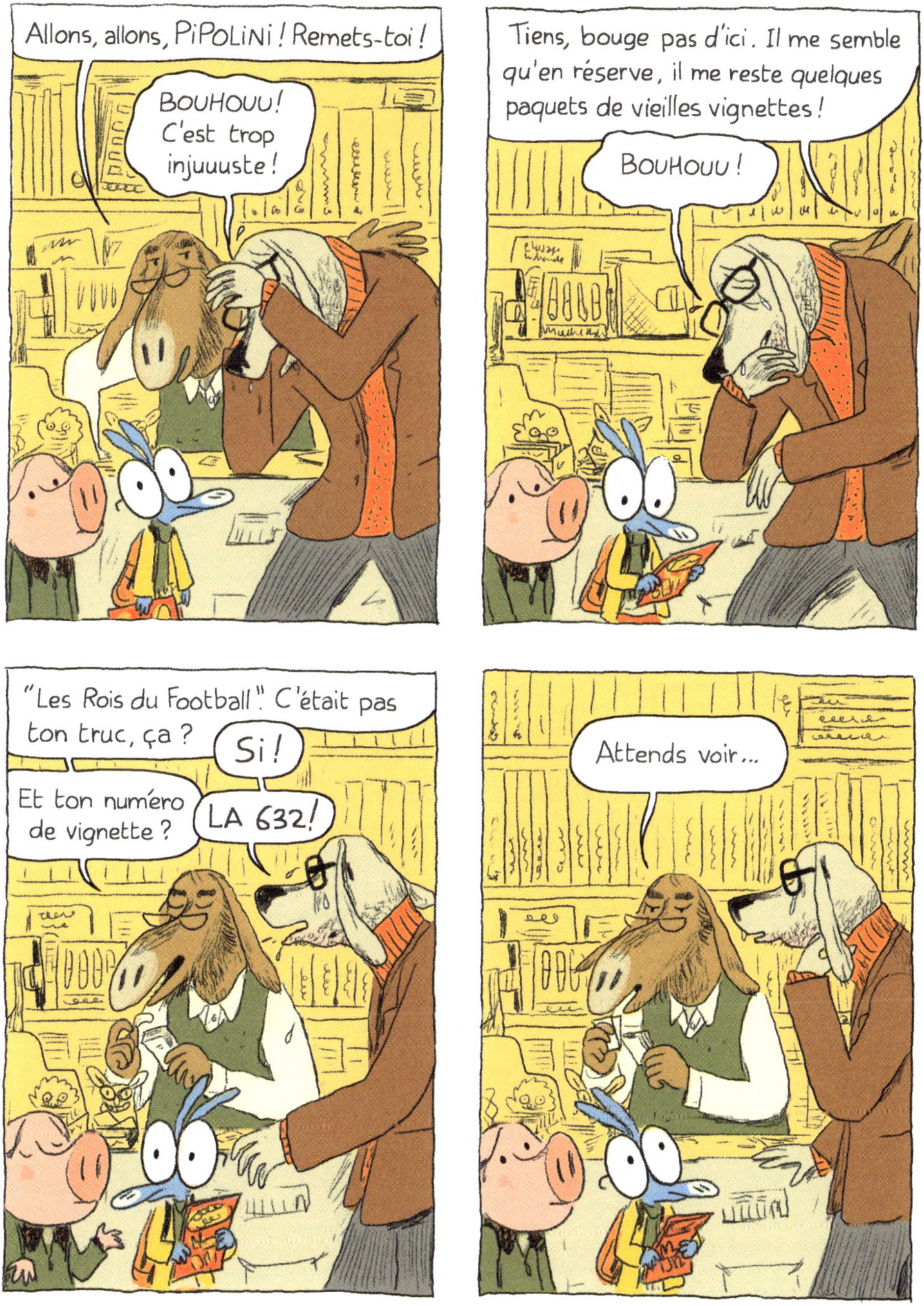
Allons, allons, PIPOLINI ! Remets-toi !
BOUHOUU ! C'est trop injuuuste !
Tiens, bouge pas d'ici. Il me semble qu'en réserve, il me reste quelques paquets de vieilles vignettes !
BOUHOUU !
"Les Rois du Football". C'était pas ton truc, ça ?
Si !
Et ton numéro de vignette ?
LA 632 !
Attends voir...

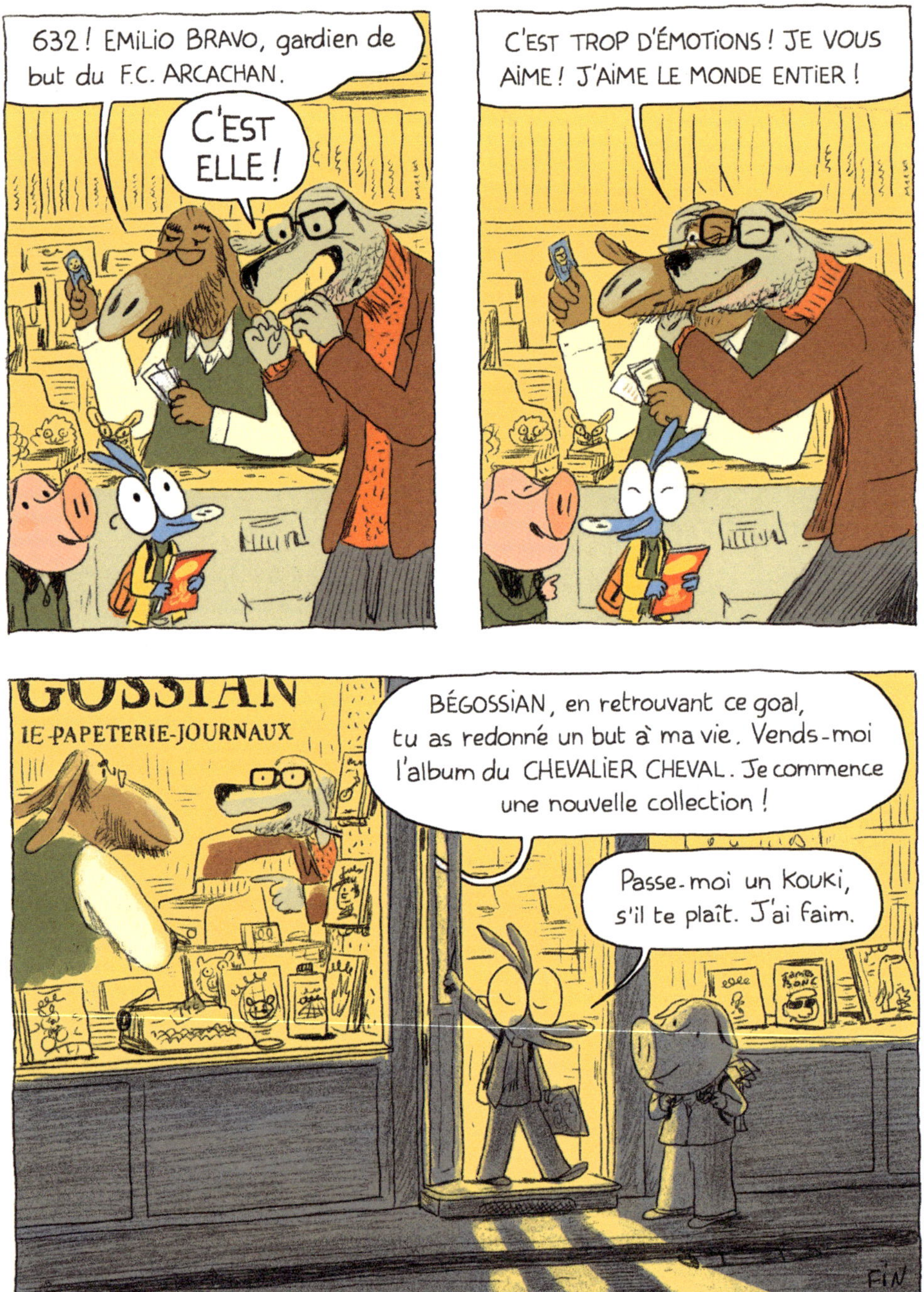
632 ! EMILIO BRAVO, gardien de but du F.C. ARCACHAN.
C'EST ELLE !
C'EST TROP D'ÉMOTIONS ! JE VOUS AIME ! J'AIME LE MONDE ENTIER !
GOSSIAN
IE-PAPETERIE-JOURNAUX
BÉGOSSIAN, en retrouvant ce goal, tu as redonné un but à ma vie. Vends-moi l'album du CHEVALIER CHEVAL. Je commence une nouvelle collection !
Passe-moi un KOUKI, s'il te plaît. J'ai faim.
FIN

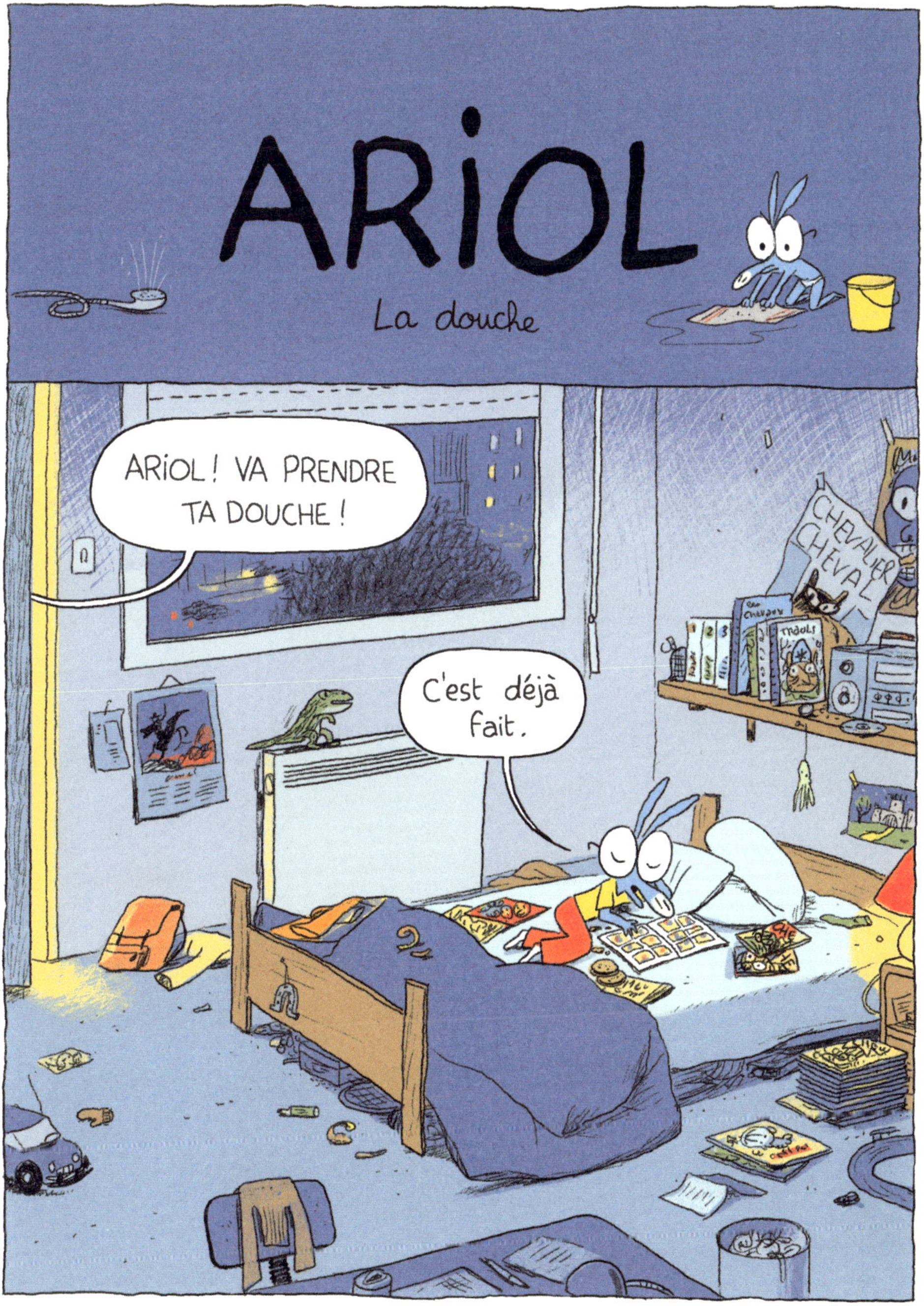
ARiOL
La douche
ARiOL! VA PRENDRE TA DOUCHE!
C'est déjà fait.
CHEVALIER CHEVAL

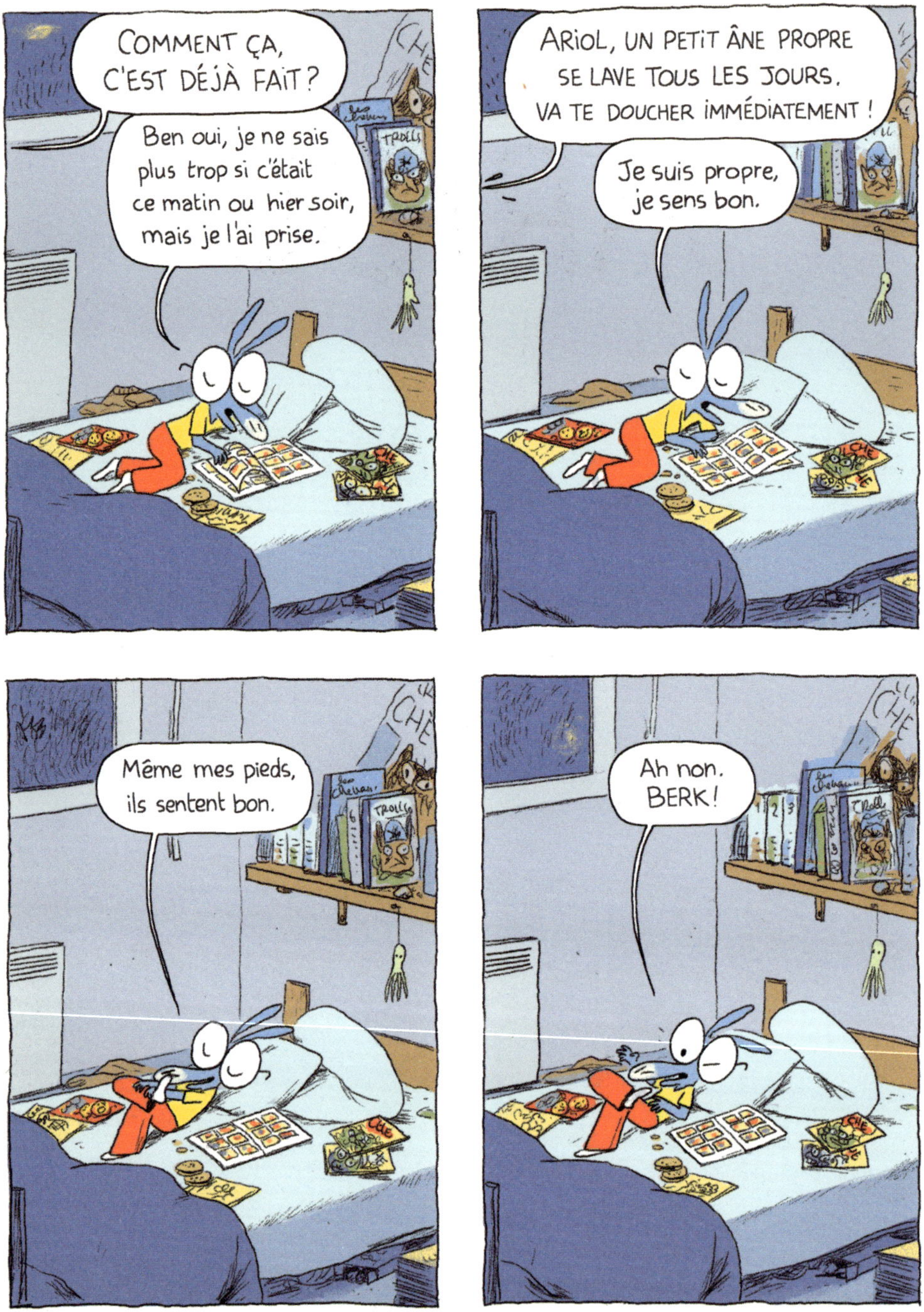
COMMENT ÇA, C'EST DÉJÀ FAIT ?
Ben oui, je ne sais plus trop si c'était ce matin ou hier soir, mais je l'ai prise.
ARIOL, UN PETIT ÂNE PROPRE SE LAVE TOUS LES JOURS. VA TE DOUCHER IMMÉDIATEMENT !
Je suis propre, je sens bon.
Même mes pieds, ils sentent bon.
Ah non. BERK !

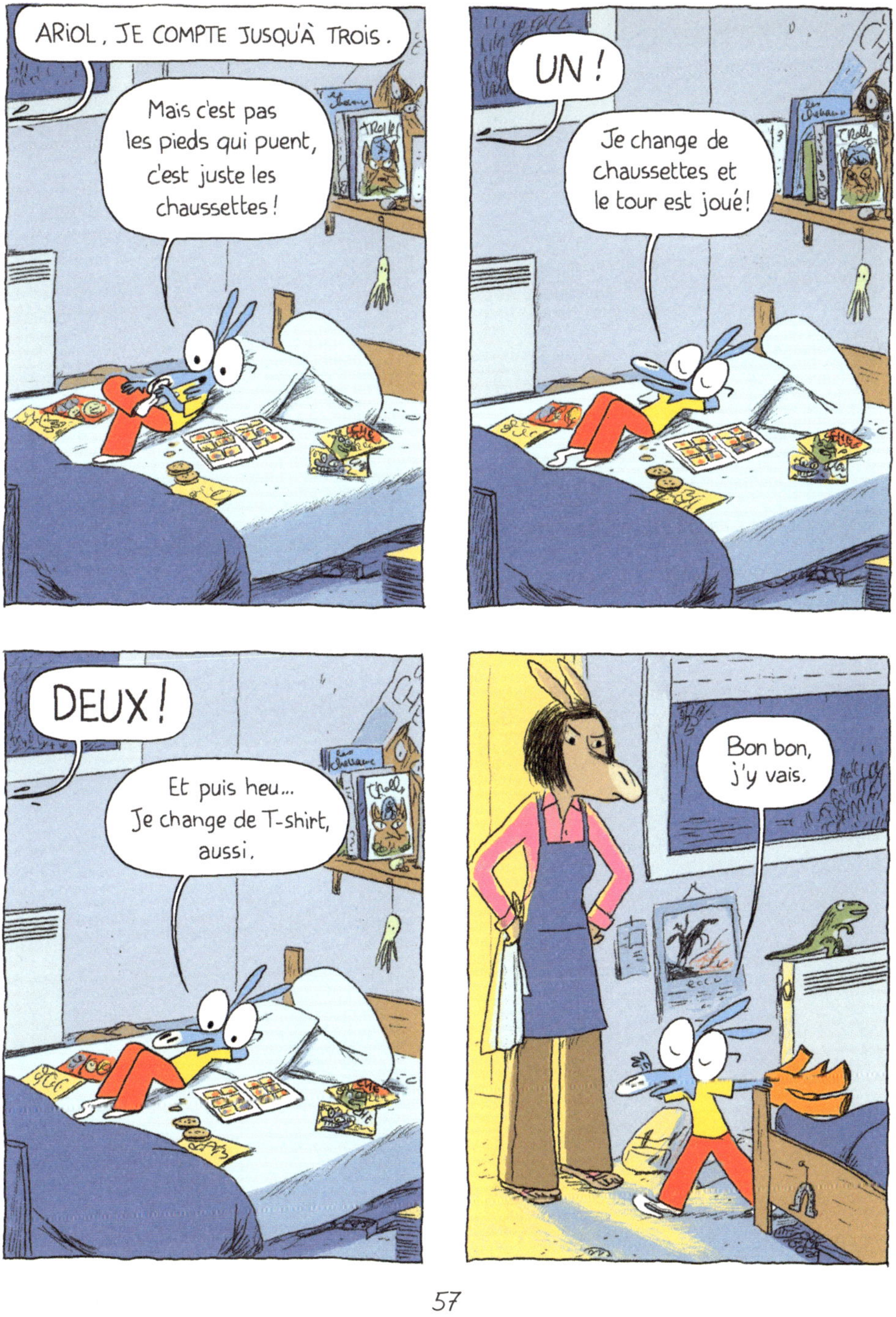
ARIOL, JE COMPTE JUSQU'À TROIS.
Mais c'est pas les pieds qui puent, c'est juste les chaussettes !
UN !
Je change de chaussettes et le tour est joué !
DEUX !
Et puis heu... Je change de T-shirt, aussi.
Bon bon, j'y vais.

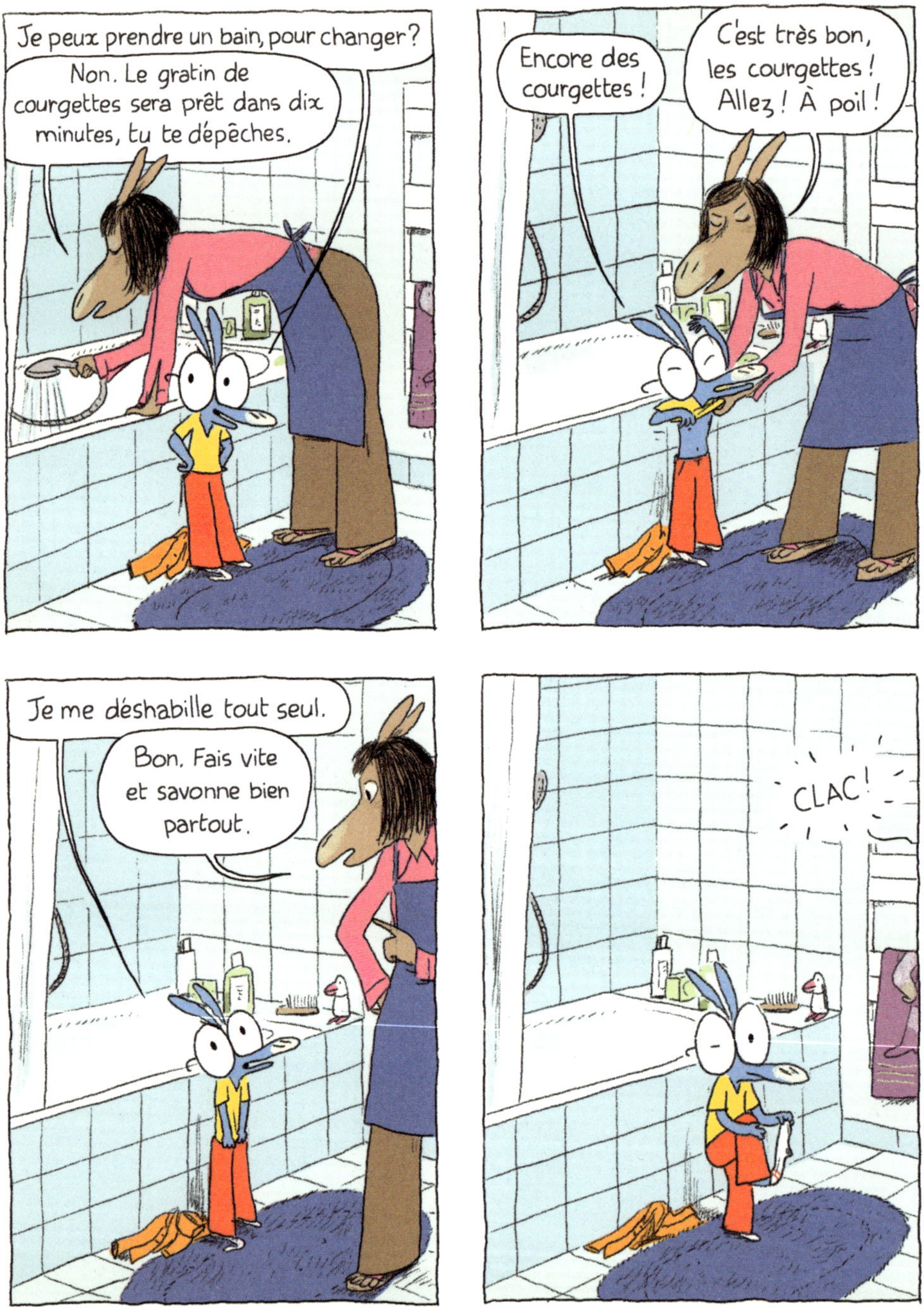
Je peux prendre un bain, pour changer?
Non. Le gratin de courgettes sera prêt dans dix minutes, tu te dépêches.
Encore des courgettes !
C'est très bon, les courgettes ! Allez ! À poil !
Je me déshabille tout seul.
Bon. Fais vite et savonne bien partout.
CLAC !

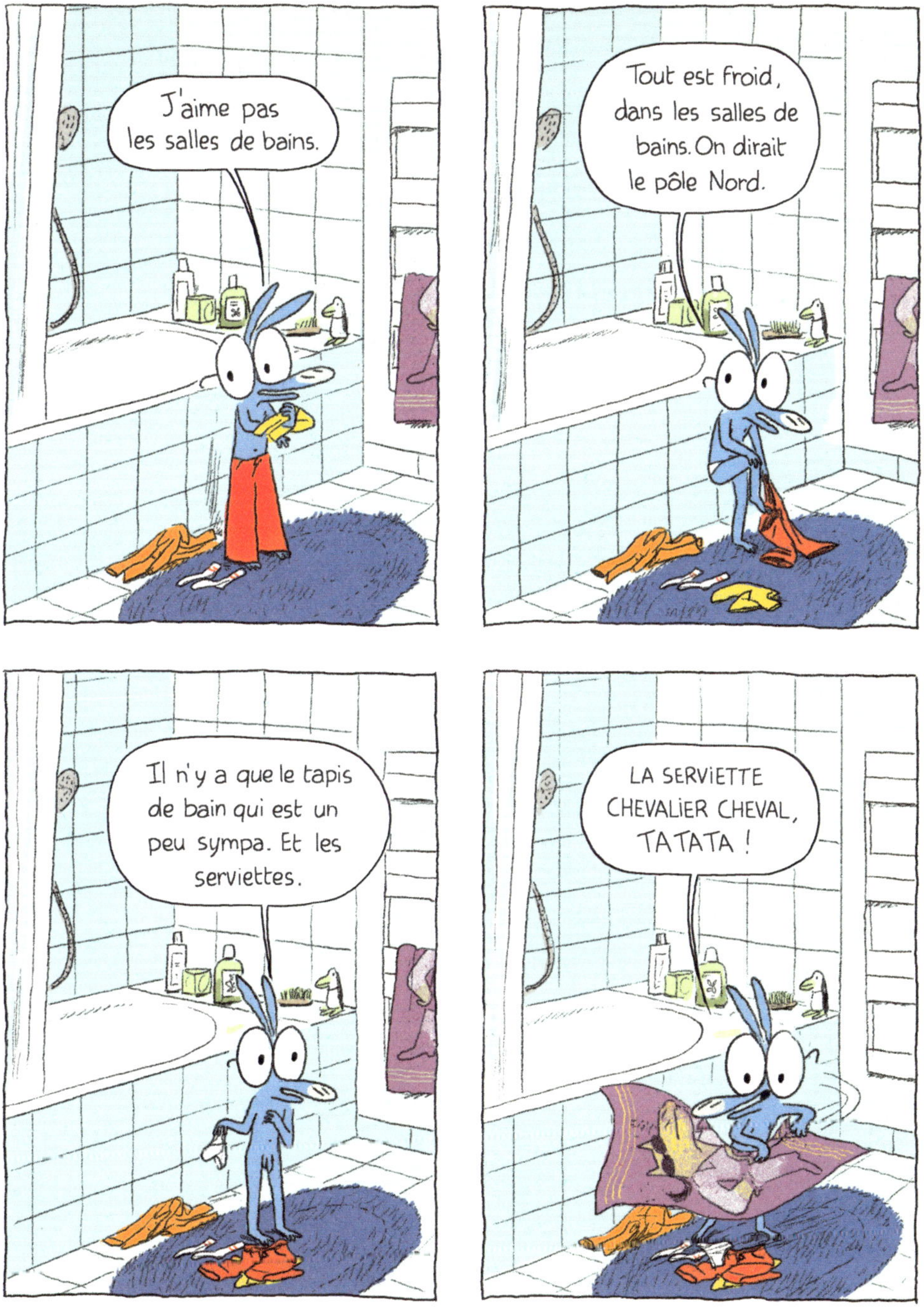
J'aime pas
les salles de bains.
Tout est froid, dans les salles de bains. On dirait le pôle Nord.
Il n'y a que le tapis de bain qui est un peu sympa. Et les serviettes.
LA SERVIETTE CHEVALIER CHEVAL, TATATA !

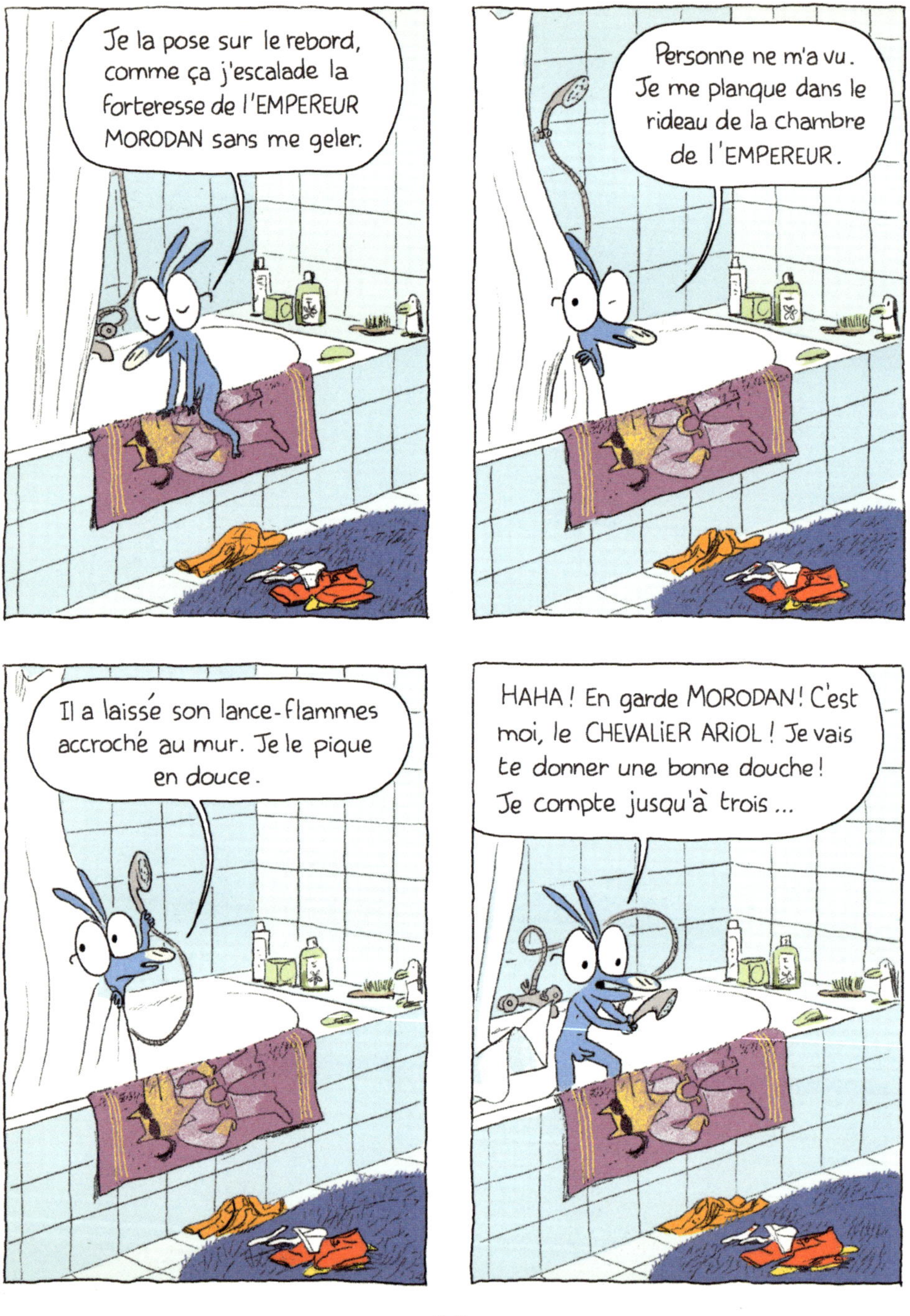
Je la pose sur le rebord, comme ça j'escalade la forteresse de l'EMPEREUR MORODAN sans me geler.
Personne ne m'a vu. Je me planque dans le rideau de la chambre de l'EMPEREUR.
Il a laissé son lance-flammes accroché au mur. Je le pique en douce.
HAHA ! En garde MORODAN ! C'est moi, le CHEVALIER ARIOL ! Je vais te donner une bonne douche ! Je compte jusqu'à trois ...

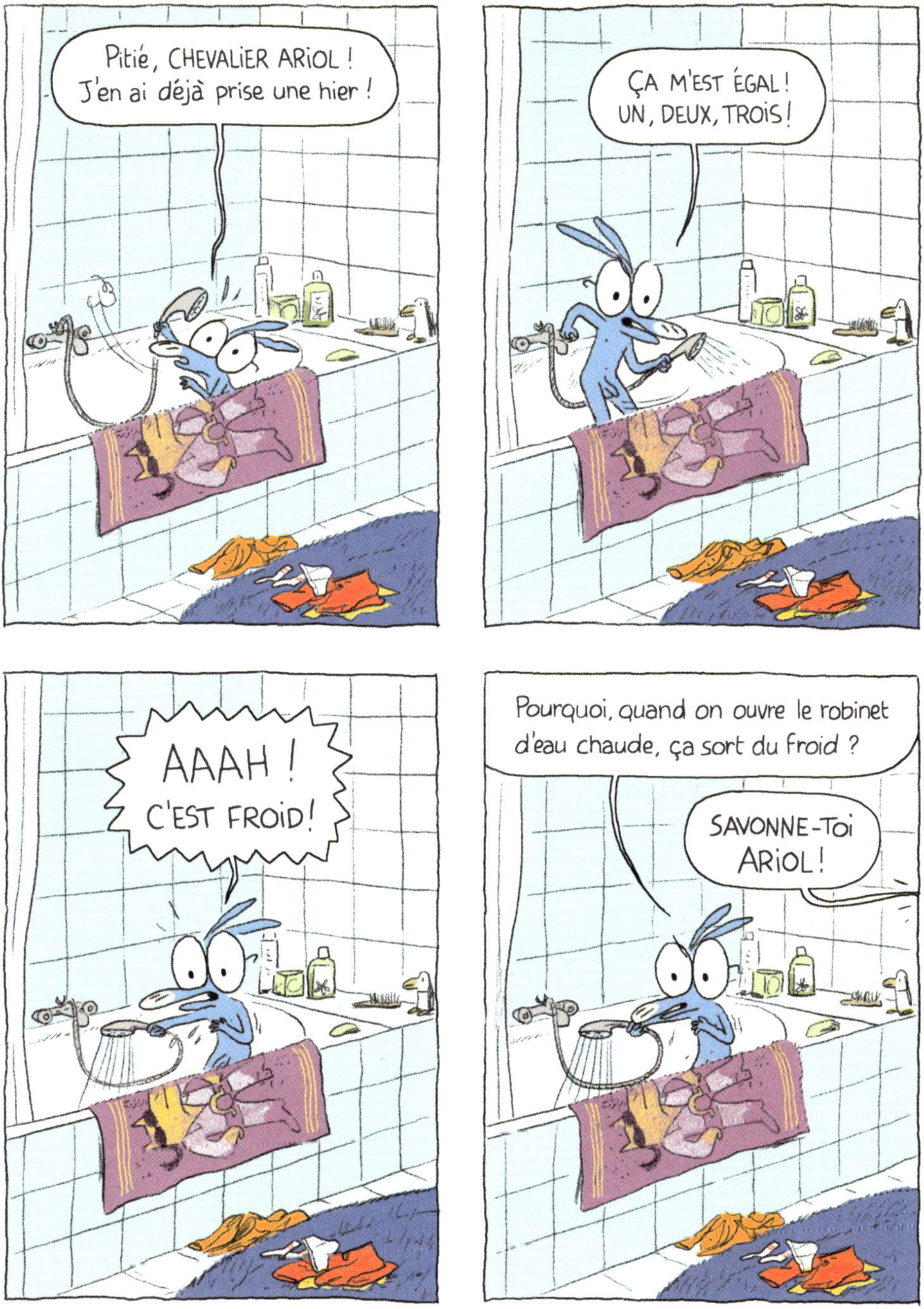
Pitié, CHEVALIER ARiOL ! J'en ai déjà prise une hier !
ÇA M'EST ÉGAL ! UN, DEUX, TROiS !
AAAH ! C'EST FROiD !
Pourquoi, quand on ouvre le robinet d'eau chaude, ça sort du froid ?
SAVONNE-Toi ARiOL !

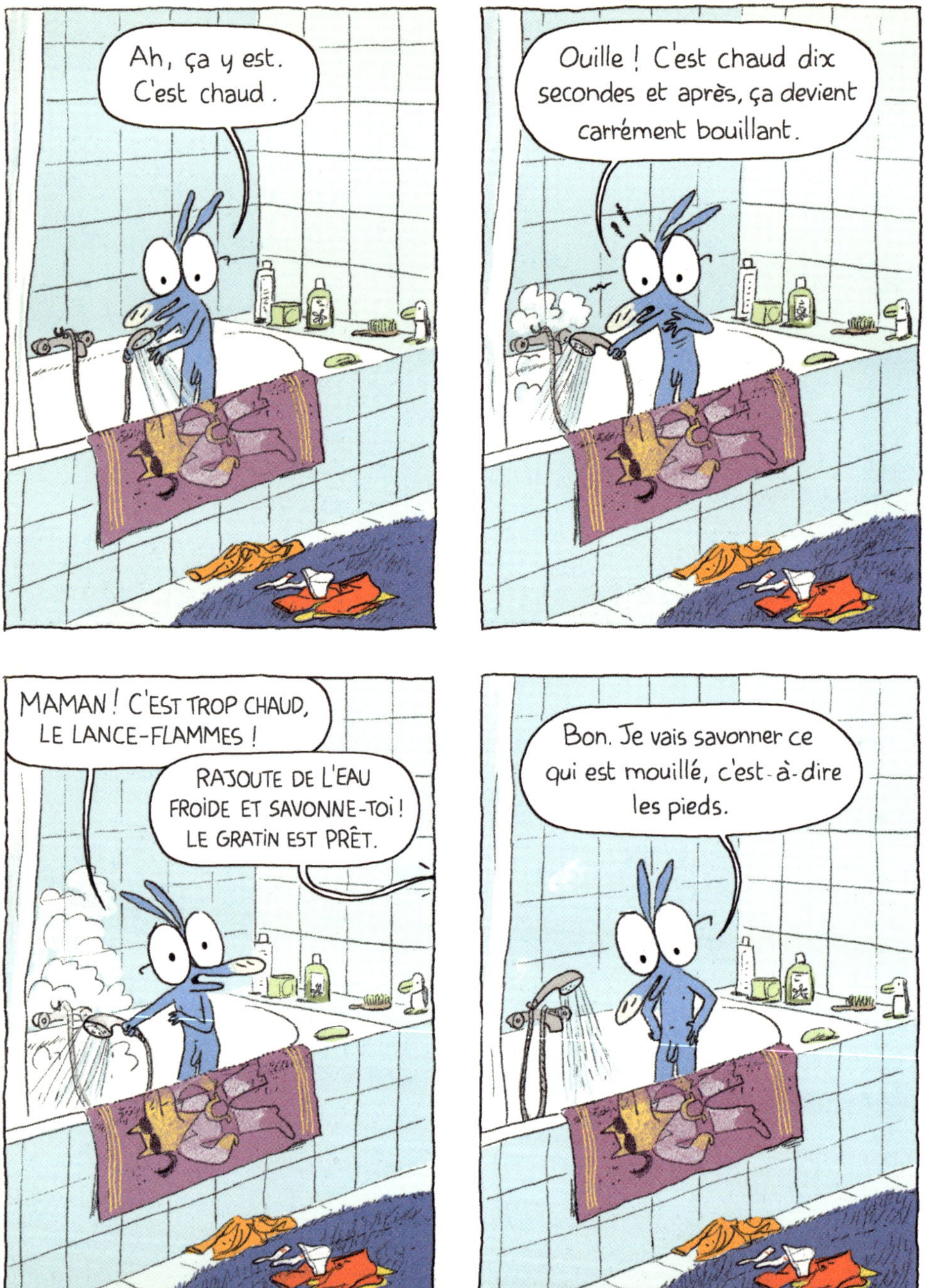
Ah, ça y est. C'est chaud.
Ouille ! C'est chaud dix secondes et après, ça devient carrément bouillant.
MAMAN ! C'EST TROP CHAUD, LE LANCE-FLAMMES !
RAJOUTE DE L'EAU FROIDE ET SAVONNE-TOI ! LE GRATIN EST PRÊT.
Bon. Je vais savonner ce qui est mouillé, c'est-à-dire les pieds.

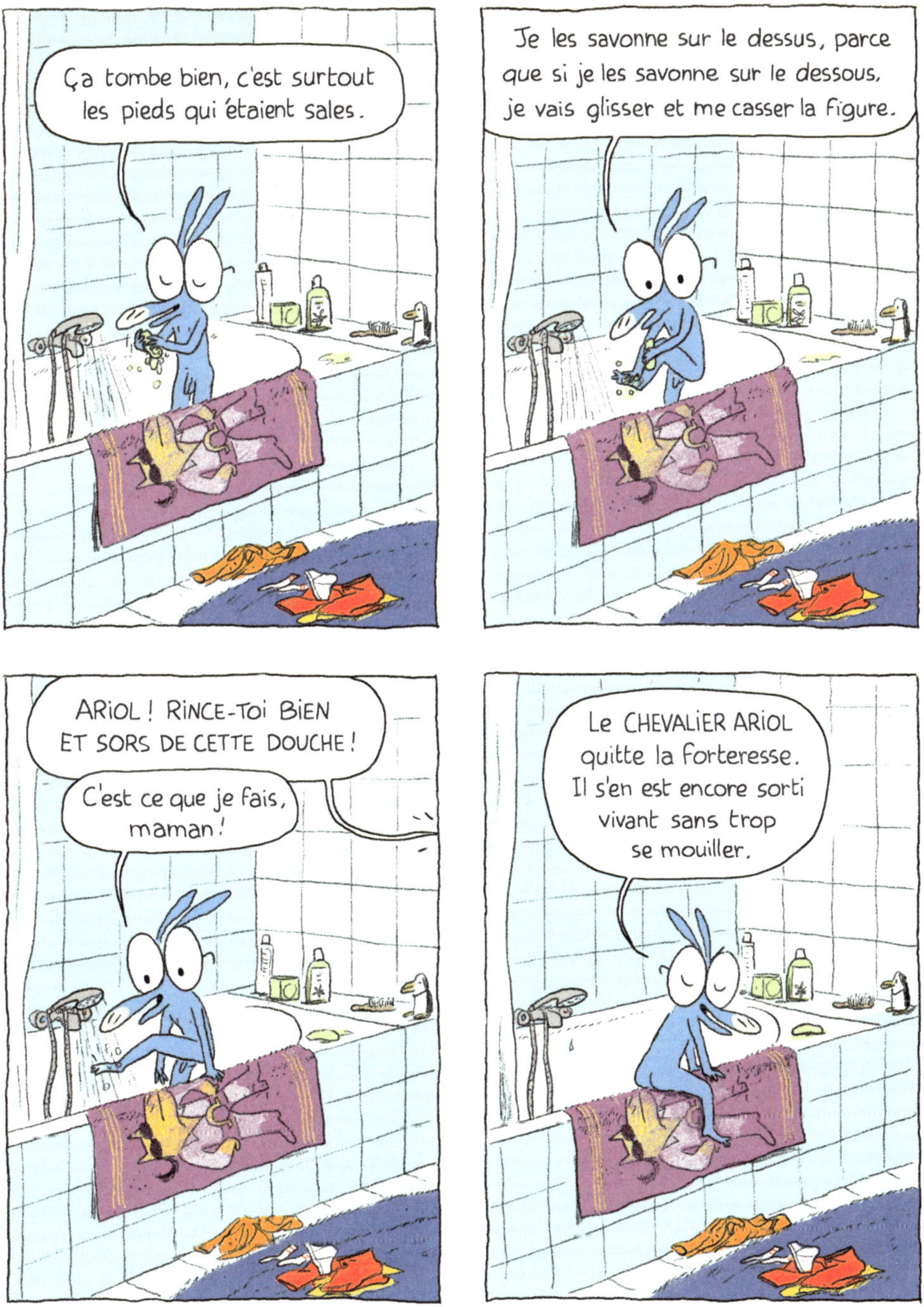
Ça tombe bien, c'est surtout les pieds qui étaient sales.
Je les savonne sur le dessus, parce que si je les savonne sur le dessous, je vais glisser et me casser la figure.
ARIOL ! RINCE-TOI BIEN ET SORS DE CETTE DOUCHE !
C'est ce que je fais, maman !
Le CHEVALIER ARIOL quitte la forteresse. Il s'en est encore sorti vivant sans trop se mouiller.

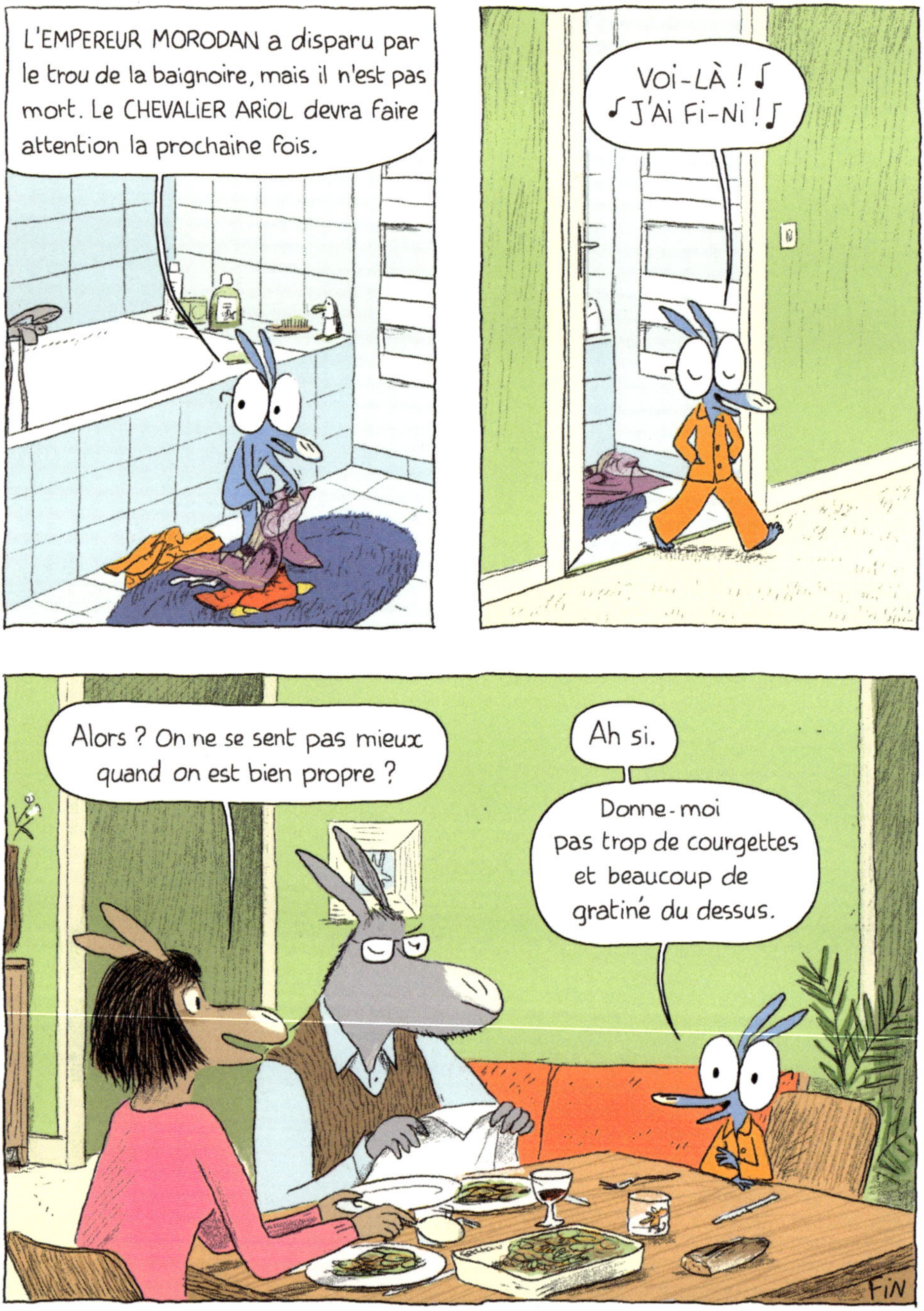
L'EMPEREUR MORODAN a disparu par le trou de la baignoire, mais il n'est pas mort. Le CHEVALIER ARIOL devra faire attention la prochaine fois.
VOI-LÀ ! ♪ ♪ J'AI FI-NI ! ♪
Alors ? On ne se sent pas mieux quand on est bien propre ?
Ah si.
Donne-moi pas trop de courgettes et beaucoup de gratiné du dessus.
FIN

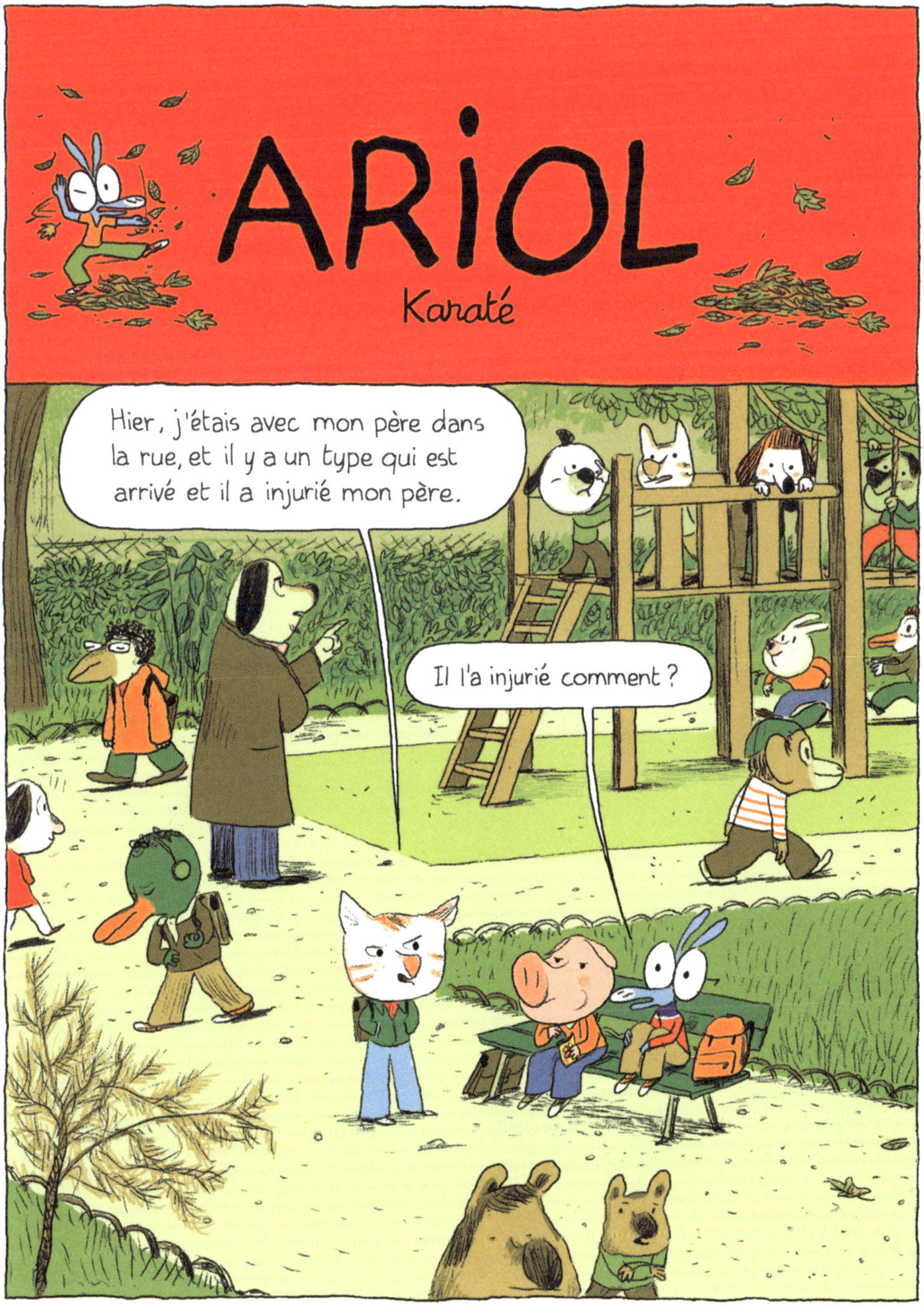
ARIOL
Karaté
Hier, j'étais avec mon père dans la rue, et il y a un type qui est arrivé et il a injurié mon père.
Il l'a injurié comment ?

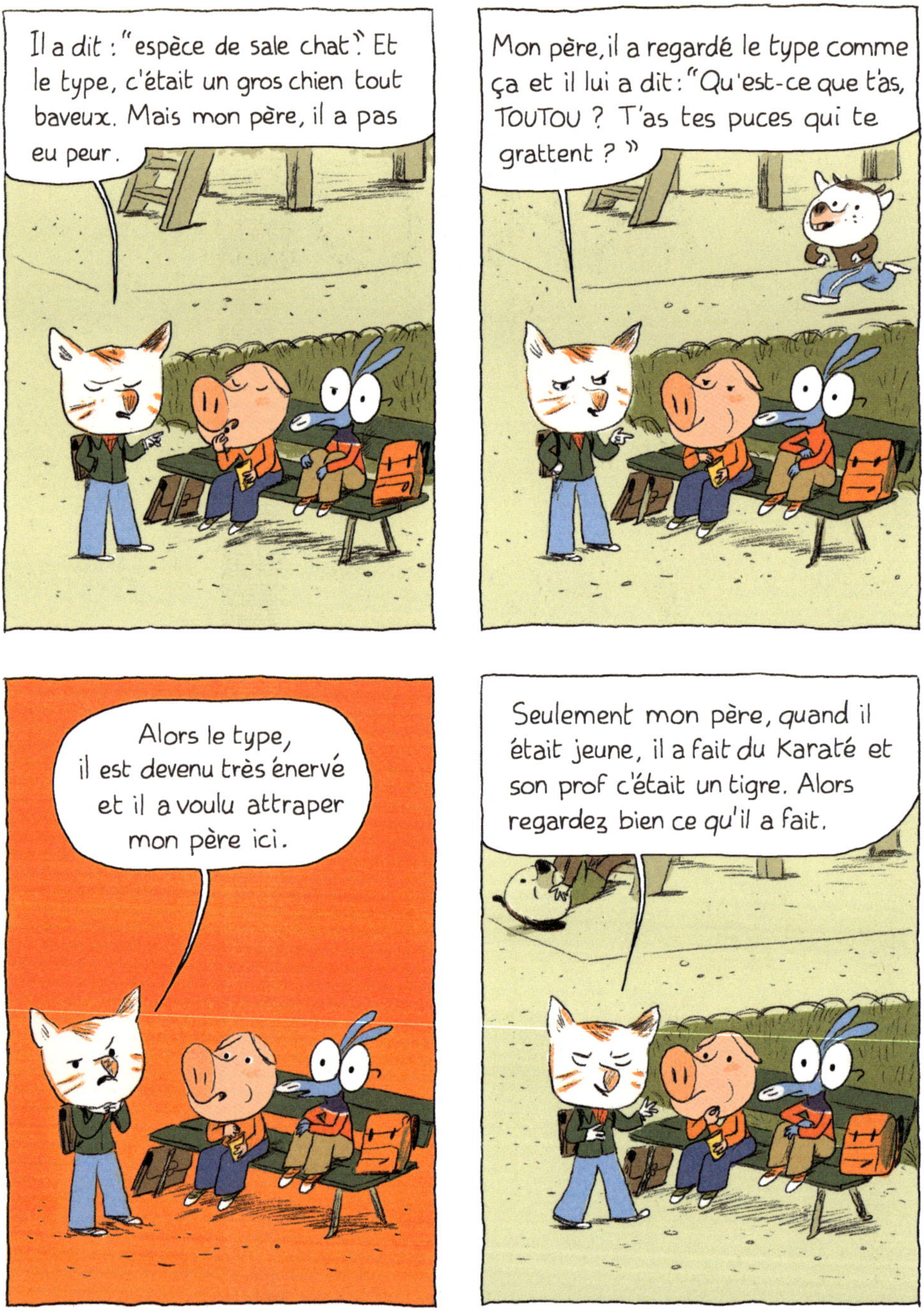
Il a dit : "espèce de sale chat". Et le type, c'était un gros chien tout baveux. Mais mon père, il a pas eu peur.
Mon père, il a regardé le type comme ça et il lui a dit : "Qu'est-ce que t'as, TOUTOU ? T'as tes puces qui te grattent ? »
Alors le type, il est devenu très énervé et il a voulu attraper mon père ici.
Seulement mon père, quand il était jeune, il a fait du Karaté et son prof c'était un tigre. Alors regardez bien ce qu'il a fait.

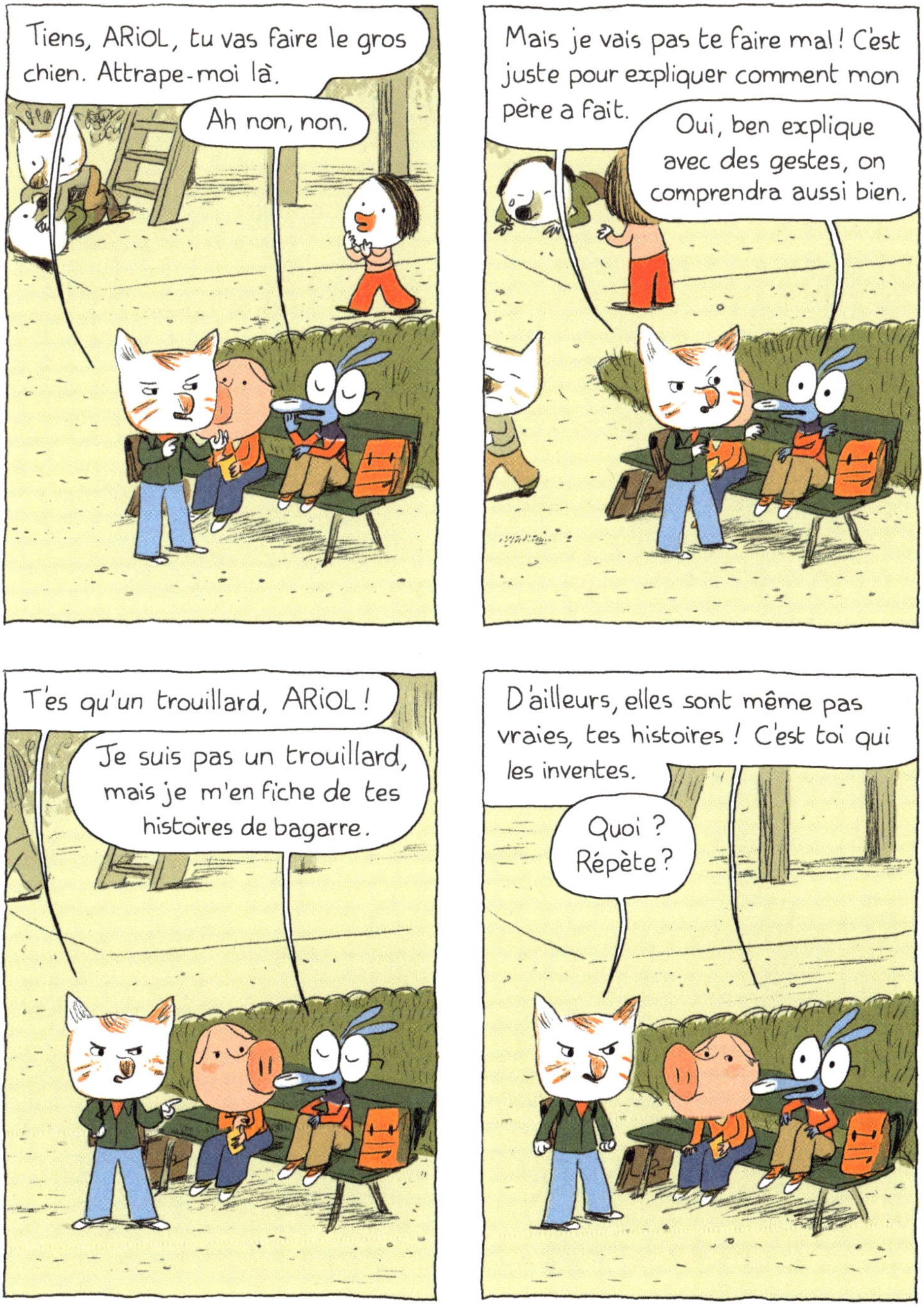
Tiens, ARiOL, tu vas faire le gros chien. Attrape-moi là.
Ah non, non.
Mais je vais pas te faire mal ! C'est juste pour expliquer comment mon père a fait.
Oui, ben explique avec des gestes, on comprendra aussi bien.
T'es qu'un trouillard, ARiOL !
Je suis pas un trouillard, mais je m'en fiche de tes histoires de bagarre.
D'ailleurs, elles sont même pas vraies, tes histoires ! C'est toi qui les inventes.
Quoi ? Répète ?

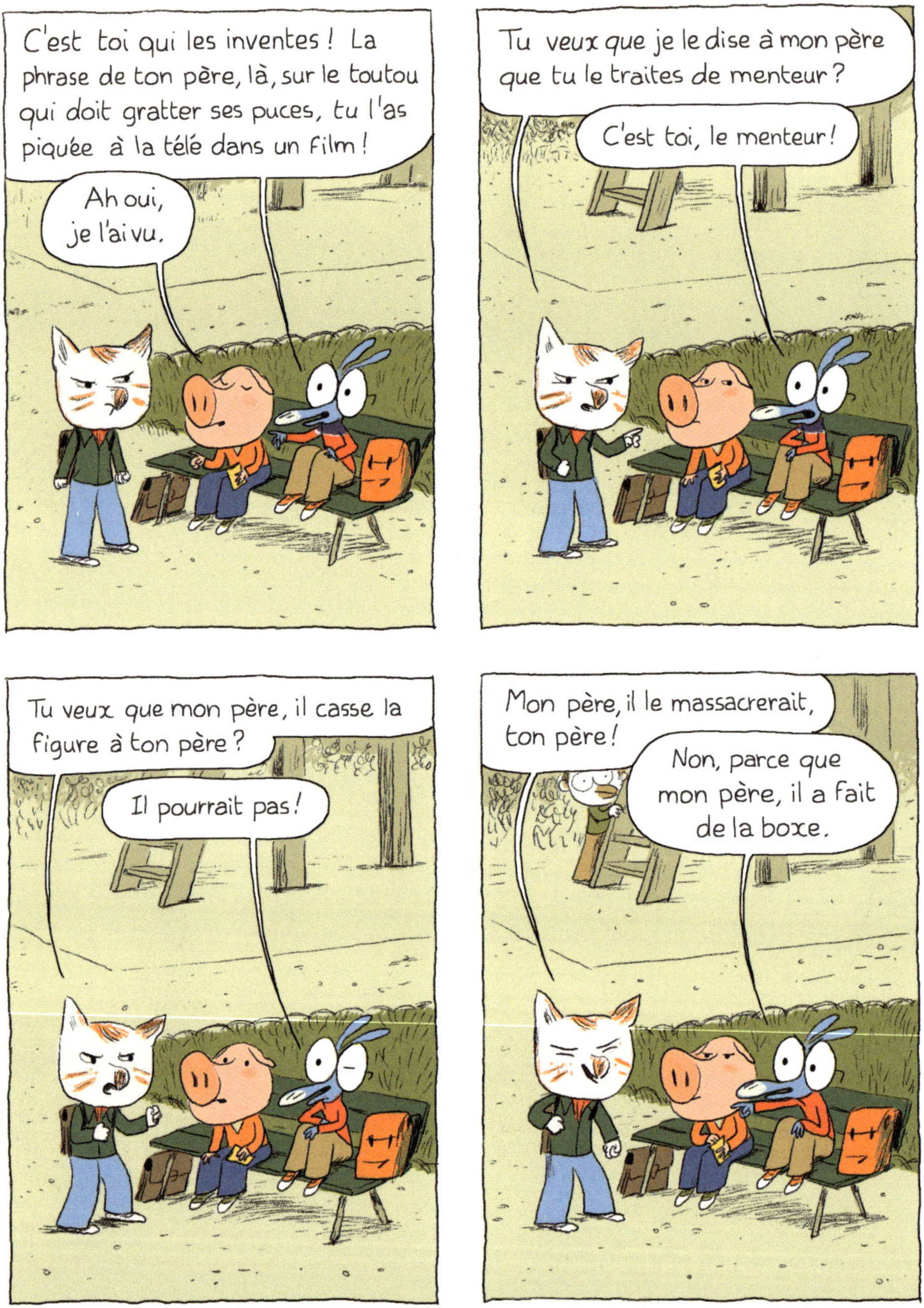
C'est toi qui les inventes ! La phrase de ton père, là, sur le toutou qui doit gratter ses puces, tu l'as piquée à la télé dans un film !
Ah oui, je l'ai vu.
Tu veux que je le dise à mon père que tu le traites de menteur ?
C'est toi, le menteur !
Tu veux que mon père, il casse la figure à ton père ?
Il pourrait pas !
Mon père, il le massacrerait, ton père !
Non, parce que mon père, il a fait de la boxe.

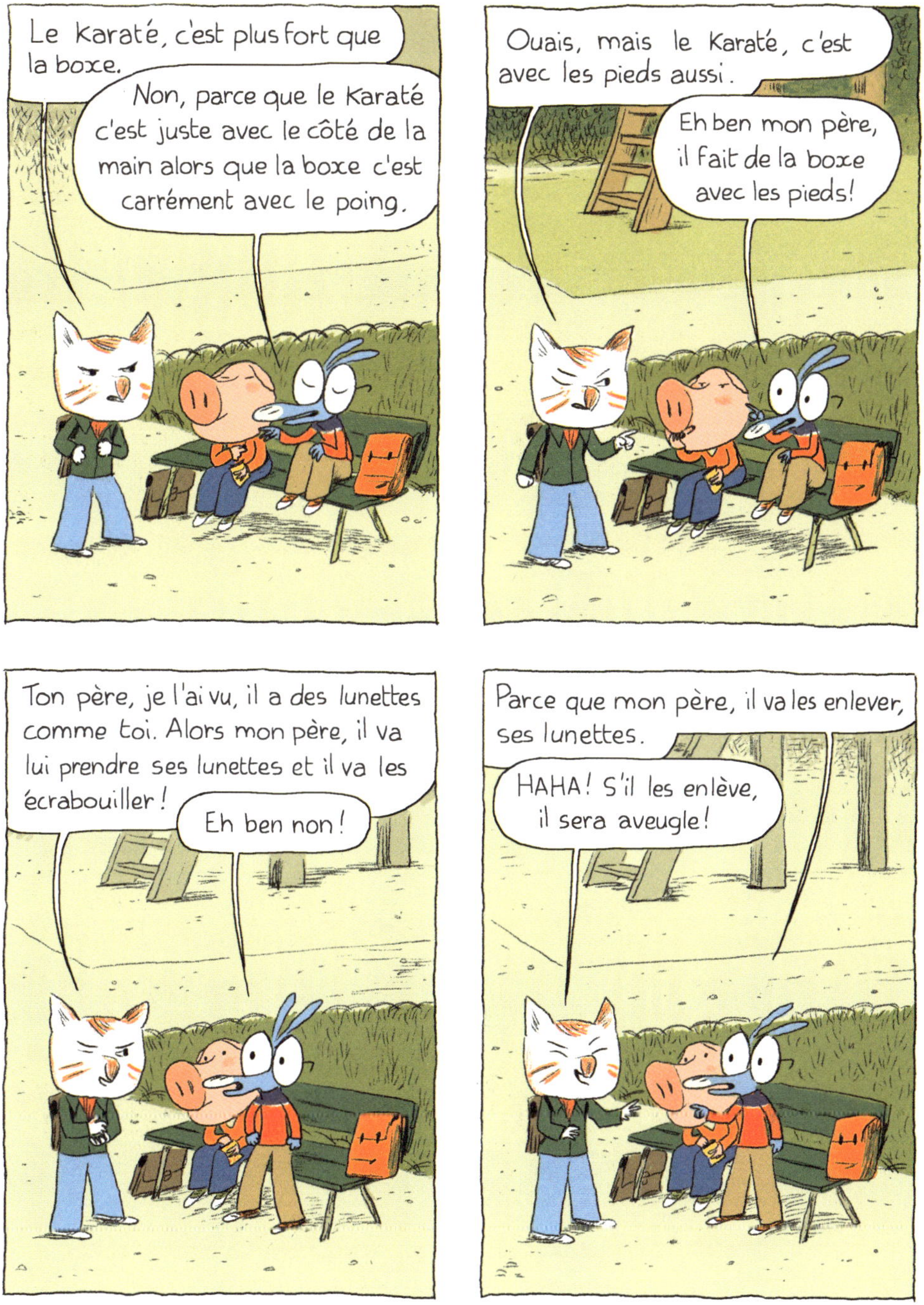
Le Karaté, c'est plus fort que la boxe.
Non, parce que le Karaté c'est juste avec le côté de la main alors que la boxe c'est carrément avec le poing.
Ouais, mais le Karaté, c'est avec les pieds aussi.
Eh ben mon père, il fait de la boxe avec les pieds!
Ton père, je l'ai vu, il a des lunettes comme toi. Alors mon père, il va lui prendre ses lunettes et il va les écrabouiller!
Eh ben non!
Parce que mon père, il va les enlever, ses lunettes.
HAHA! S'il les enlève, il sera aveugle!

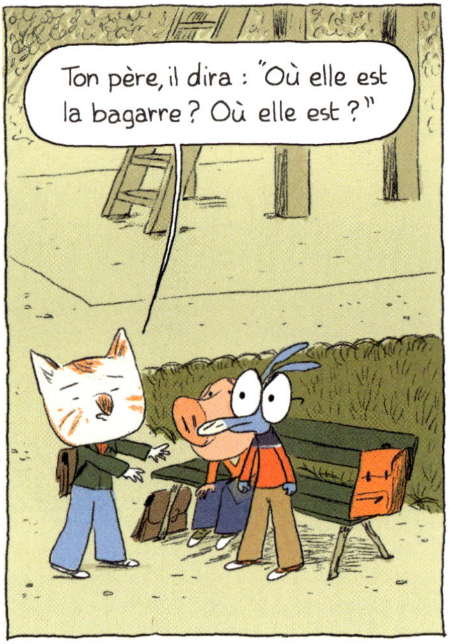
Ton père, il dira : "Où elle est la bagarre ? Où elle est ?"

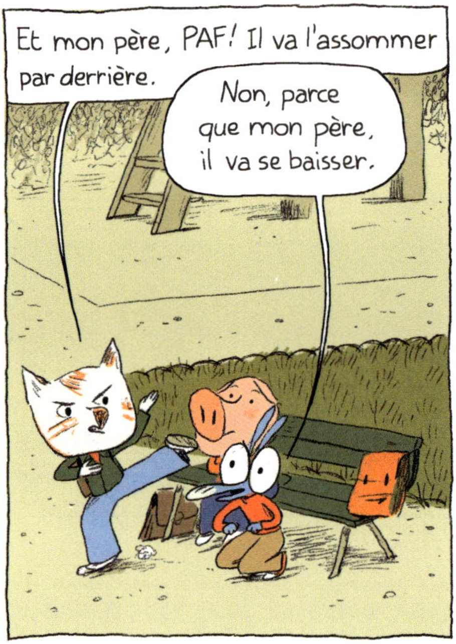
Et mon père, PAF! Il va l'assommer par derrière.
Non, parce que mon père, il va se baisser.

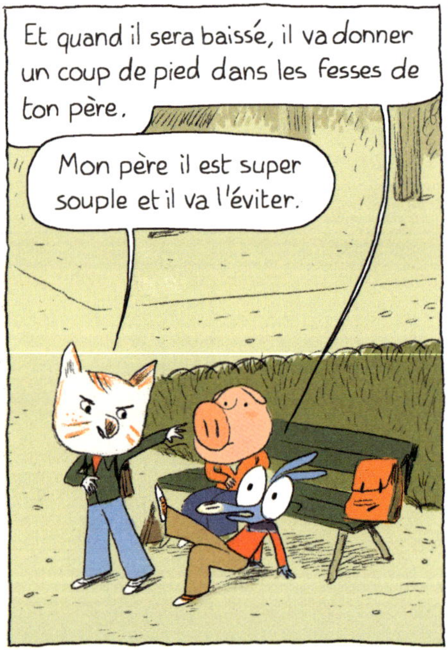
Et quand il sera baissé, il va donner un coup de pied dans les fesses de ton père.
Mon père il est super souple et il va l'éviter.

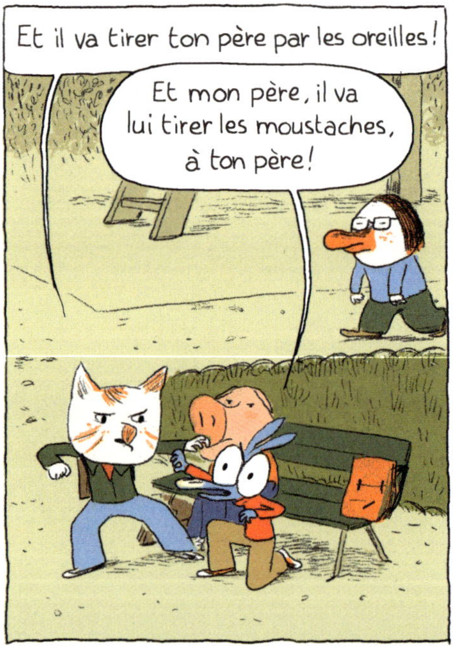
Et il va tirer ton père par les oreilles!
Et mon père, il va lui tirer les moustaches, à ton père!

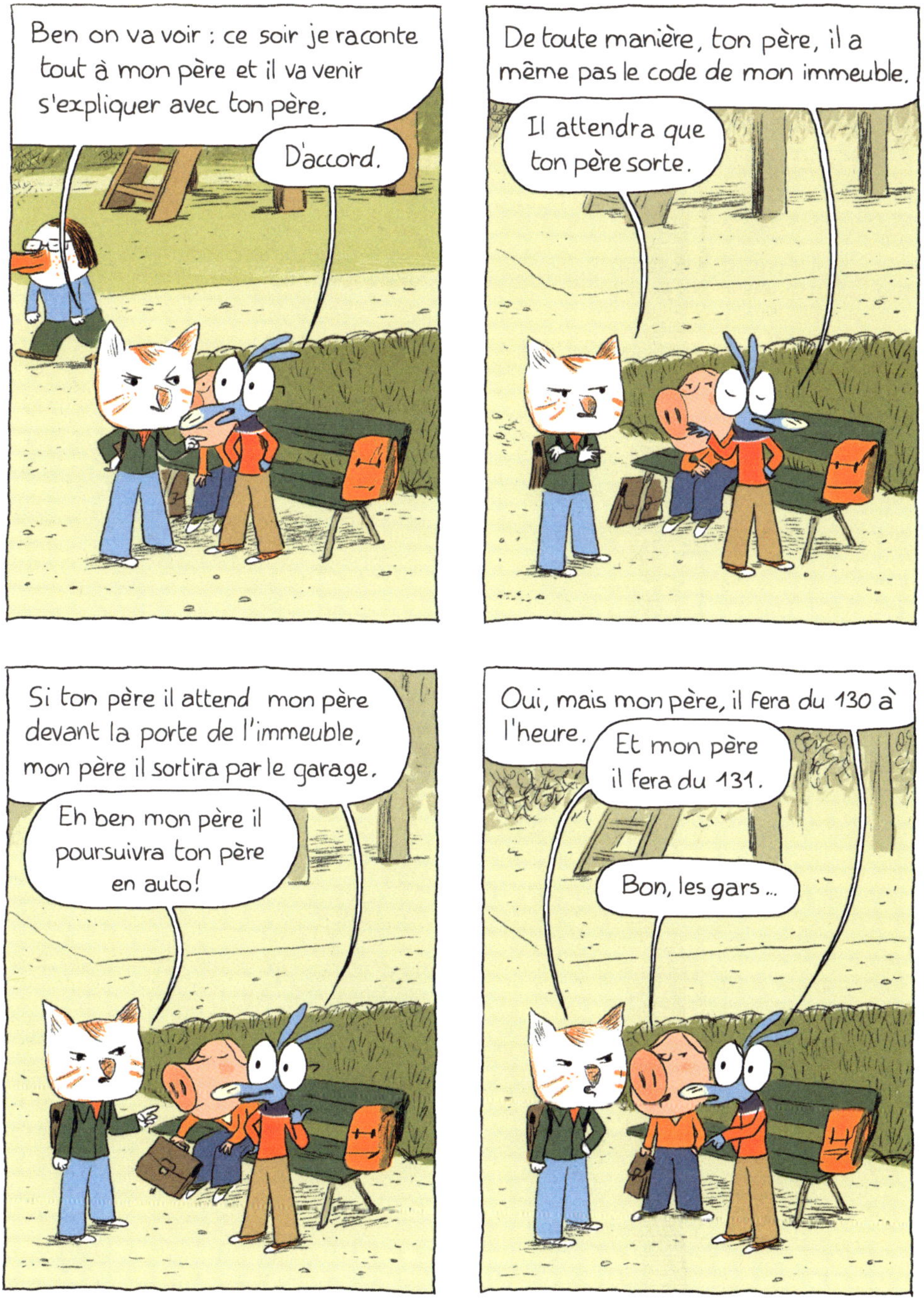
Ben on va voir : ce soir je raconte tout à mon père et il va venir s'expliquer avec ton père.
D'accord.
De toute manière, ton père, il a même pas le code de mon immeuble.
Il attendra que ton père sorte.
Si ton père il attend mon père devant la porte de l'immeuble, mon père il sortira par le garage.
Eh ben mon père il poursuivra ton père en auto!
Oui, mais mon père, il fera du 130 à l'heure.
Et mon père il fera du 131.
Bon, les gars ...

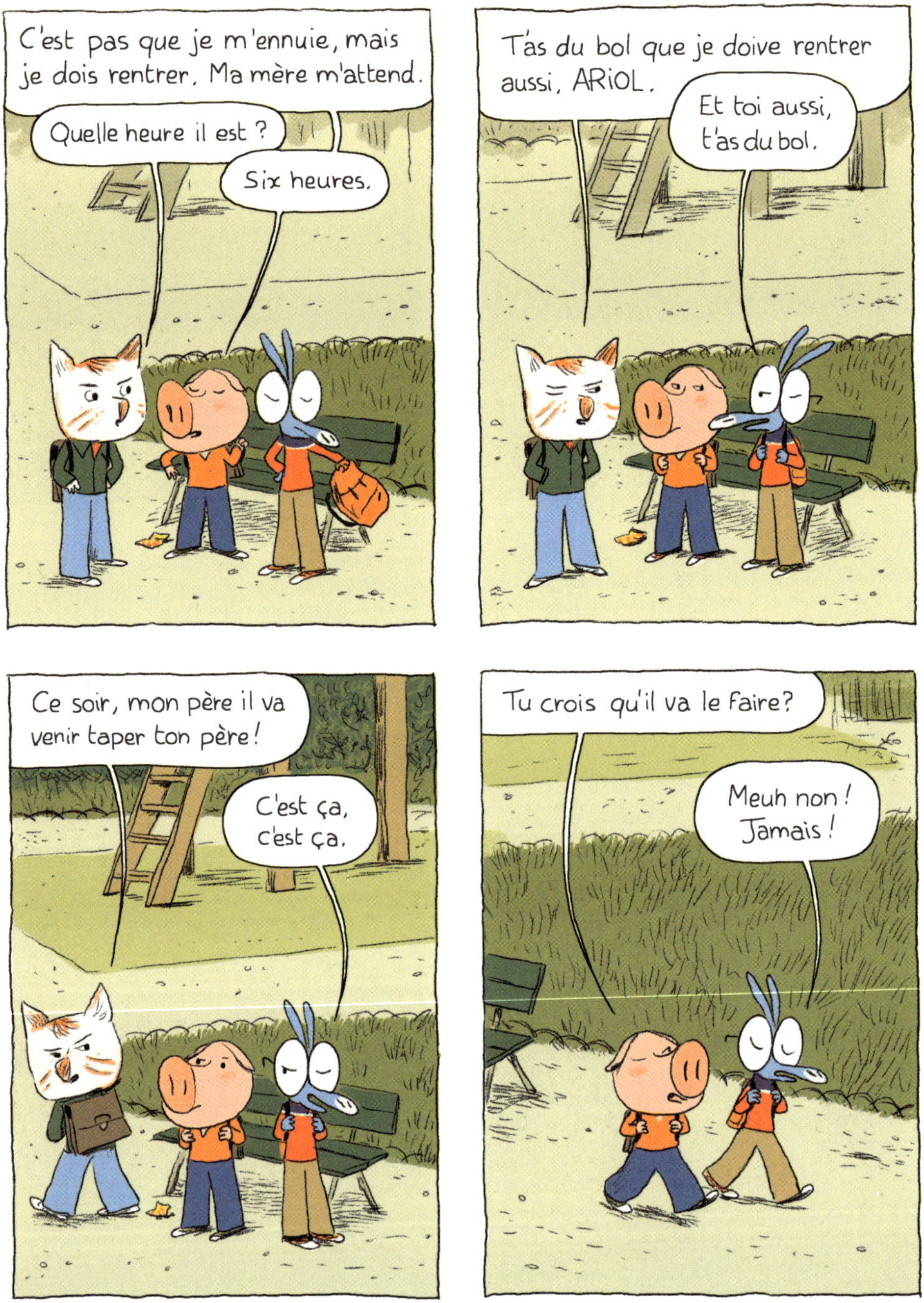
C'est pas que je m'ennuie, mais je dois rentrer. Ma mère m'attend.
Quelle heure il est ?
Six heures.
T'as du bol que je doive rentrer aussi, ARIOL.
Et toi aussi, t'as du bol.
Ce soir, mon père il va venir taper ton père !
C'est ça, c'est ça.
Tu crois qu'il va le faire?
Meuh non ! Jamais !

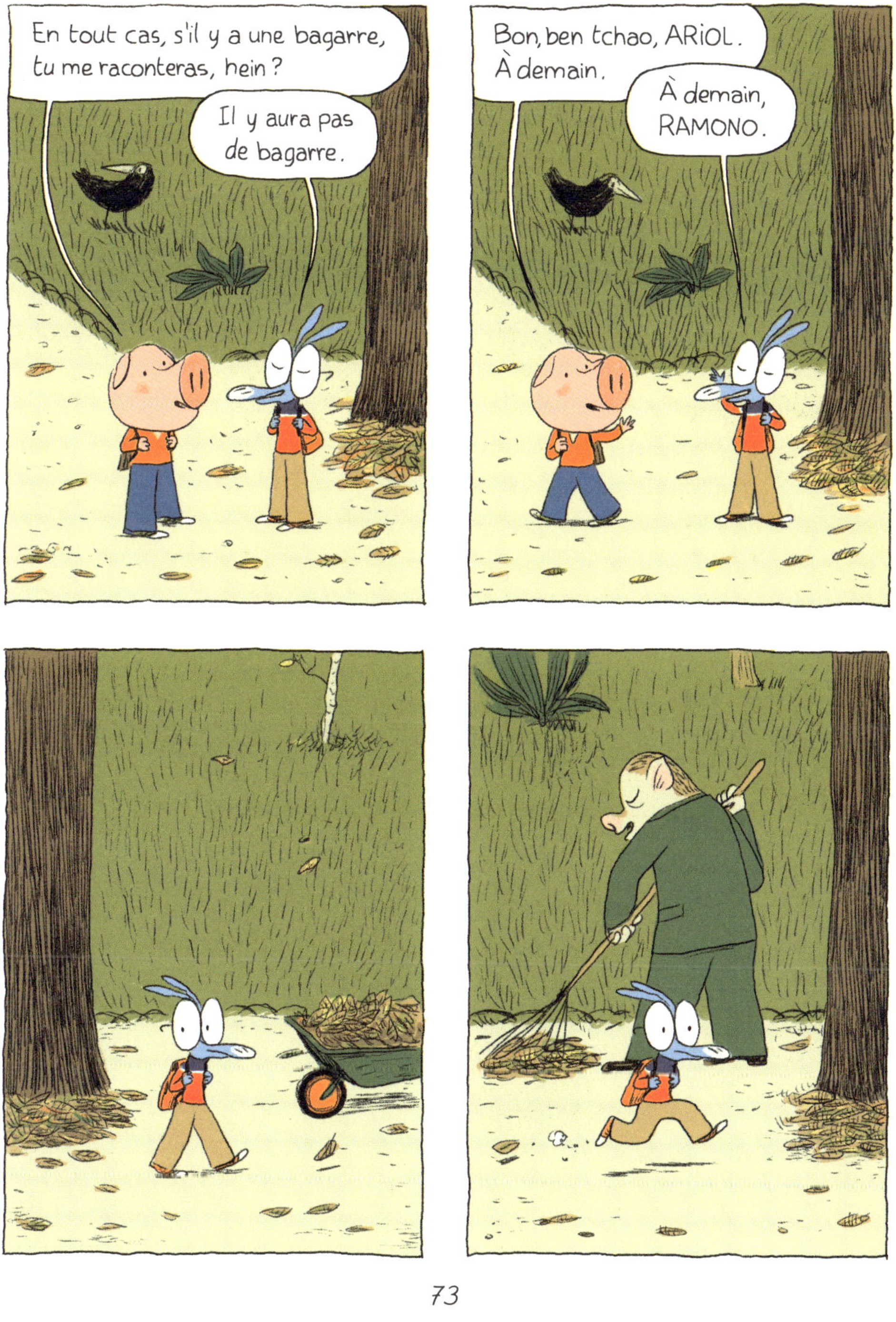

En tout cas, s'il y a une bagarre, tu me raconteras, hein ?
Il y aura pas de bagarre.
Bon, ben tchao, ARIOL. À demain.
À demain, RAMONO.

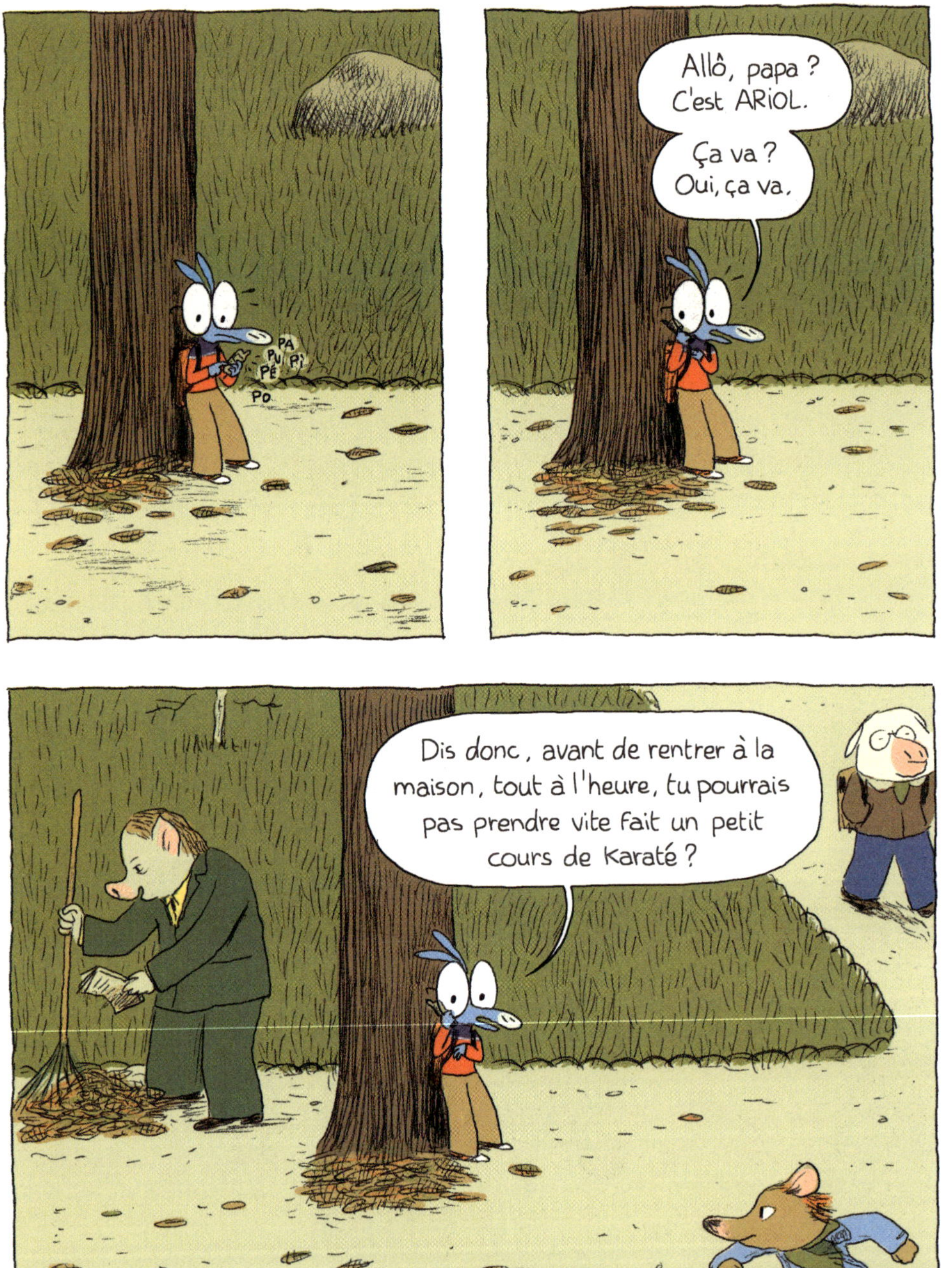
PA
PU
Pi
PÉ
PO
Allô, papa ? C'est ARIOL.
Ça va ? Oui, ça va.
Dis donc, avant de rentrer à la maison, tout à l'heure, tu pourrais pas prendre vite fait un petit cours de karaté ?
FIN

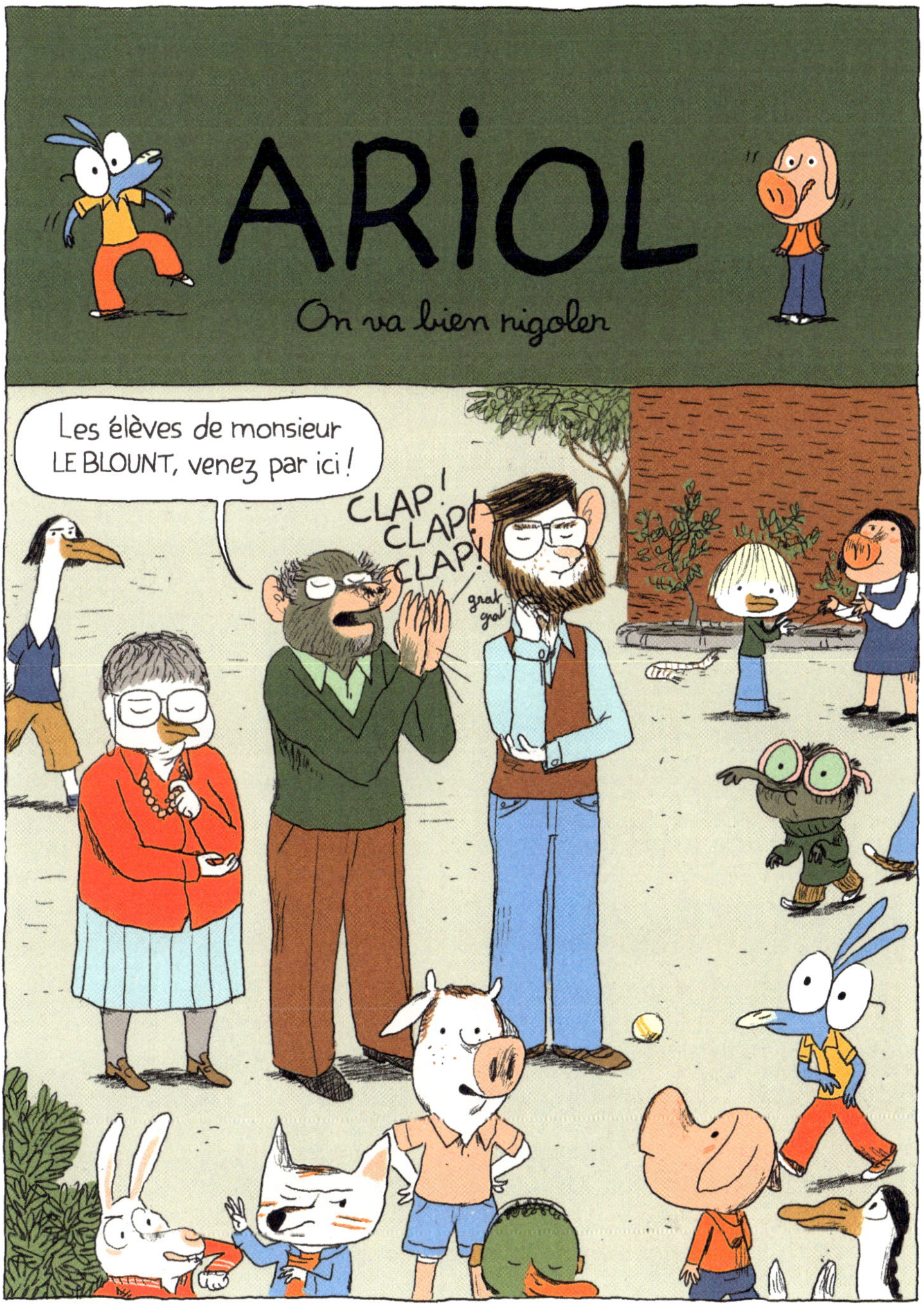
ARIOL
On va bien rigoler
Les élèves de monsieur LE BLOUNT, venez par ici !
CLAP ! CLAP ! CLAP !
grat grat

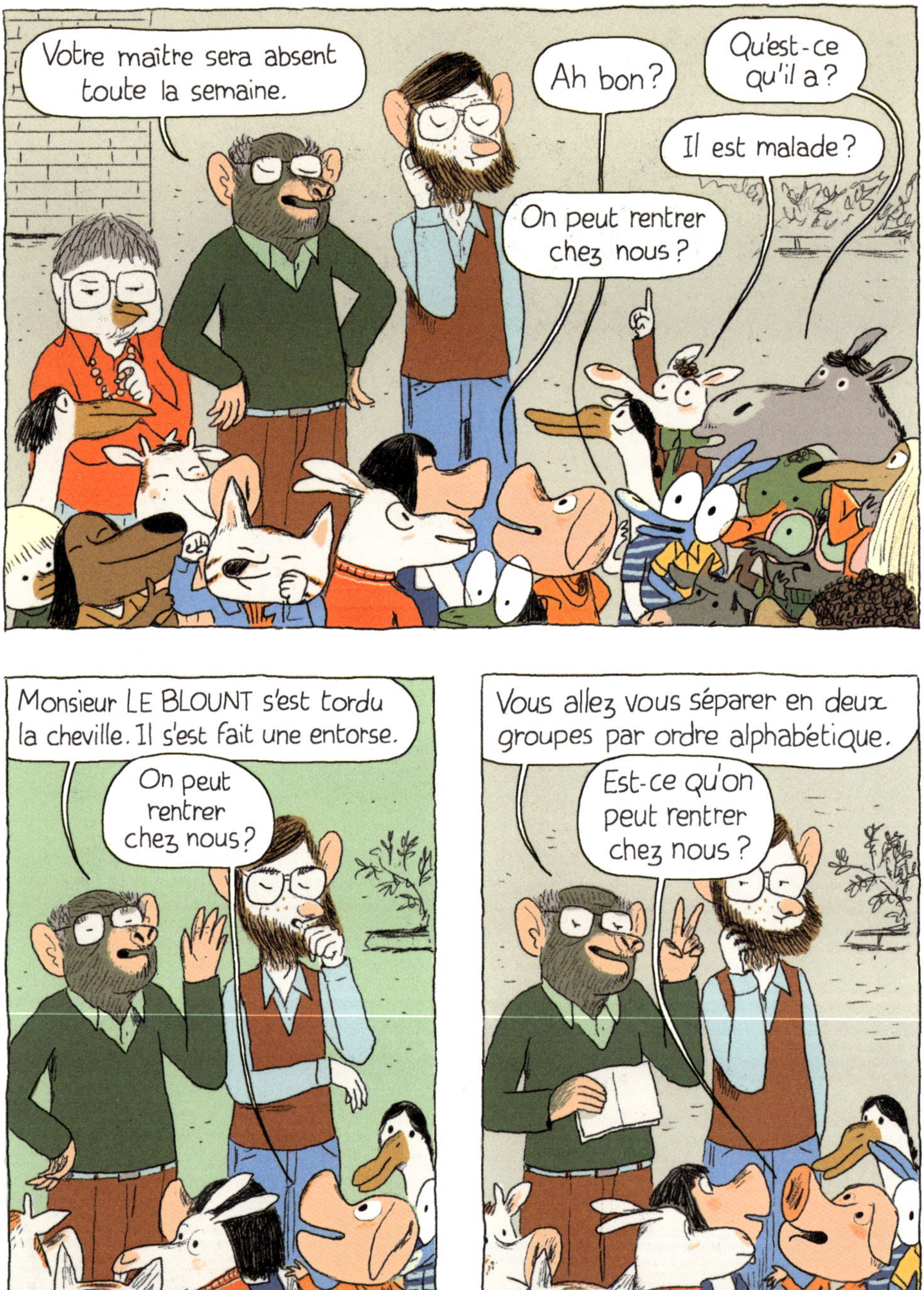
Votre maître sera absent toute la semaine.
Ah bon ?
Qu'est-ce qu'il a ?
Il est malade ?
On peut rentrer chez nous ?
Monsieur LE BLOUNT s'est tordu la cheville. Il s'est fait une entorse.
On peut rentrer chez nous ?
Vous allez vous séparer en deux groupes par ordre alphabétique.
Est-ce qu'on peut rentrer chez nous ?

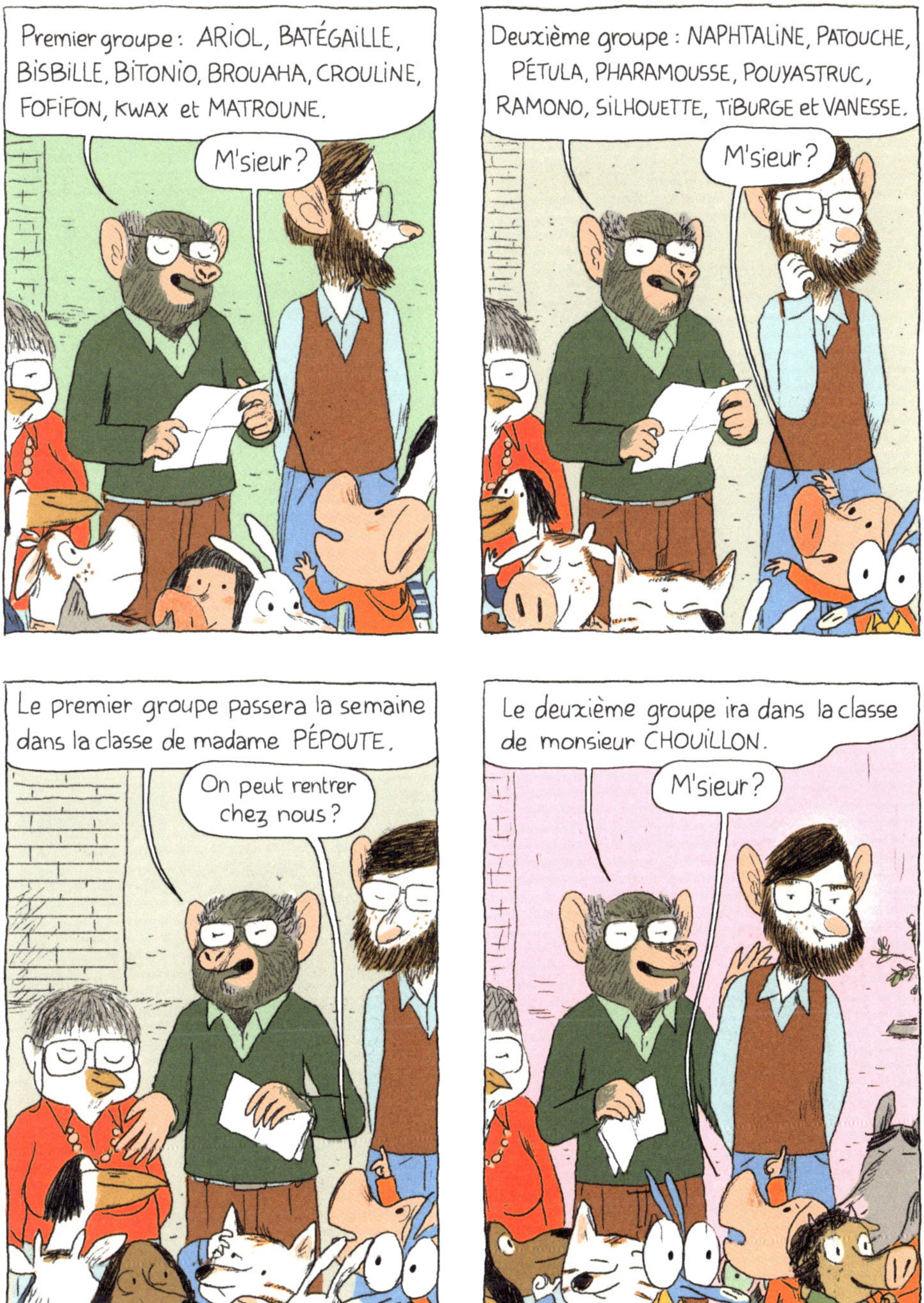
Premier groupe : ARIOL, BATÉGAILLE, BISBILLE, BITONIO, BROUAHA, CROULINE, FOFIFON, KWAX et MATROUNE.
M'sieur ?
Deuxième groupe : NAPHTALINE, PATOUCHE, PÉTULA, PHARAMOUSSE, POUYASTRUC, RAMONO, SILHOUETTE, TIBURGE et VANESSE.
M'sieur ?
Le premier groupe passera la semaine dans la classe de madame PÉPOUTE.
On peut rentrer chez nous ?
Le deuxième groupe ira dans la classe de monsieur CHOUILLON.
M'sieur ?

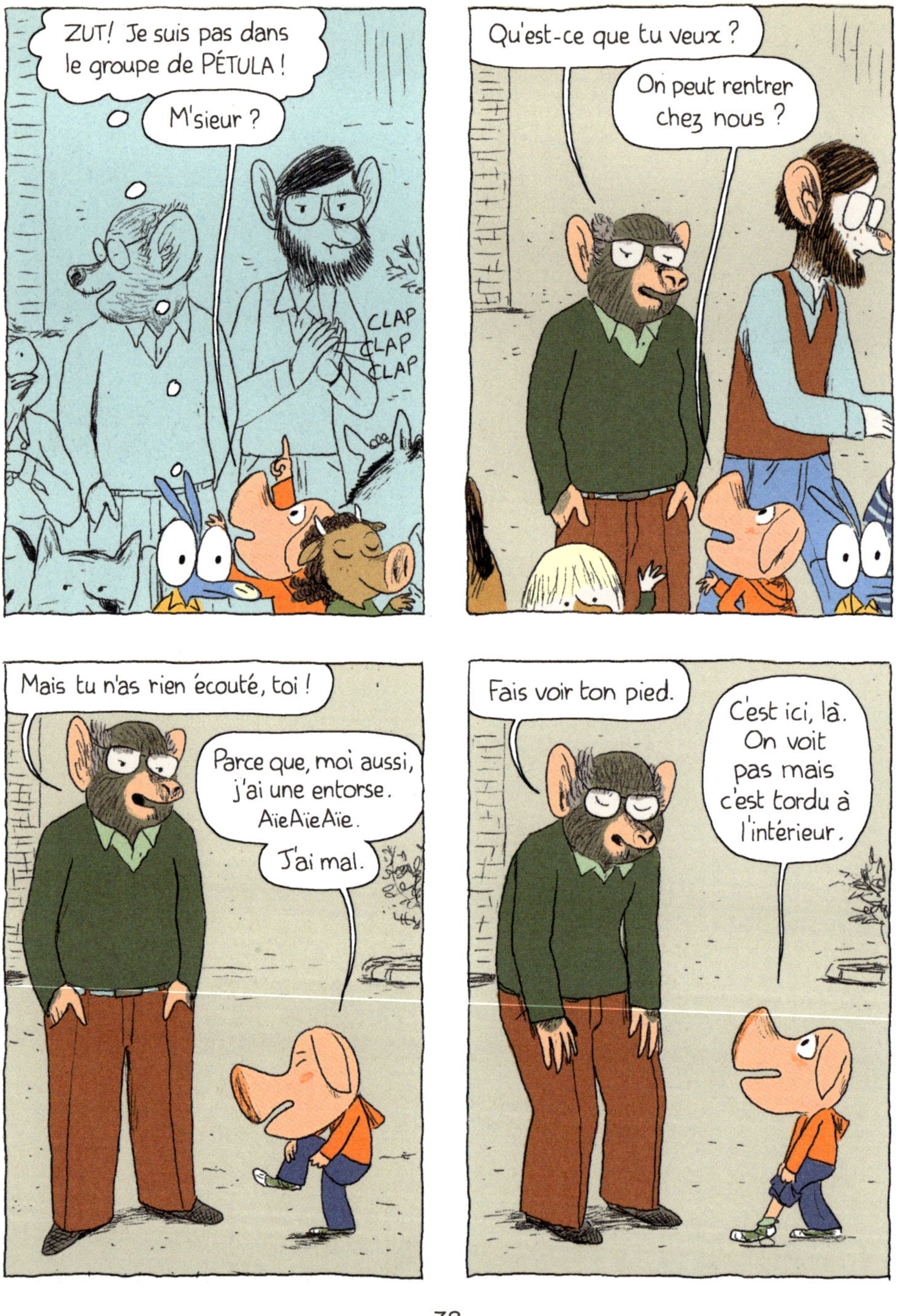
ZUT! Je suis pas dans le groupe de PÉTULA!
M'sieur ?
CLAP
CLAP
CLAP
Qu'est-ce que tu veux ?
On peut rentrer chez nous ?
Mais tu n'as rien écouté, toi !
Parce que, moi aussi, j'ai une entorse. AïeAïeAïe.
J'ai mal.
Fais voir ton pied.
C'est ici, là. On voit pas mais c'est tordu à l'intérieur.

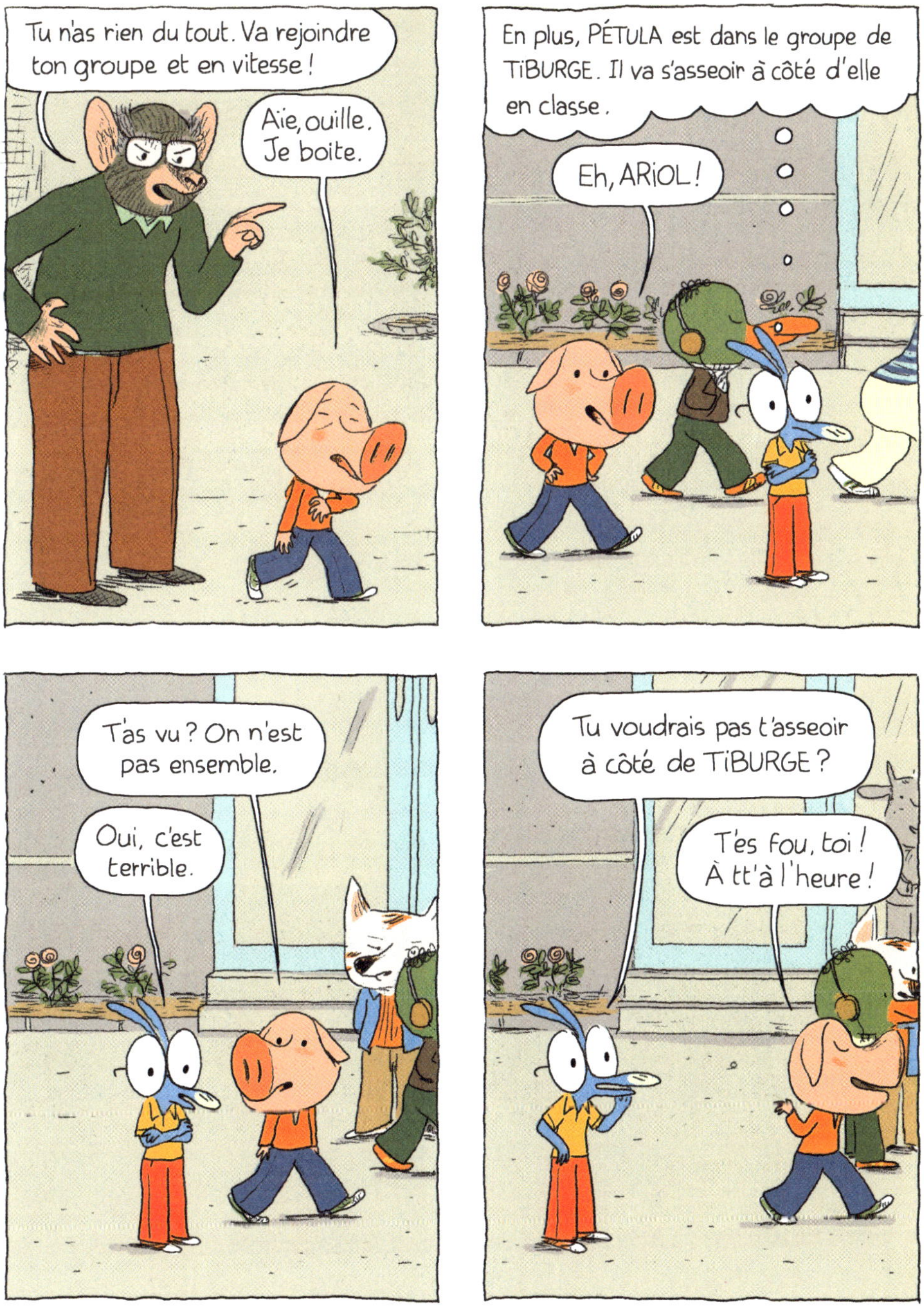
Tu n'as rien du tout. Va rejoindre ton groupe et en vitesse !
Aïe, ouille. Je boite.
En plus, PÉTULA est dans le groupe de TiBURGE. Il va s'asseoir à côté d'elle en classe.
Eh, ARiOL !
T'as vu ? On n'est pas ensemble.
Oui, c'est terrible.
Tu voudrais pas t'asseoir à côté de TiBURGE ?
T'es fou, toi ! À tt'à l'heure !

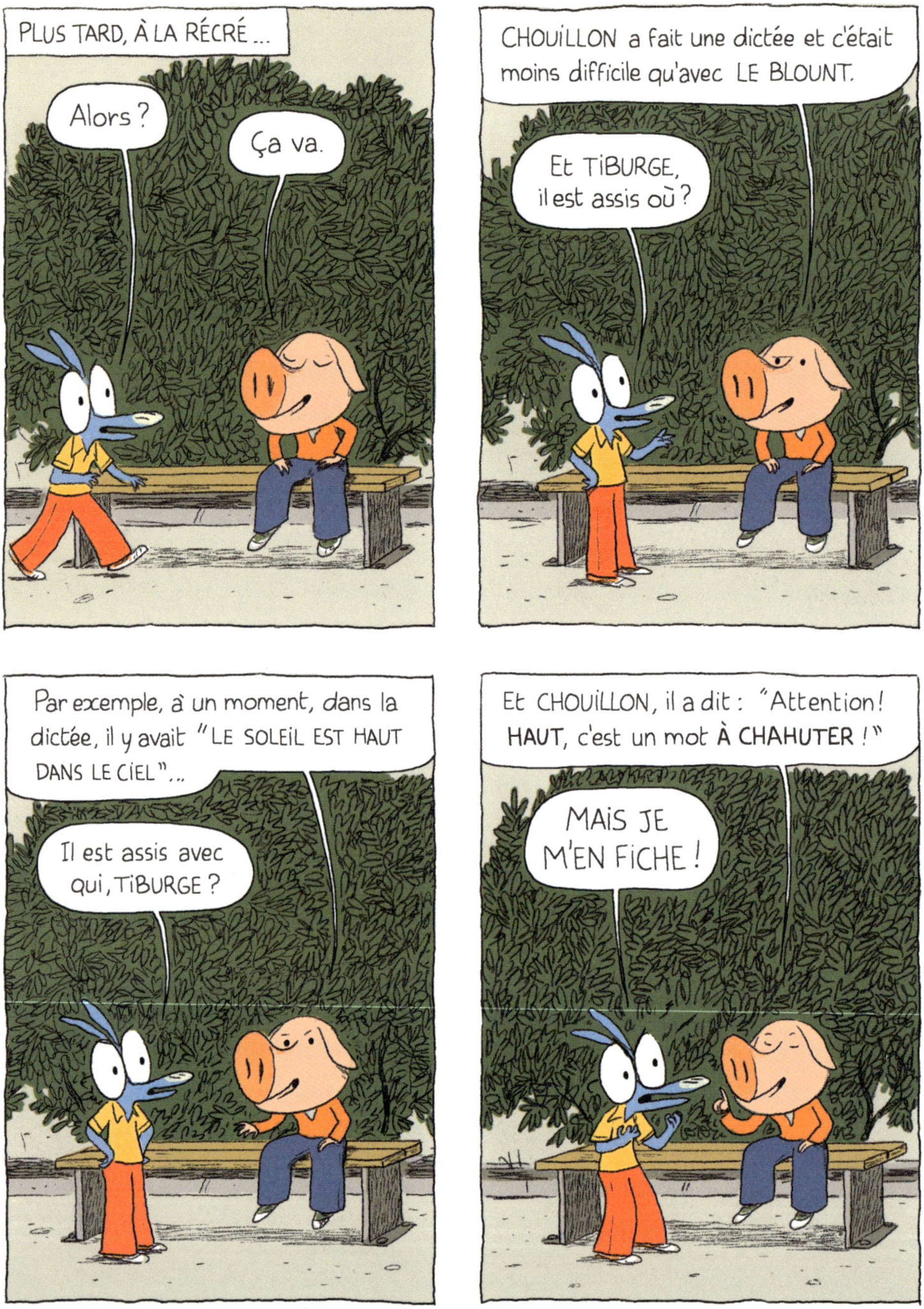
PLUS TARD, À LA RÉCRÉ...
Alors ?
Ça va.
CHOUILLON a fait une dictée et c'était moins difficile qu'avec LE BLOUNT.
Et TIBURGE, il est assis où ?
Par exemple, à un moment, dans la dictée, il y avait "LE SOLEIL EST HAUT DANS LE CIEL"...
Il est assis avec qui, TIBURGE ?
Et CHOUILLON, il a dit : "Attention ! **HAUT**, c'est un mot **À CHAHUTER** !"
MAIS JE M'EN FICHE !

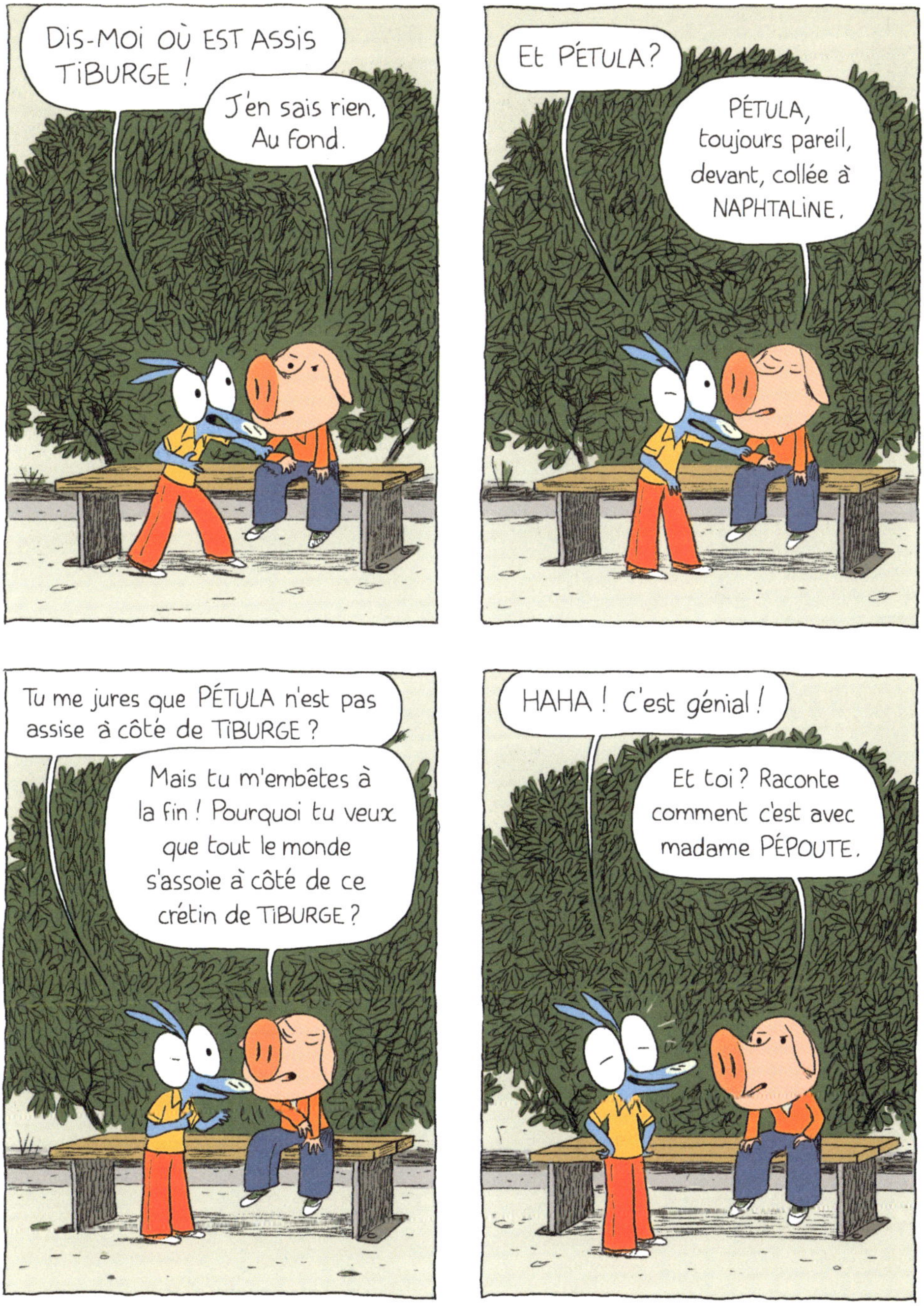
DIS-MOI OÙ EST ASSIS TIBURGE !
J'en sais rien. Au fond.
Et PÉTULA ?
PÉTULA, toujours pareil, devant, collée à NAPHTALINE.
Tu me jures que PÉTULA n'est pas assise à côté de TIBURGE ?
Mais tu m'embêtes à la fin ! Pourquoi tu veux que tout le monde s'assoie à côté de ce crétin de TIBURGE ?
HAHA ! C'est génial !
Et toi ? Raconte comment c'est avec madame PÉPOUTE.

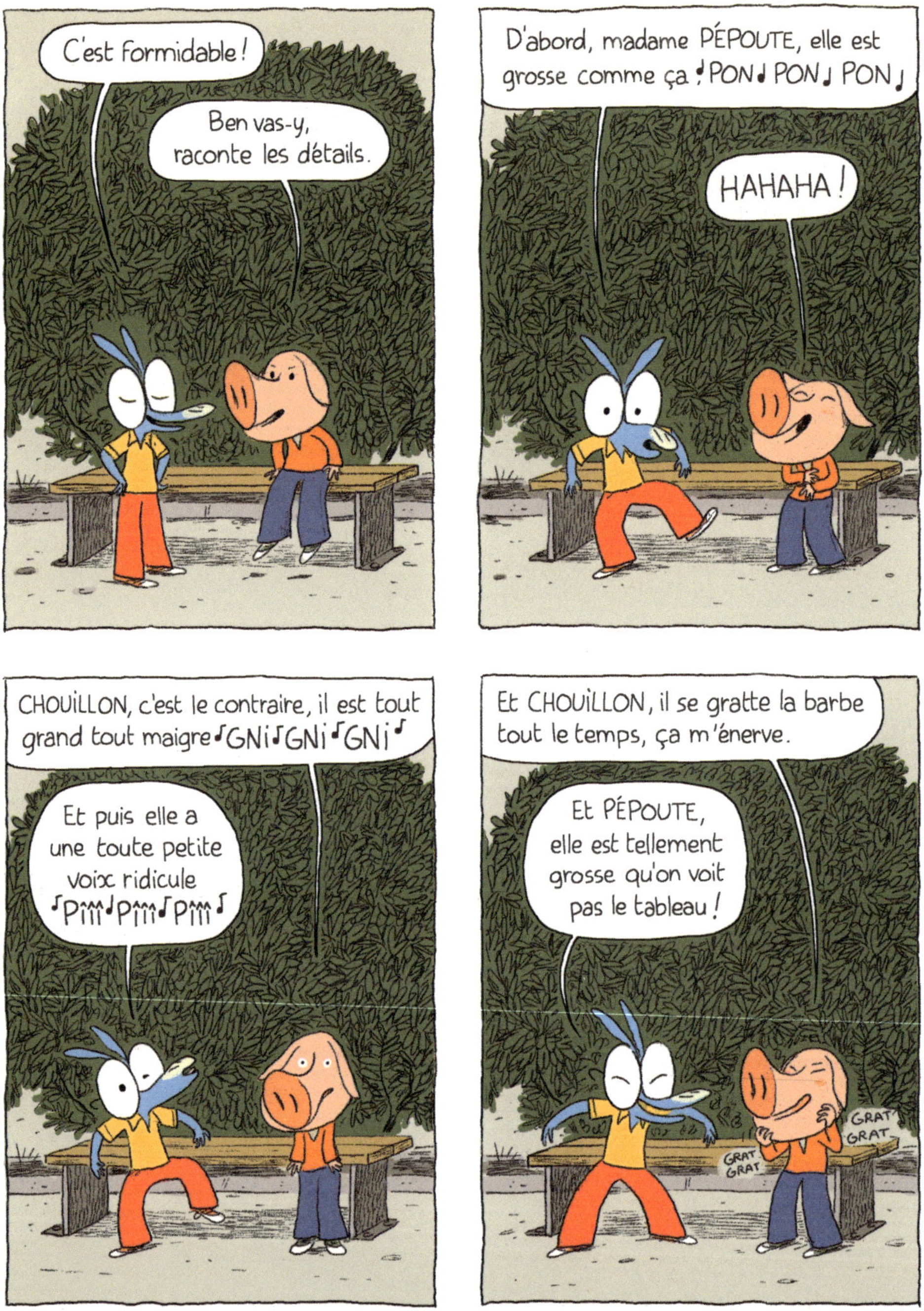
C'est formidable !
Ben vas-y, raconte les détails.
D'abord, madame PÉPOUTE, elle est grosse comme ça PON PON PON
HAHAHA !
CHOUILLON, c'est le contraire, il est tout grand tout maigre GNi GNi GNi
Et puis elle a une toute petite voix ridicule Pîîî Pîîî Pîîî
Et CHOUILLON, il se gratte la barbe tout le temps, ça m'énerve.
Et PÉPOUTE, elle est tellement grosse qu'on voit pas le tableau !
GRAT GRAT
GRAT GRAT

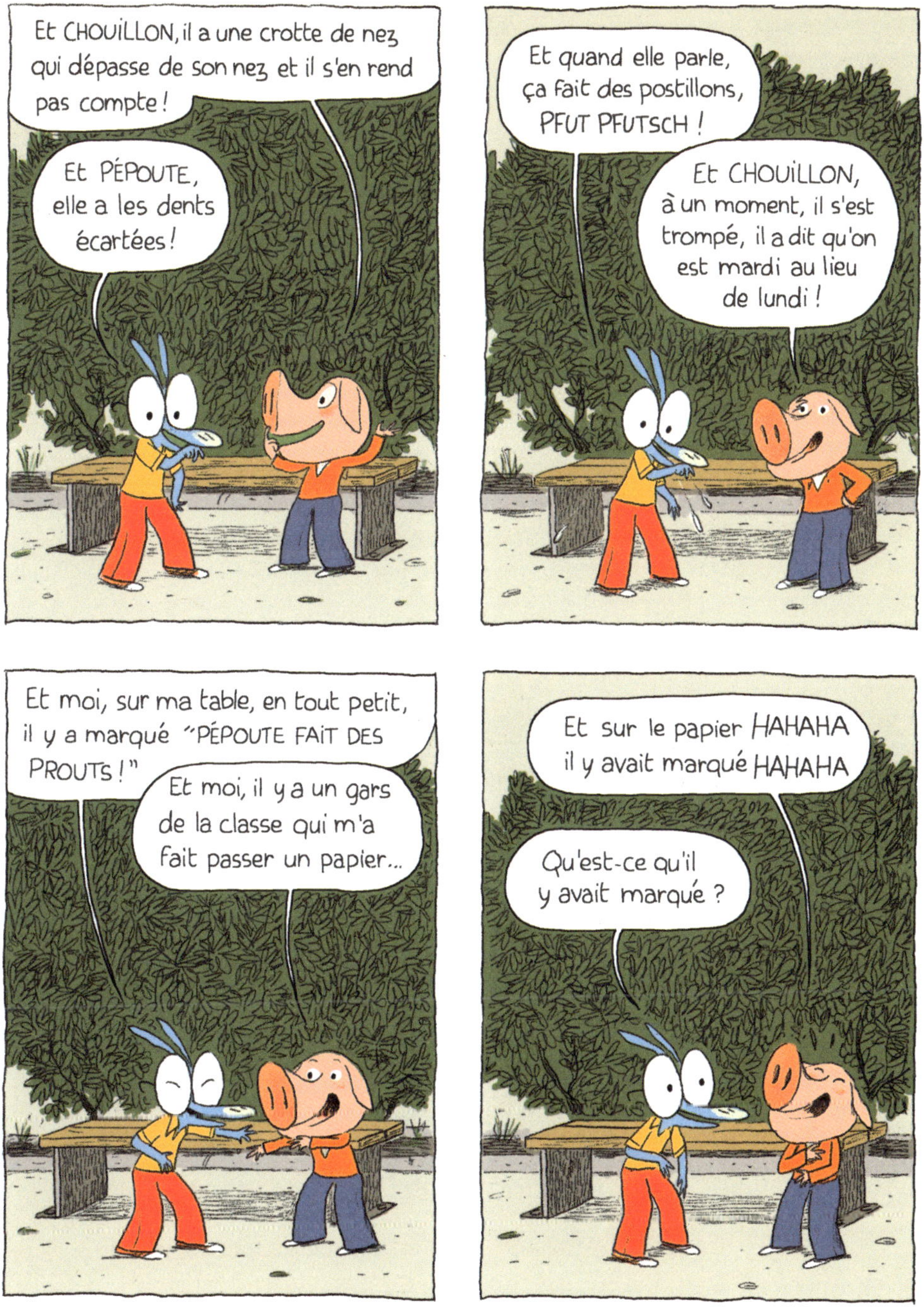
Et CHOUiLLON, il a une crotte de nez qui dépasse de son nez et il s'en rend pas compte !
Et PÉPOUTE, elle a les dents écartées !
Et quand elle parle, ça fait des postillons, PFUT PFUTSCH !
Et CHOUiLLON, à un moment, il s'est trompé, il a dit qu'on est mardi au lieu de lundi !
Et moi, sur ma table, en tout petit, il y a marqué "PÉPOUTE FAiT DES PROUTS !"
Et moi, il y a un gars de la classe qui m'a fait passer un papier...
Et sur le papier HAHAHA il y avait marqué HAHAHA
Qu'est-ce qu'il y avait marqué ?

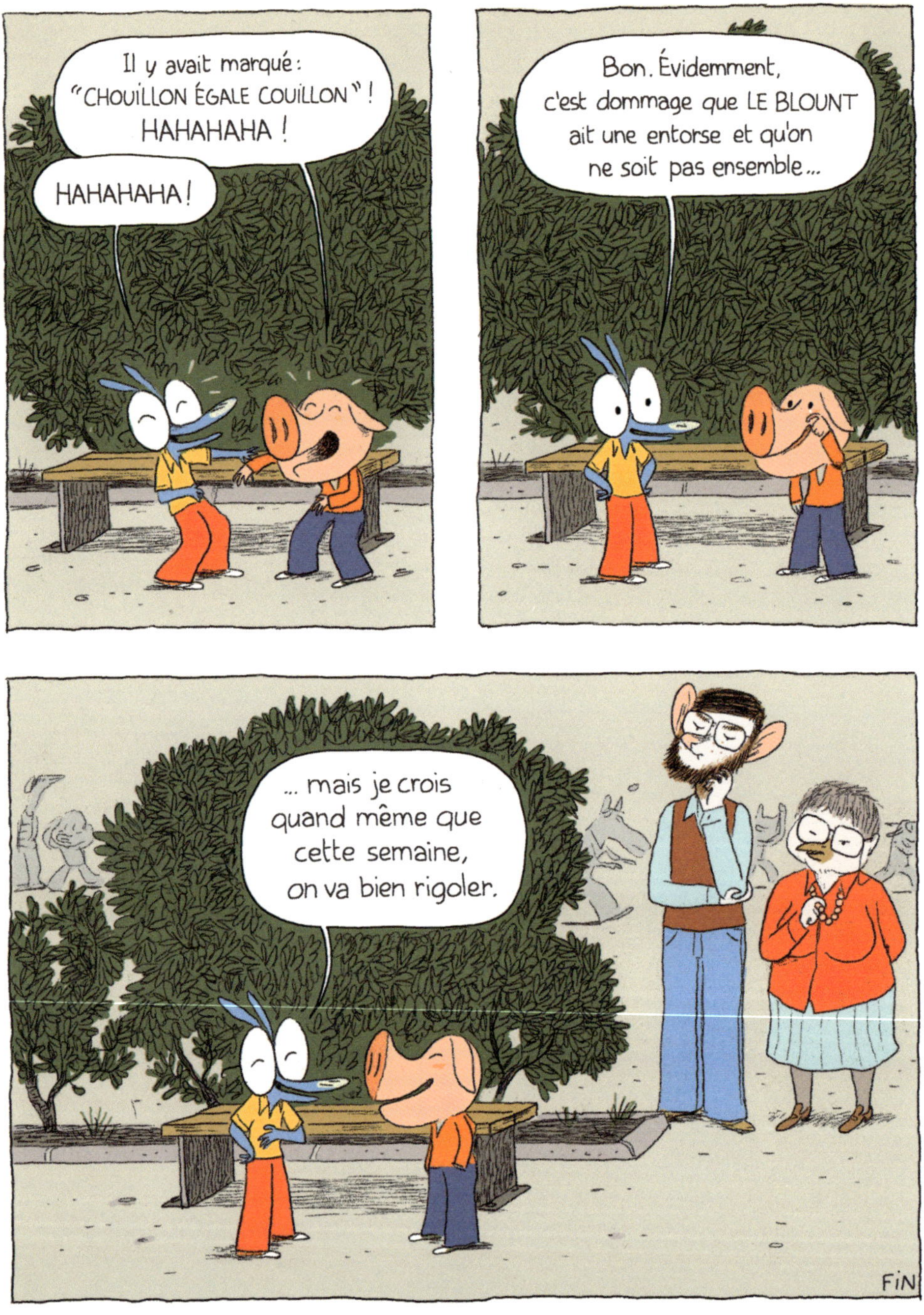
Il y avait marqué : "CHOUILLON ÉGALE COUILLON" ! HAHAHAHA !
HAHAHAHA !
Bon. Évidemment, c'est dommage que LE BLOUNT ait une entorse et qu'on ne soit pas ensemble...
... mais je crois quand même que cette semaine, on va bien rigoler.
FIN

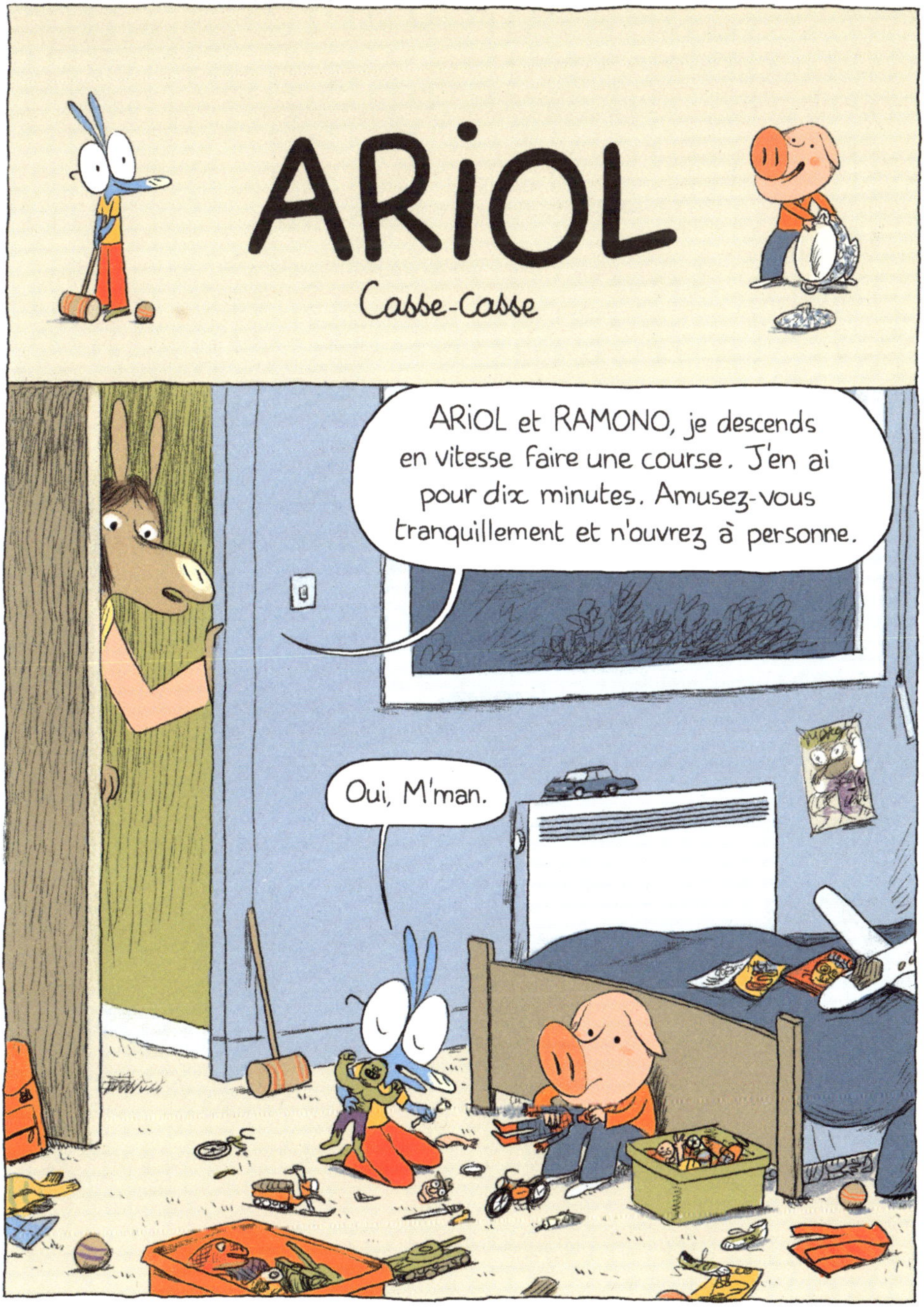
ARiOL
Casse-Casse
ARiOL et RAMONO, je descends en vitesse faire une course. J'en ai pour dix minutes. Amusez-vous tranquillement et n'ouvrez à personne.
Oui, M'man.

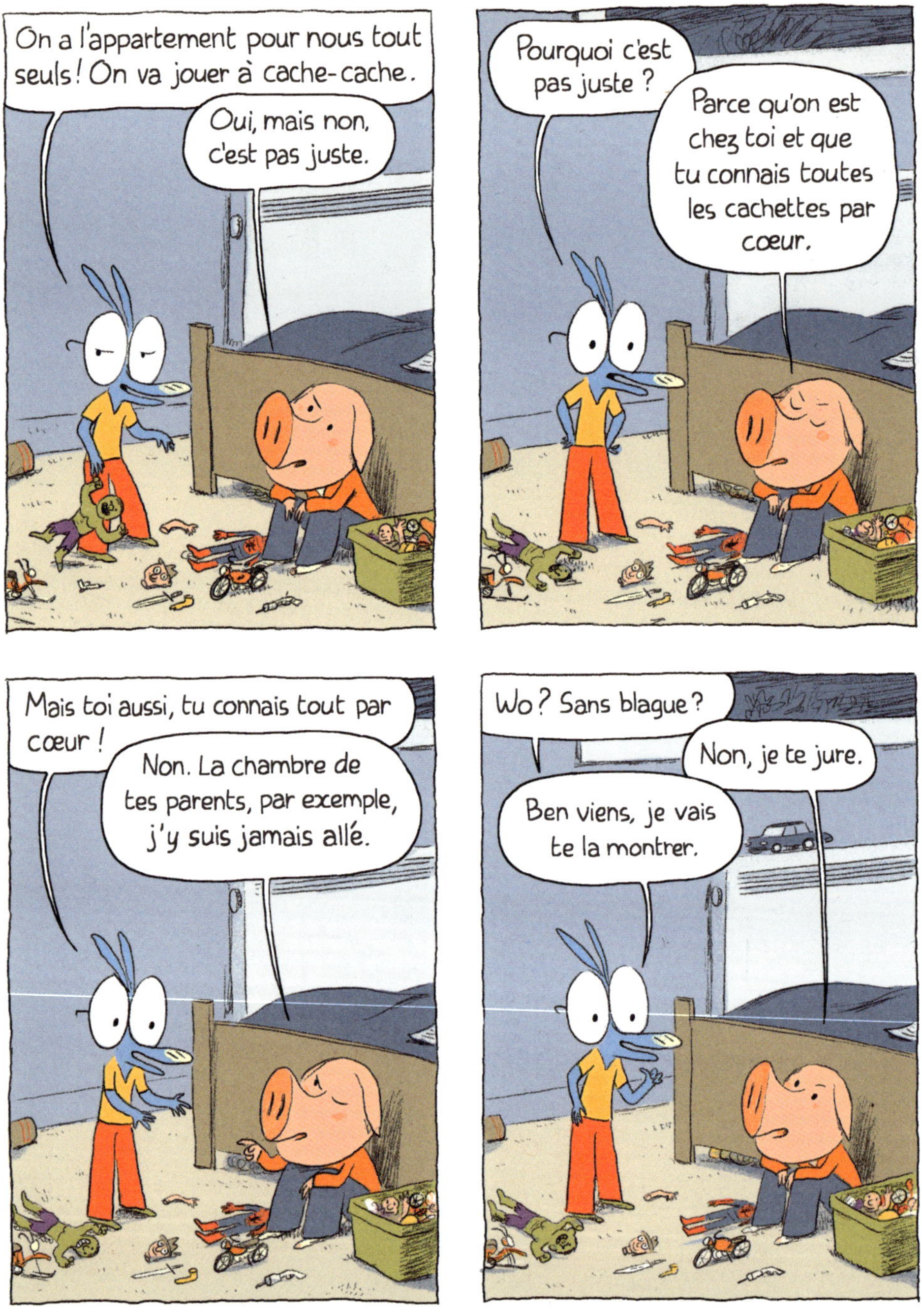
On a l'appartement pour nous tout seuls ! On va jouer à cache-cache.
Oui, mais non, c'est pas juste.
Pourquoi c'est pas juste ?
Parce qu'on est chez toi et que tu connais toutes les cachettes par cœur.
Mais toi aussi, tu connais tout par cœur !
Non. La chambre de tes parents, par exemple, j'y suis jamais allé.
Wo ? Sans blague ?
Non, je te jure.
Ben viens, je vais te la montrer.

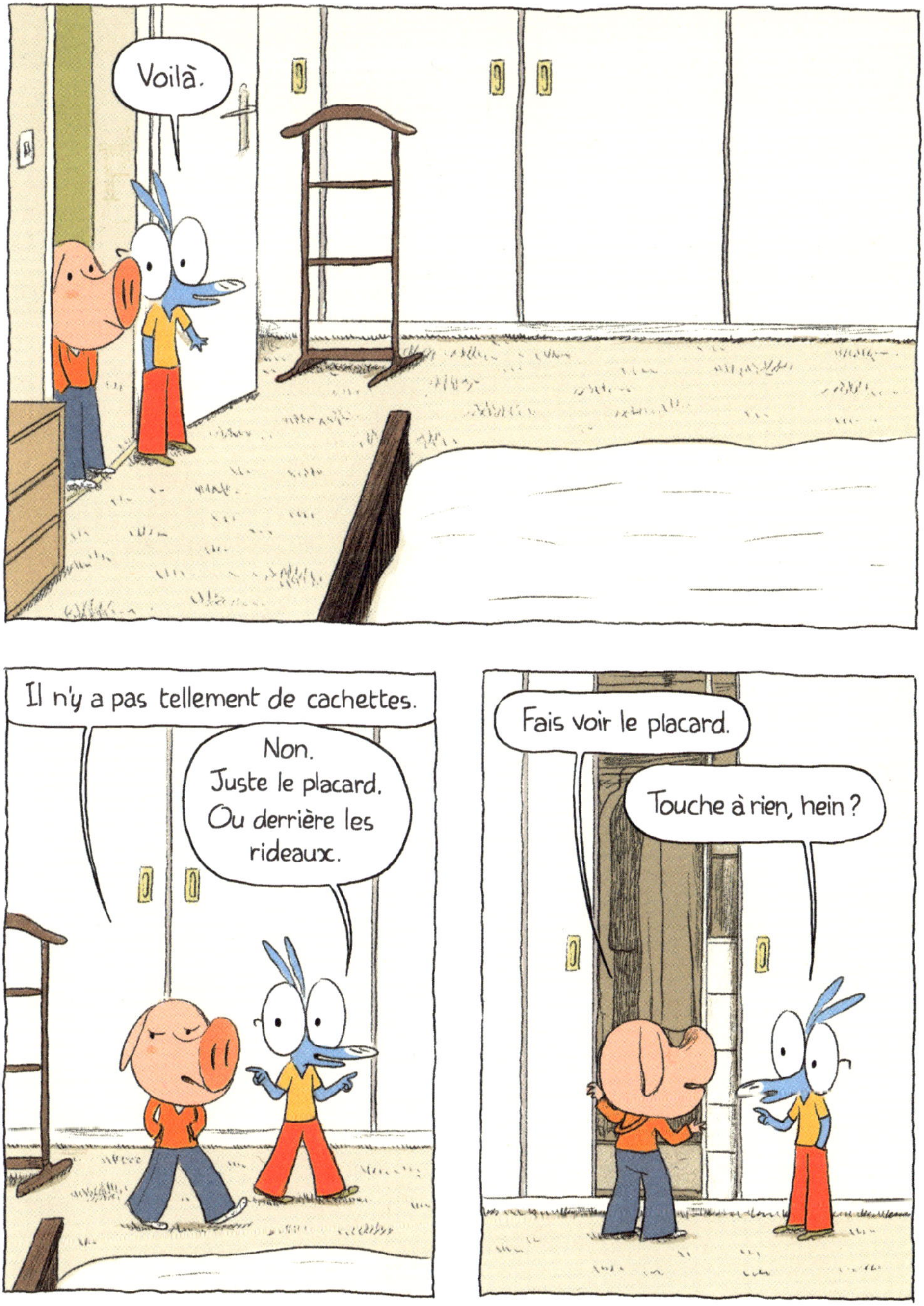
Voilà.
Il n'y a pas tellement de cachettes.
Non. Juste le placard. Ou derrière les rideaux.
Fais voir le placard.
Touche à rien, hein ?

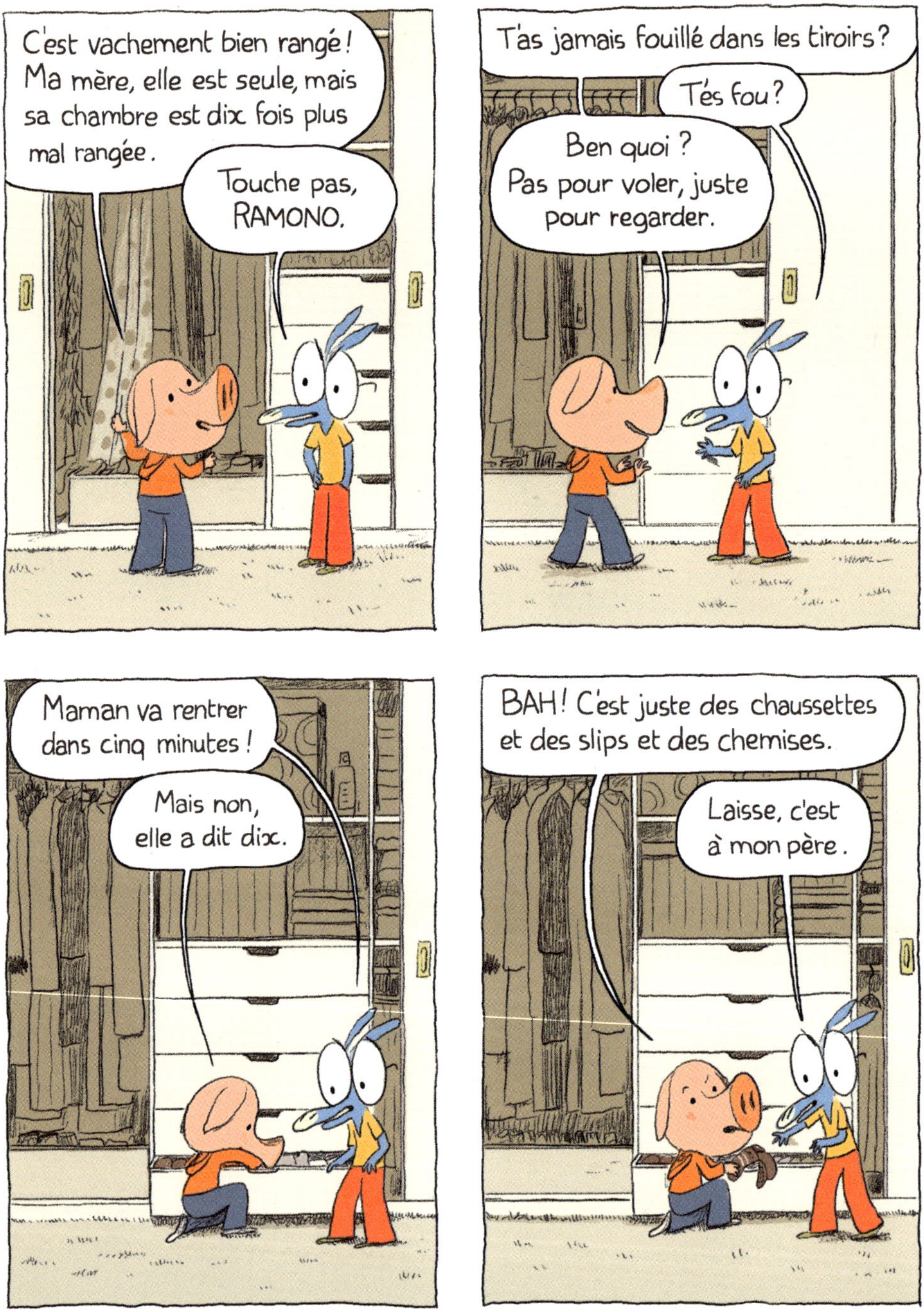

C'est vachement bien rangé! Ma mère, elle est seule, mais sa chambre est dix fois plus mal rangée.
Touche pas, RAMONO.
T'as jamais fouillé dans les tiroirs?
T'es fou?
Ben quoi ? Pas pour voler, juste pour regarder.
Maman va rentrer dans cinq minutes!
Mais non, elle a dit dix.
BAH! C'est juste des chaussettes et des slips et des chemises.
Laisse, c'est à mon père.

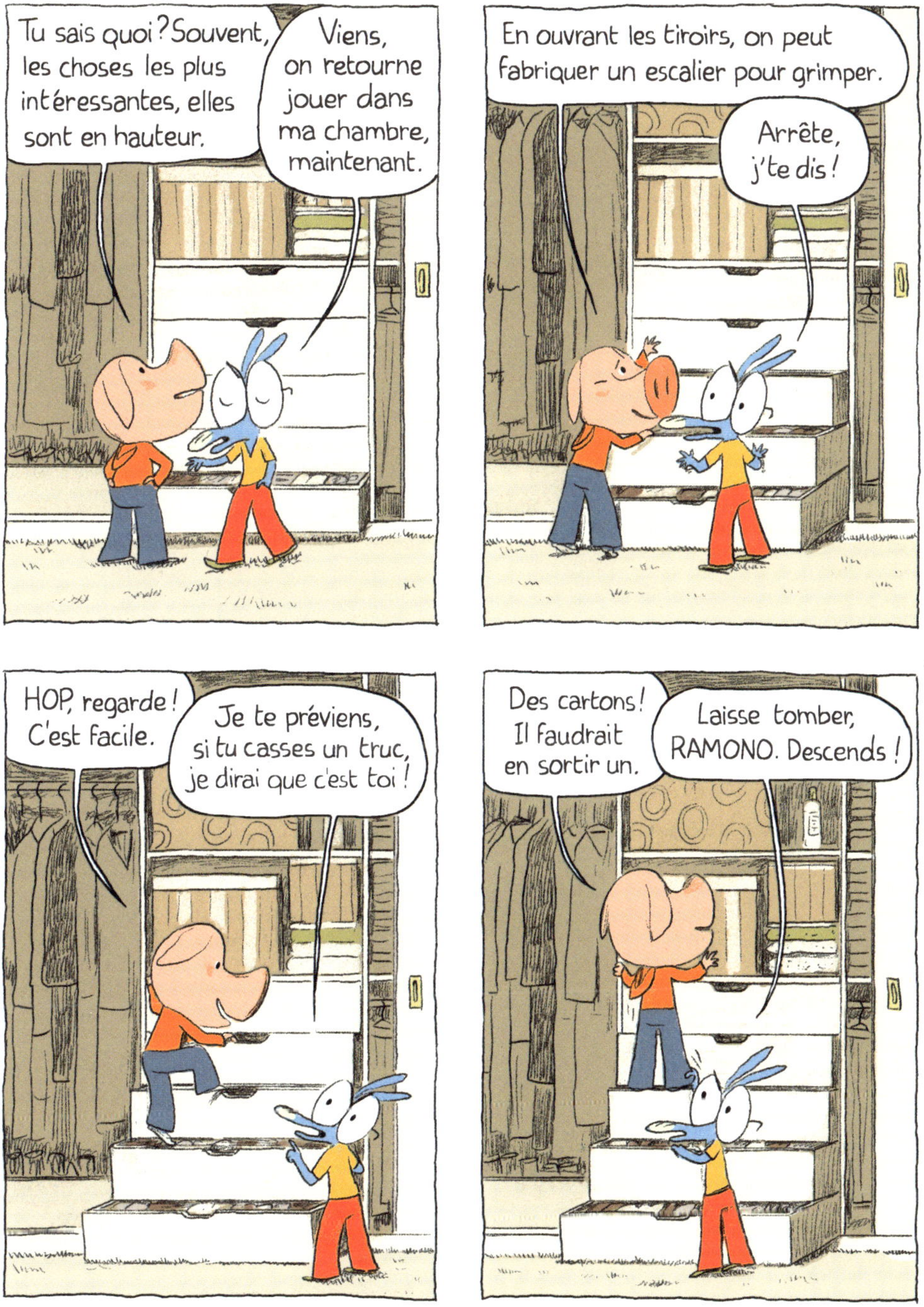
Tu sais quoi ? Souvent, les choses les plus intéressantes, elles sont en hauteur.
Viens, on retourne jouer dans ma chambre, maintenant.
En ouvrant les tiroirs, on peut fabriquer un escalier pour grimper.
Arrête, j'te dis !
HOP, regarde ! C'est facile.
Je te préviens, si tu casses un truc, je dirai que c'est toi !
Des cartons ! Il faudrait en sortir un.
Laisse tomber, RAMONO. Descends !

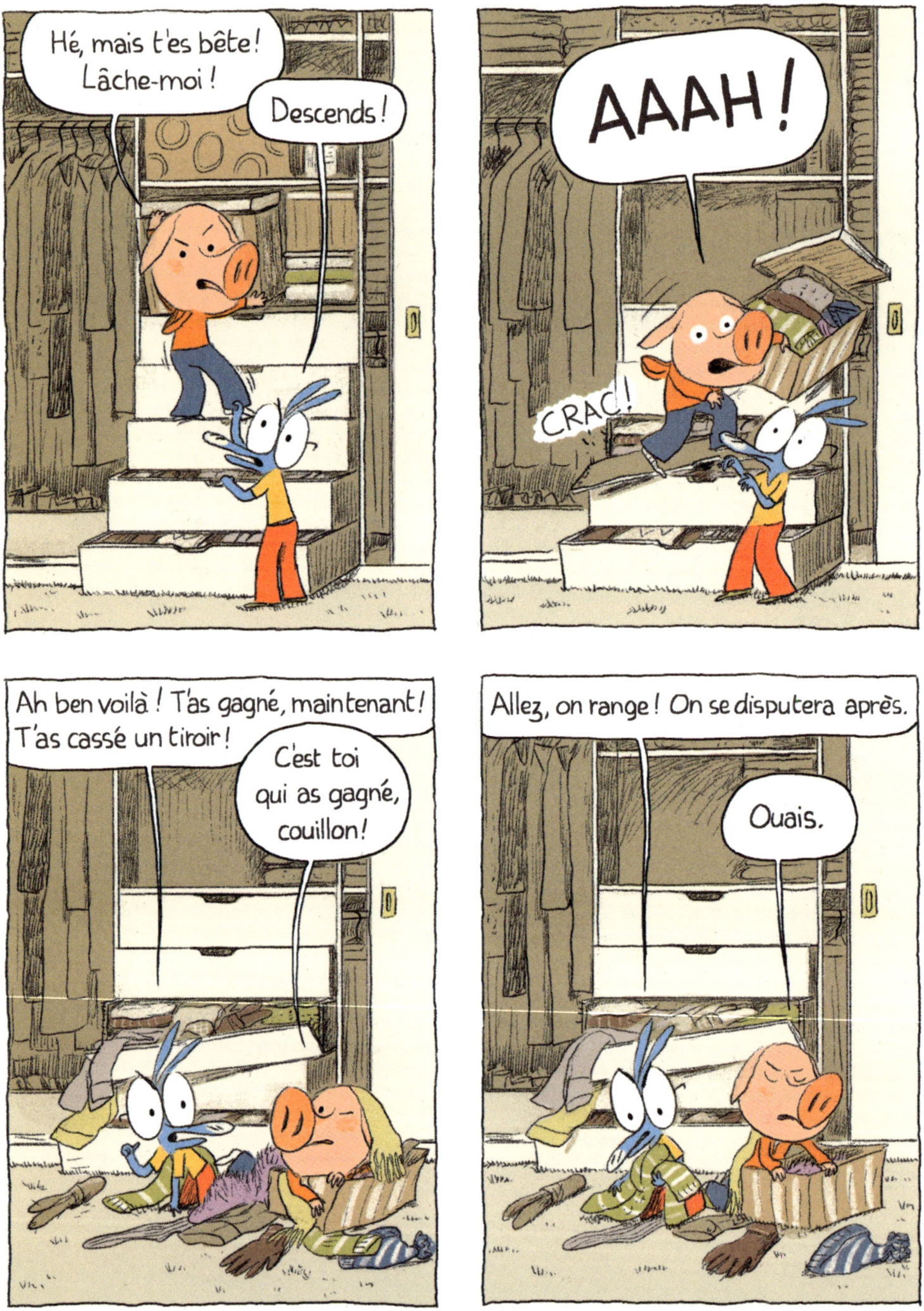
Hé, mais t'es bête! Lâche-moi!
Descends!
AAAH!
CRAC!
Ah ben voilà! T'as gagné, maintenant! T'as cassé un tiroir!
C'est toi qui as gagné, couillon!
Allez, on range! On se disputera après.
Ouais.

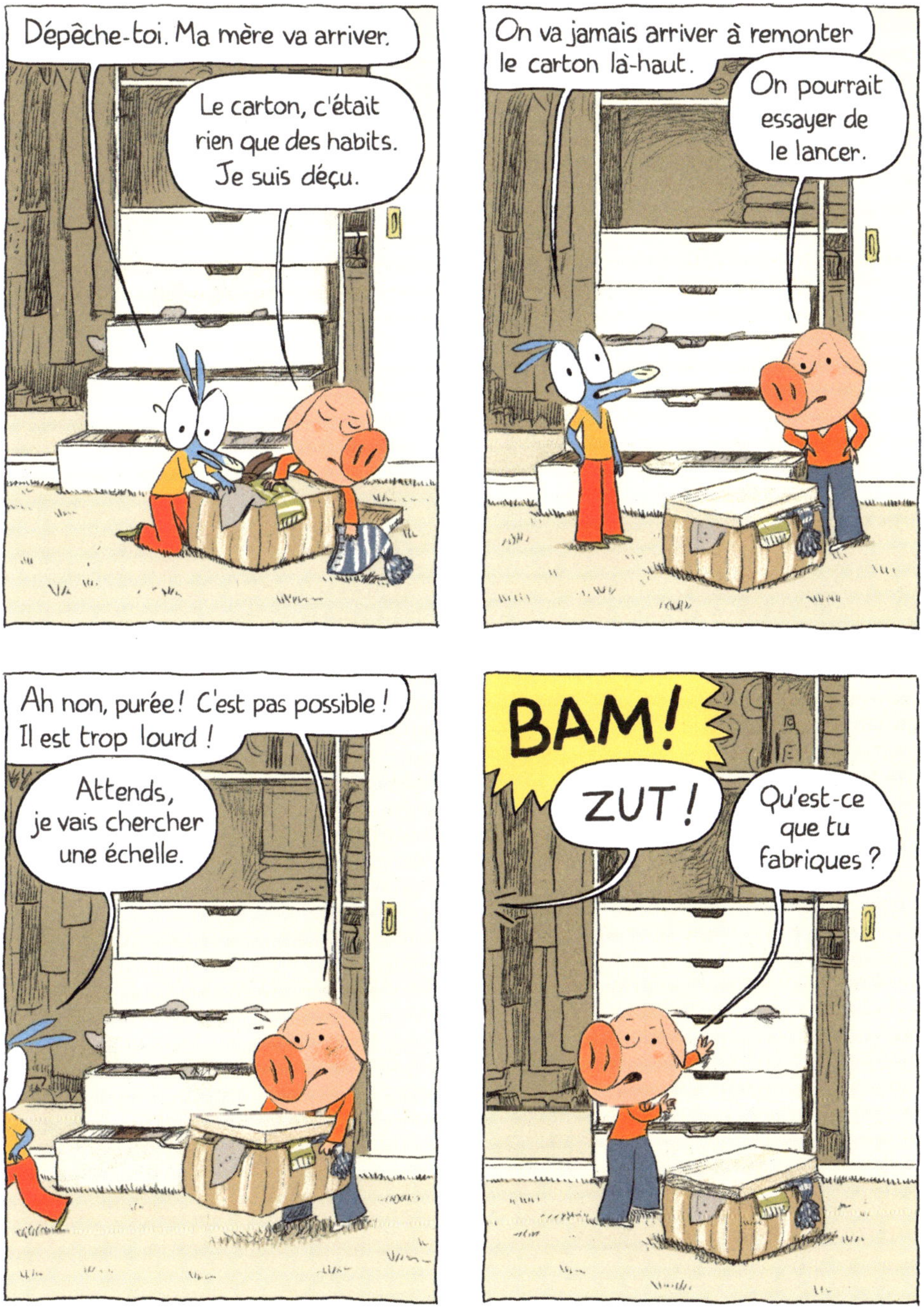
Dépêche-toi. Ma mère va arriver.
Le carton, c'était rien que des habits. Je suis déçu.
On va jamais arriver à remonter le carton là-haut.
On pourrait essayer de le lancer.
Ah non, purée ! C'est pas possible ! Il est trop lourd !
Attends, je vais chercher une échelle.
BAM !
ZUT !
Qu'est-ce que tu fabriques ?

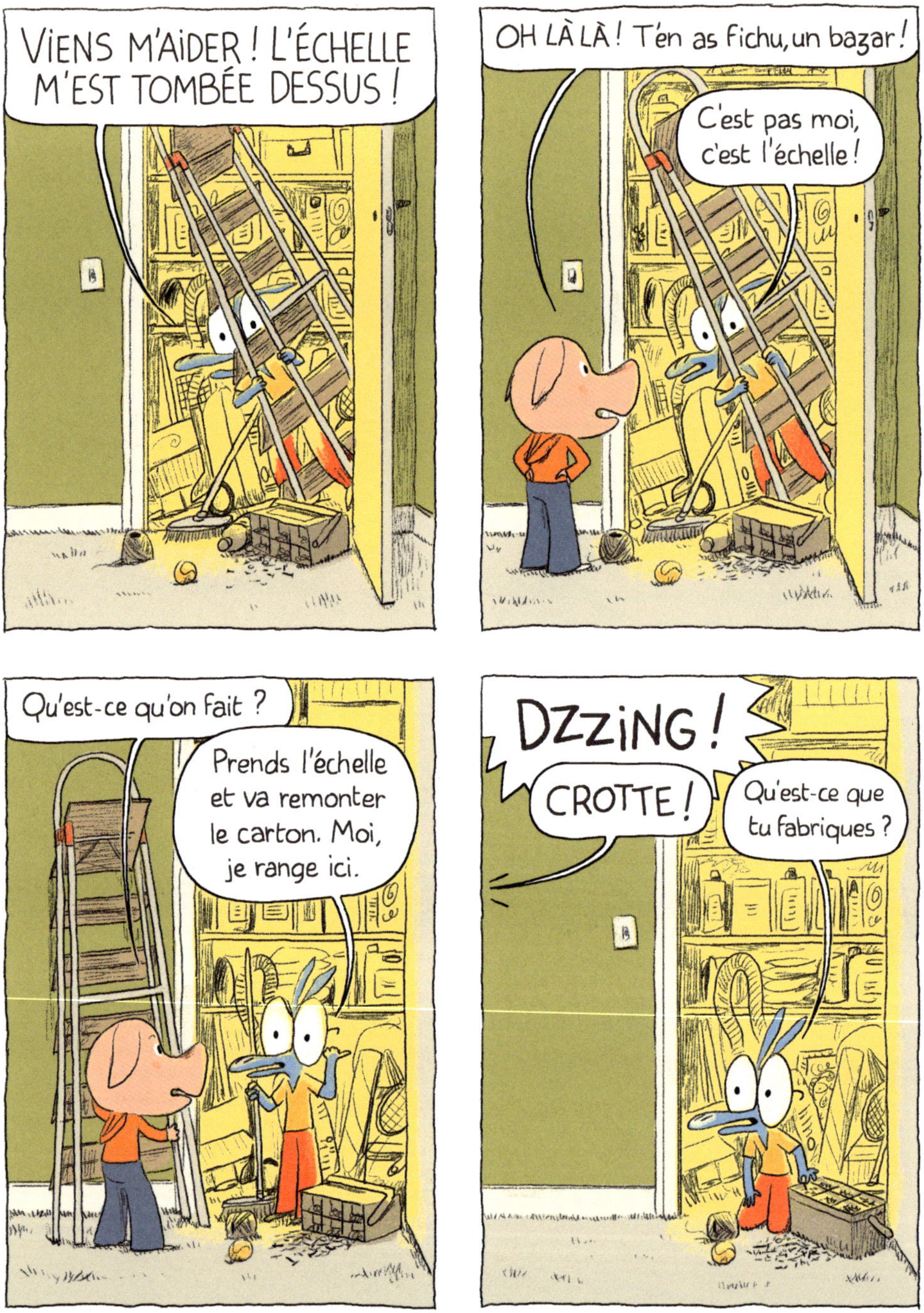
VIENS M'AIDER ! L'ÉCHELLE M'EST TOMBÉE DESSUS !
OH LÀ LÀ ! T'en as fichu, un bazar !
C'est pas moi, c'est l'échelle !
Qu'est-ce qu'on fait ?
Prends l'échelle et va remonter le carton. Moi, je range ici.
DZZING !
CROTTE !
Qu'est-ce que tu fabriques ?

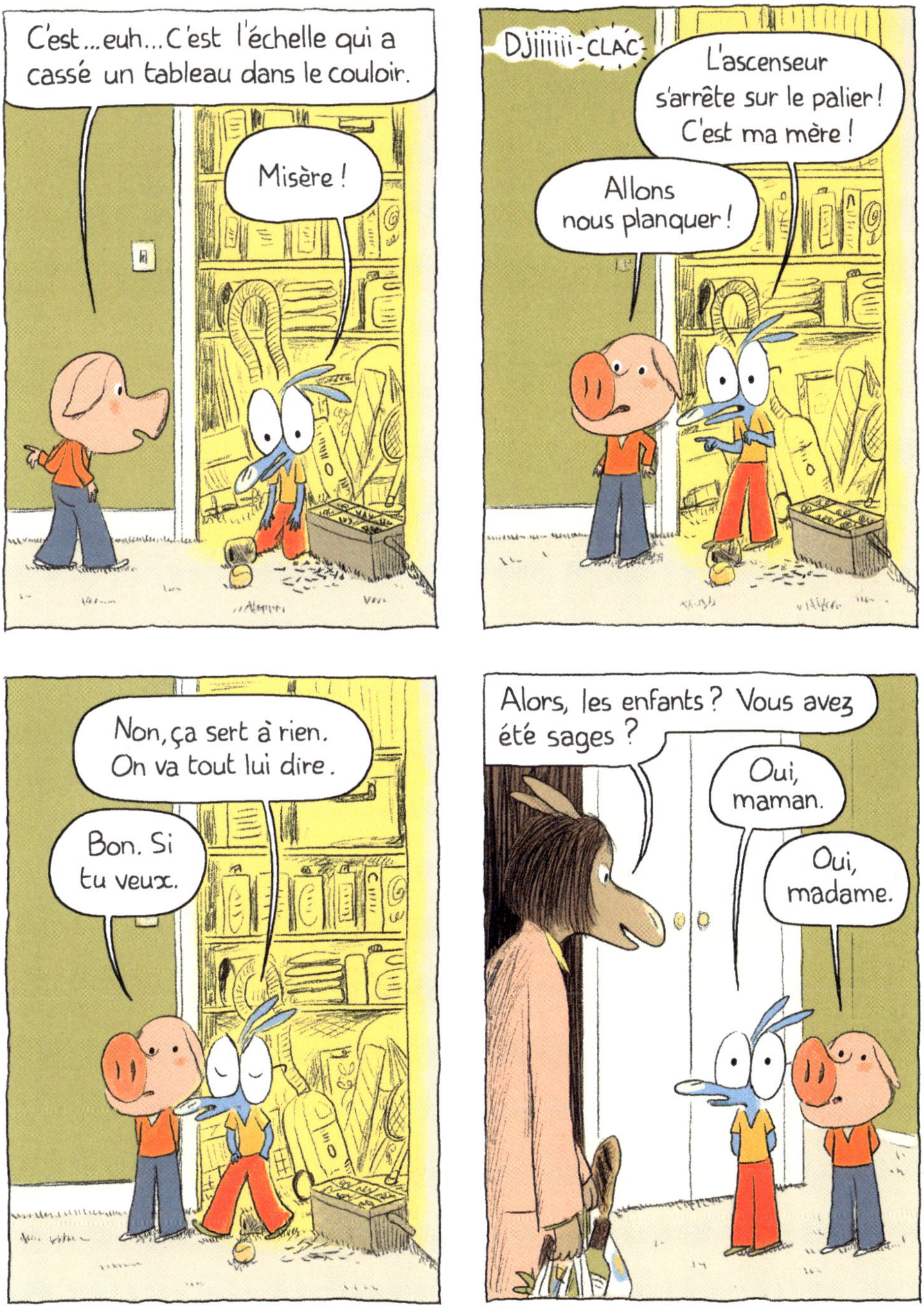

C'est... euh... C'est l'échelle qui a cassé un tableau dans le couloir.
Misère !
DJiiiiii-CLAC
L'ascenseur s'arrête sur le palier ! C'est ma mère !
Allons nous planquer !
Non, ça sert à rien. On va tout lui dire.
Bon. Si tu veux.
Alors, les enfants ? Vous avez été sages ?
Oui, maman.
Oui, madame.

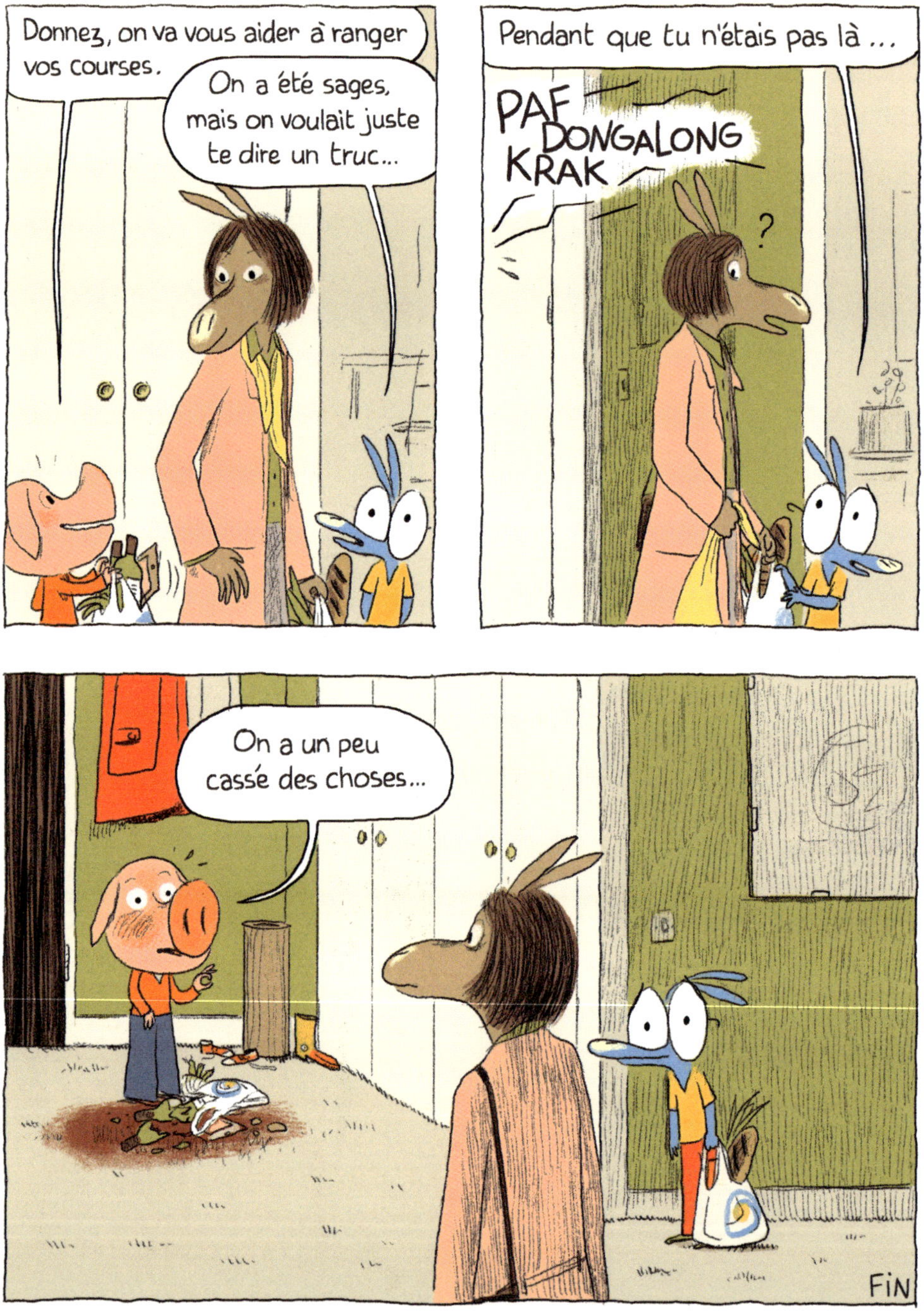
Donnez, on va vous aider à ranger vos courses.
On a été sages, mais on voulait juste te dire un truc...
Pendant que tu n'étais pas là ...
PAF
DONGALONG
KRAK
?
On a un peu cassé des choses...
FIN

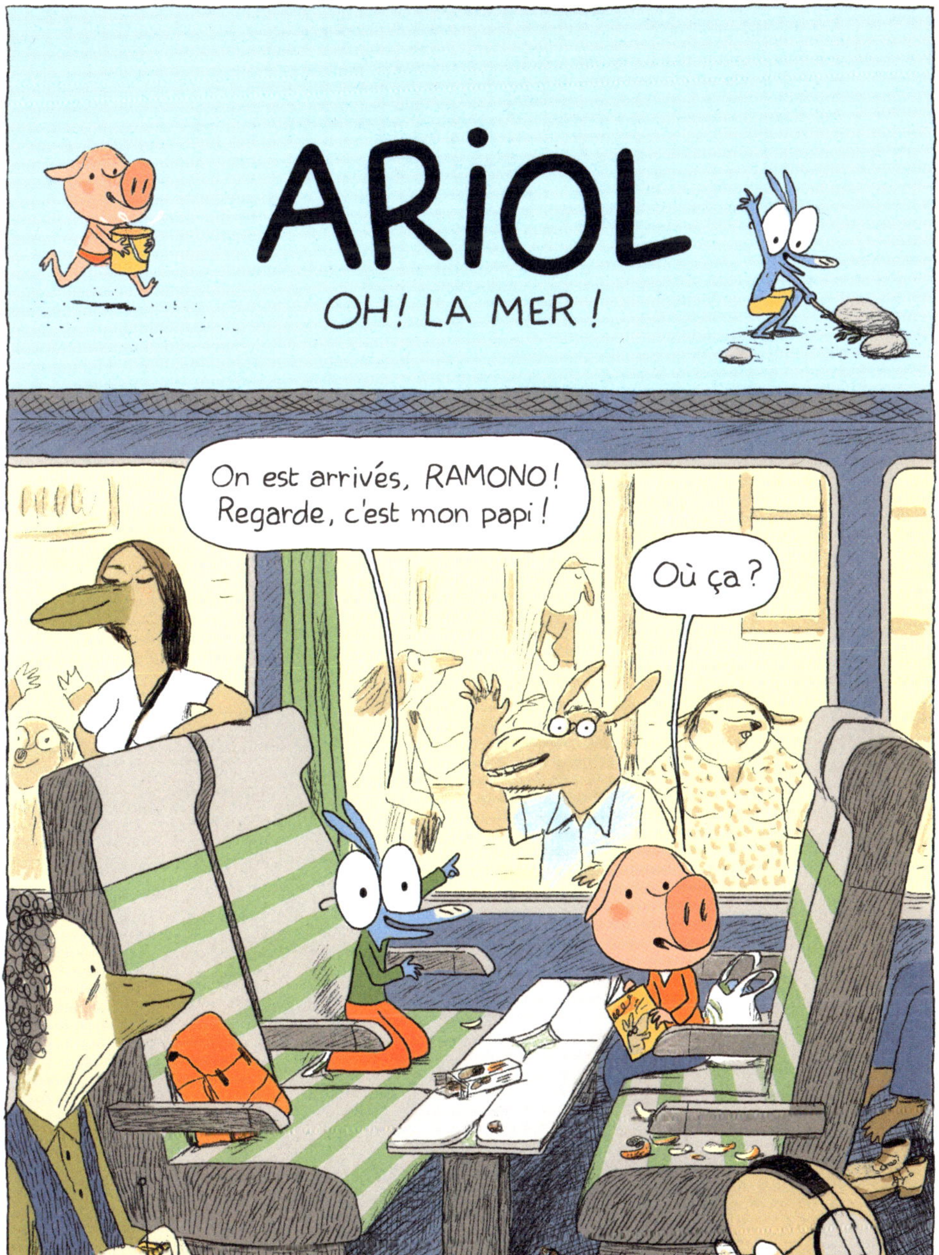
ARiOL
OH! LA MER !
On est arrivés, RAMONO ! Regarde, c'est mon papi !
Où ça ?

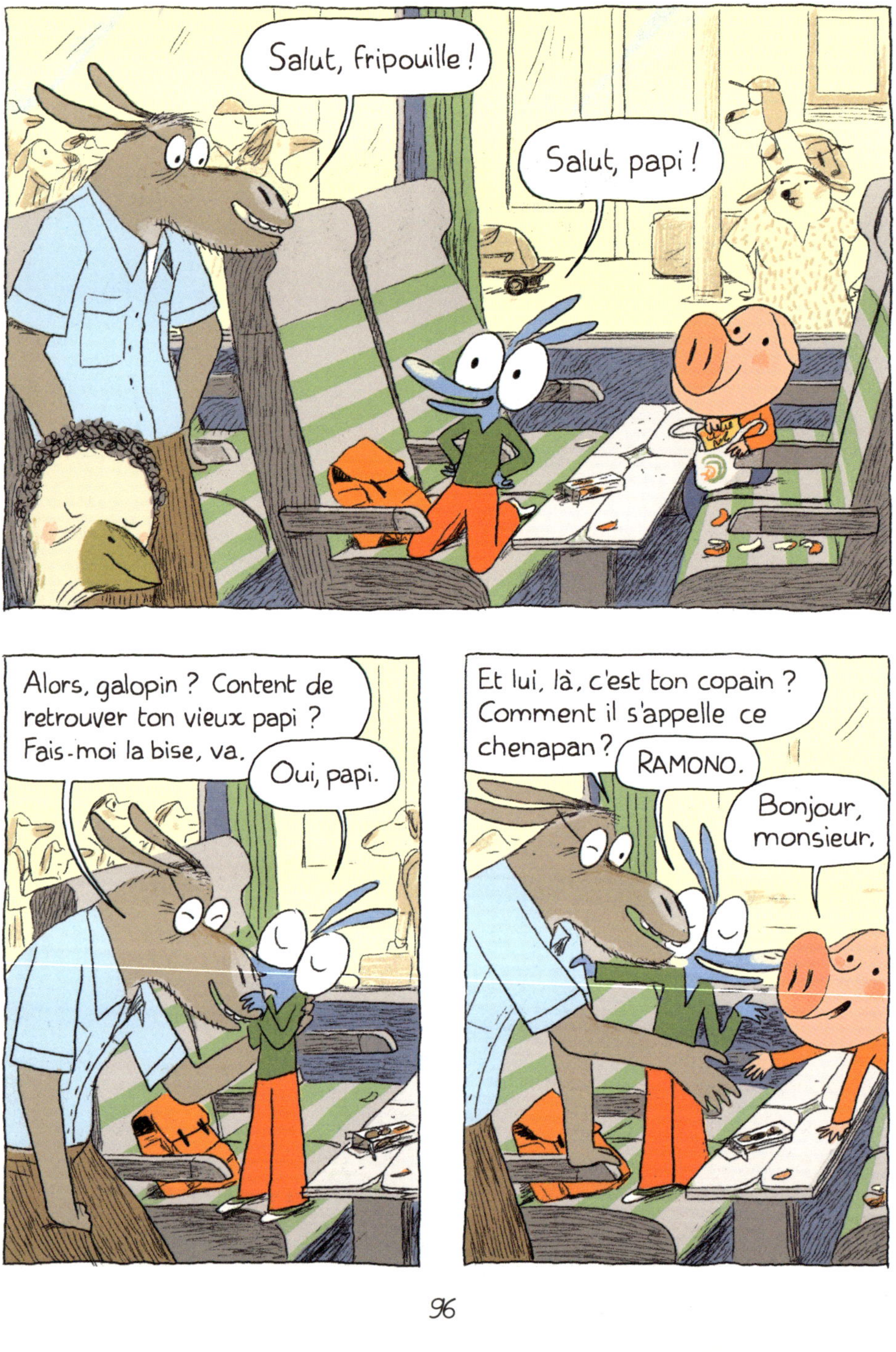
Salut, fripouille !
Salut, papi !
Alors, galopin ? Content de retrouver ton vieux papi ? Fais-moi la bise, va.
Oui, papi.
Et lui, là, c'est ton copain ? Comment il s'appelle ce chenapan ?
RAMONO.
Bonjour, monsieur.

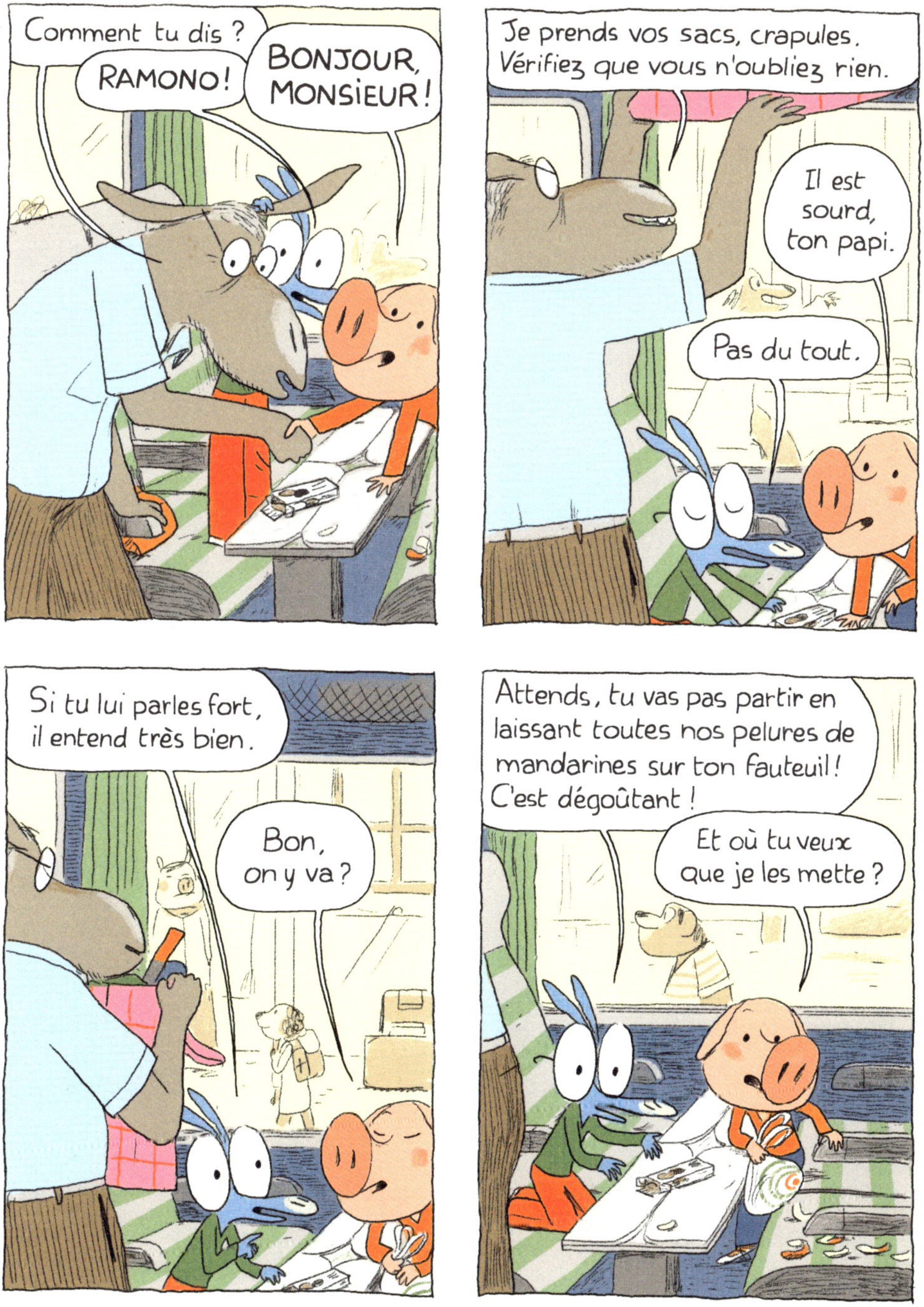
Comment tu dis ?
RAMONO !
BONJOUR, MONSIEUR !
Je prends vos sacs, crapules. Vérifiez que vous n'oubliez rien.
Il est sourd, ton papi.
Pas du tout.
Si tu lui parles fort, il entend très bien.
Bon, on y va ?
Attends, tu vas pas partir en laissant toutes nos pelures de mandarines sur ton fauteuil ! C'est dégoûtant !
Et où tu veux que je les mette ?

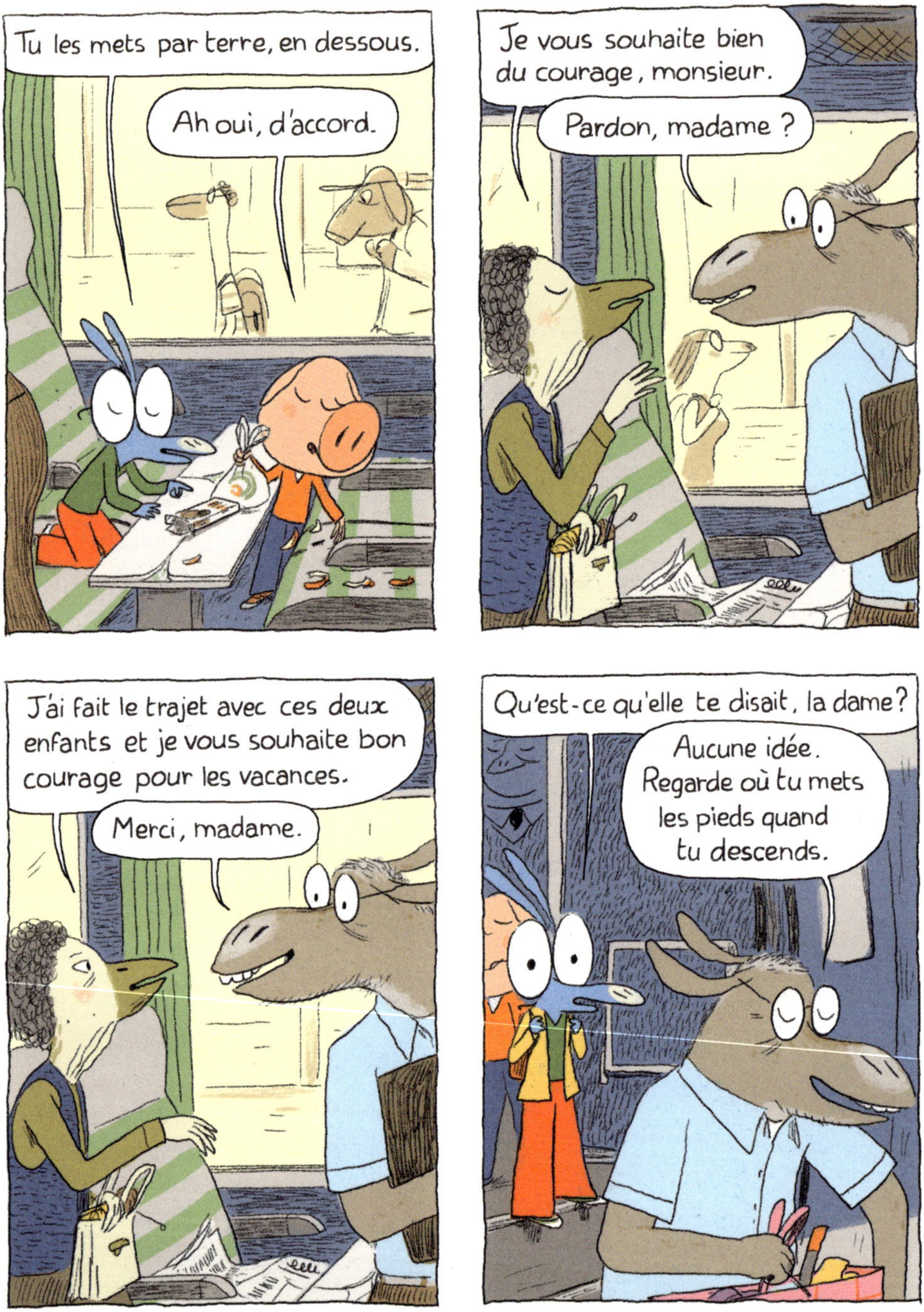
Tu les mets par terre, en dessous.
Ah oui, d'accord.
Je vous souhaite bien du courage, monsieur.
Pardon, madame ?
J'ai fait le trajet avec ces deux enfants et je vous souhaite bon courage pour les vacances.
Merci, madame.
Qu'est-ce qu'elle te disait, la dame ?
Aucune idée. Regarde où tu mets les pieds quand tu descends.

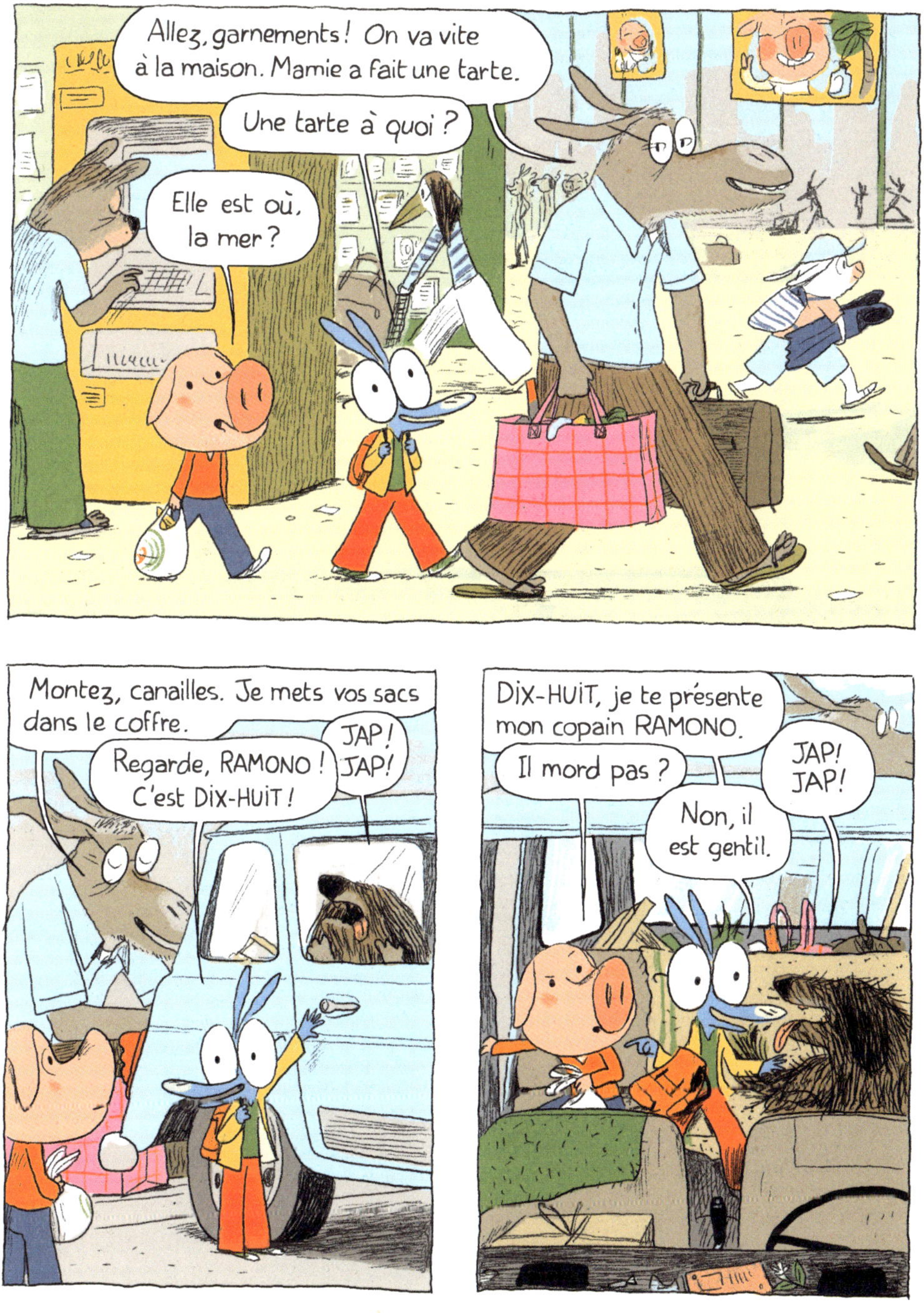

Allez, garnements ! On va vite à la maison. Mamie a fait une tarte.
Une tarte à quoi ?
Elle est où, la mer ?
Montez, canailles. Je mets vos sacs dans le coffre.
Regarde, RAMONO ! C'est DIX-HUIT !
JAP ! JAP !
DIX-HUIT, je te présente mon copain RAMONO.
Il mord pas ?
JAP ! JAP !
Non, il est gentil.

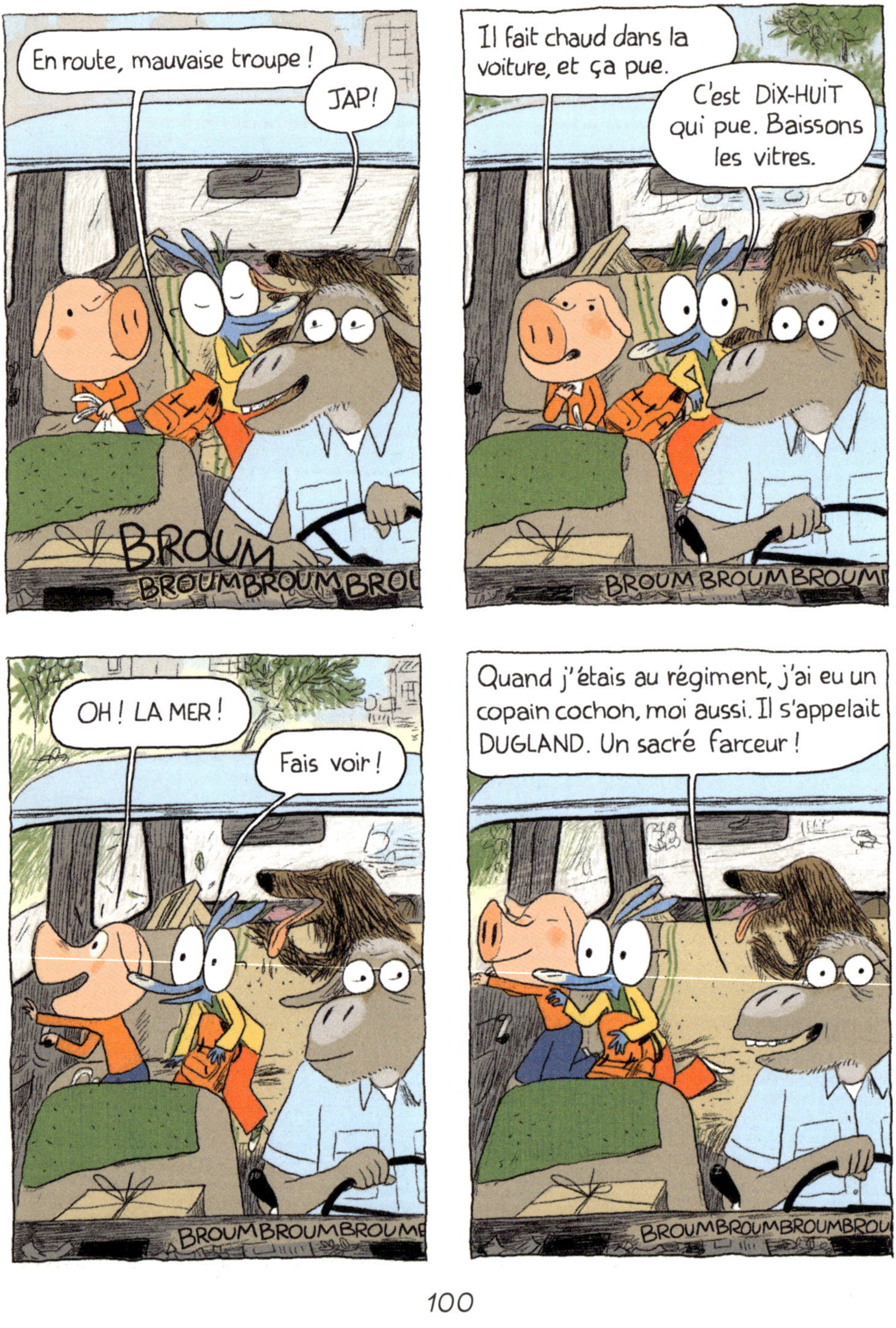
En route, mauvaise troupe !
JAP!
BROUM
BROUMBROUMBROU
Il fait chaud dans la voiture, et ça pue.
C'est DIX-HUIT qui pue. Baissons les vitres.
BROUM BROUM BROUM
OH ! LA MER !
Fais voir !
BROUMBROUMBROUM
Quand j'étais au régiment, j'ai eu un copain cochon, moi aussi. Il s'appelait DUGLAND. Un sacré farceur !
BROUMBROUMBROUMBROU

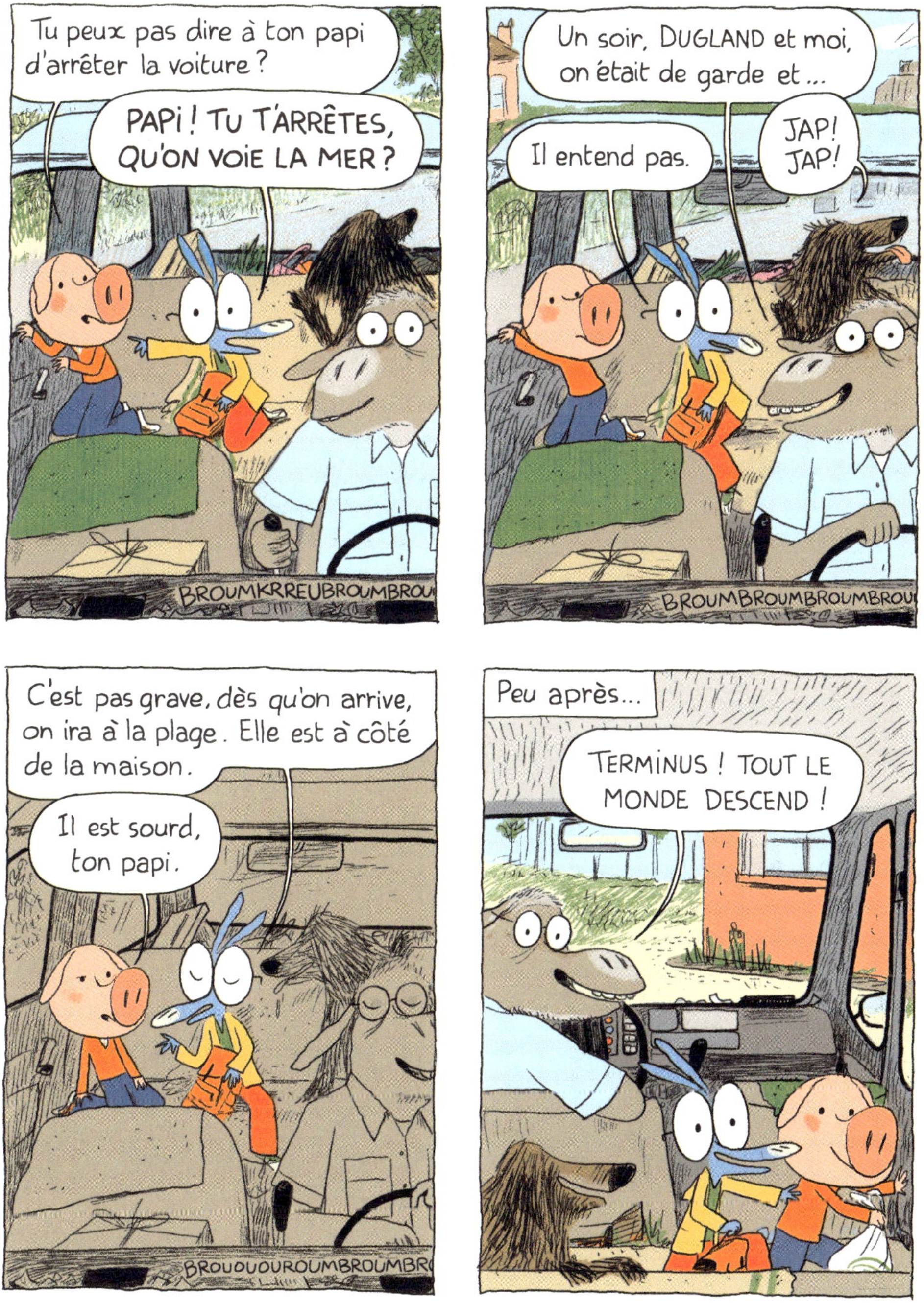
Tu peux pas dire à ton papi d'arrêter la voiture ?
PAPi ! TU T'ARRÊTES, QU'ON VOIE LA MER ?
BROUMKRREUBROUMBROU
Un soir, DUGLAND et moi, on était de garde et ...
Il entend pas.
JAP! JAP!
BROUMBROUMBROUMBROU
C'est pas grave, dès qu'on arrive, on ira à la plage. Elle est à côté de la maison.
Il est sourd, ton papi.
BROUOUOUROUMBROUMBR
Peu après...
TERMINUS ! TOUT LE MONDE DESCEND !

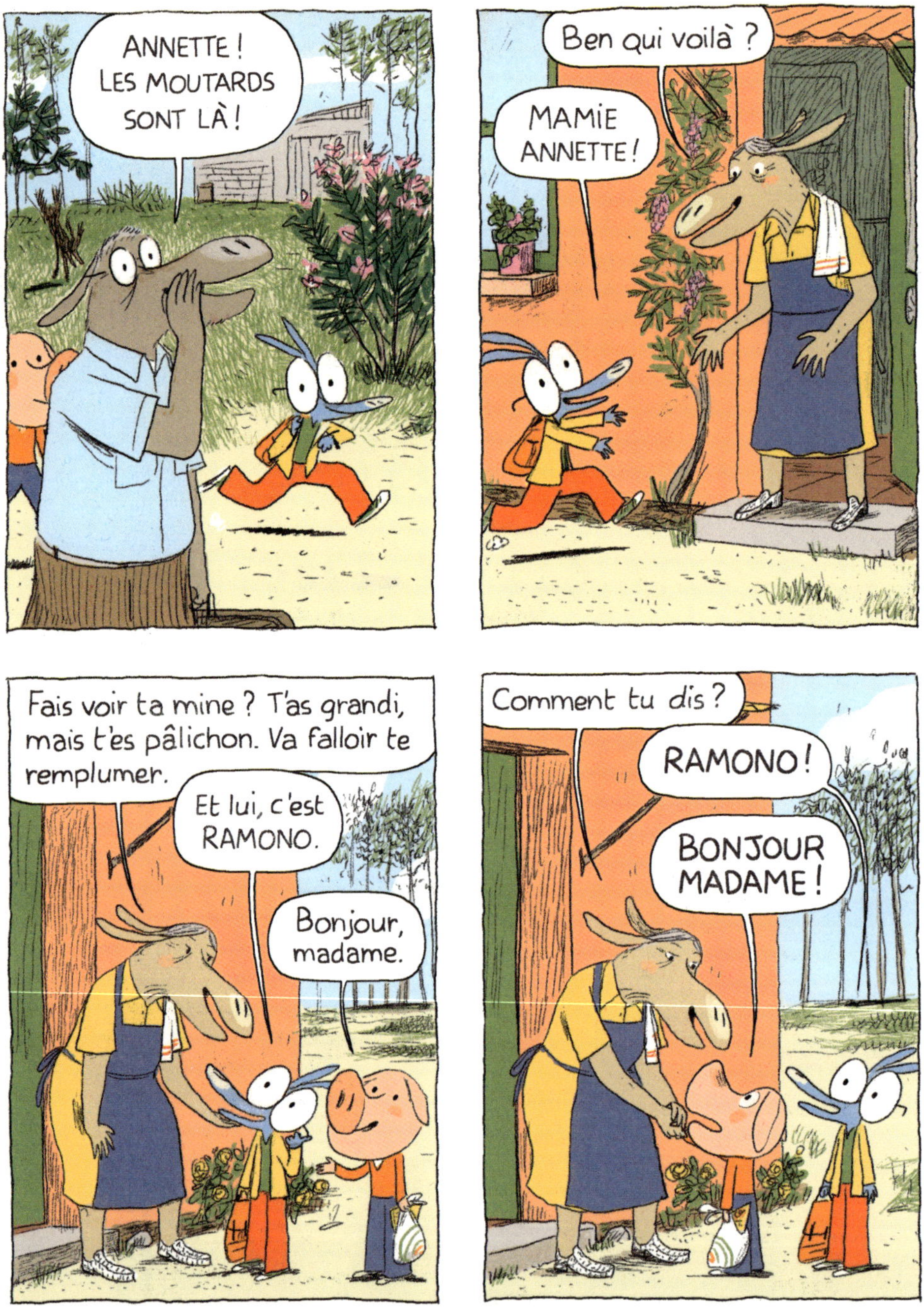
ANNETTE ! LES MOUTARDS SONT LÀ !
Ben qui voilà ?
MAMIE ANNETTE !
Fais voir ta mine ? T'as grandi, mais t'es pâlichon. Va falloir te remplumer.
Et lui, c'est RAMONO.
Bonjour, madame.
Comment tu dis ?
RAMONO !
BONJOUR MADAME !

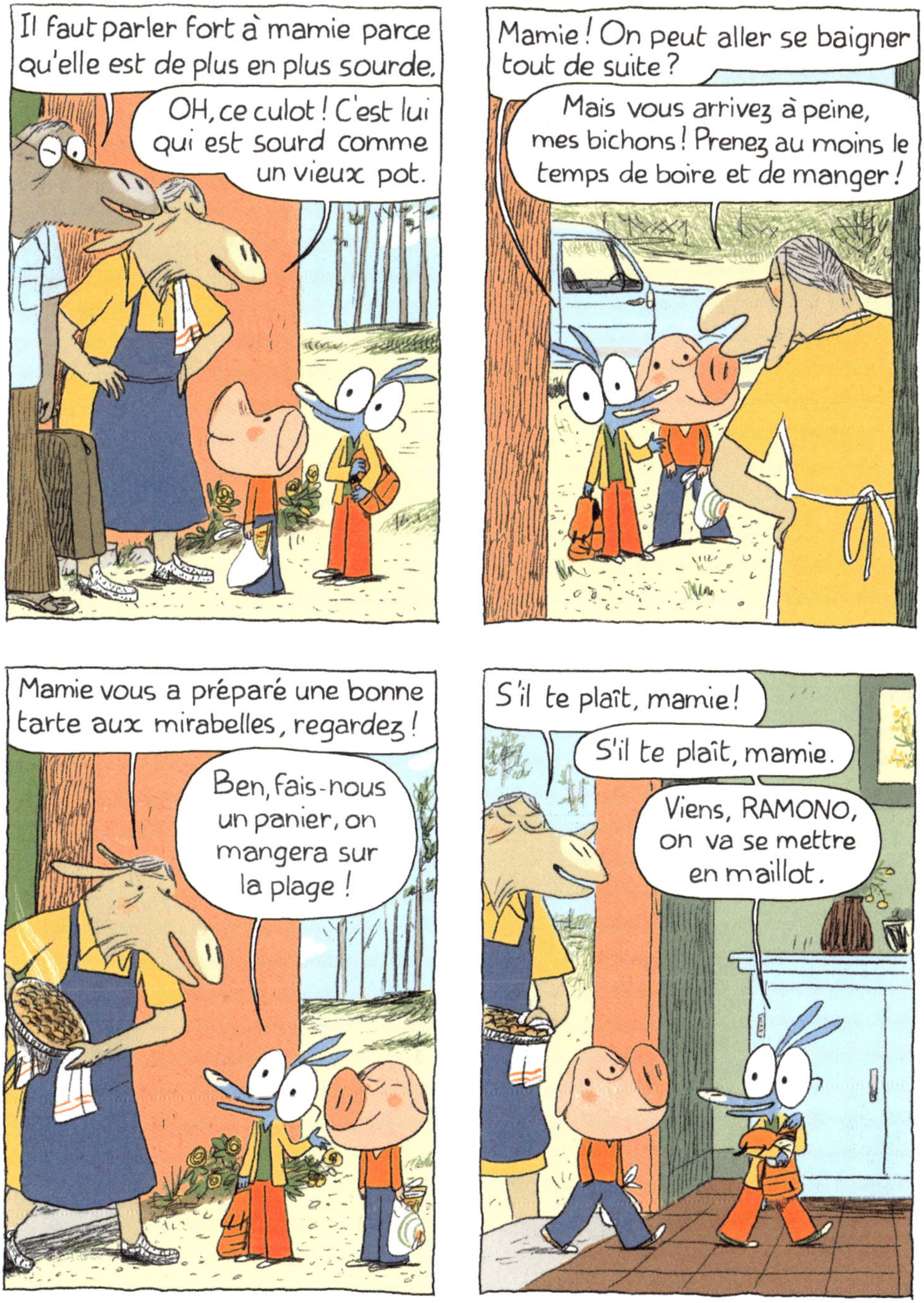
Il faut parler fort à mamie parce qu'elle est de plus en plus sourde.
OH, ce culot ! C'est lui qui est sourd comme un vieux pot.
Mamie ! On peut aller se baigner tout de suite ?
Mais vous arrivez à peine, mes bichons ! Prenez au moins le temps de boire et de manger !
Mamie vous a préparé une bonne tarte aux mirabelles, regardez !
Ben, fais-nous un panier, on mangera sur la plage !
S'il te plaît, mamie !
S'il te plaît, mamie.
Viens, RAMONO, on va se mettre en maillot.

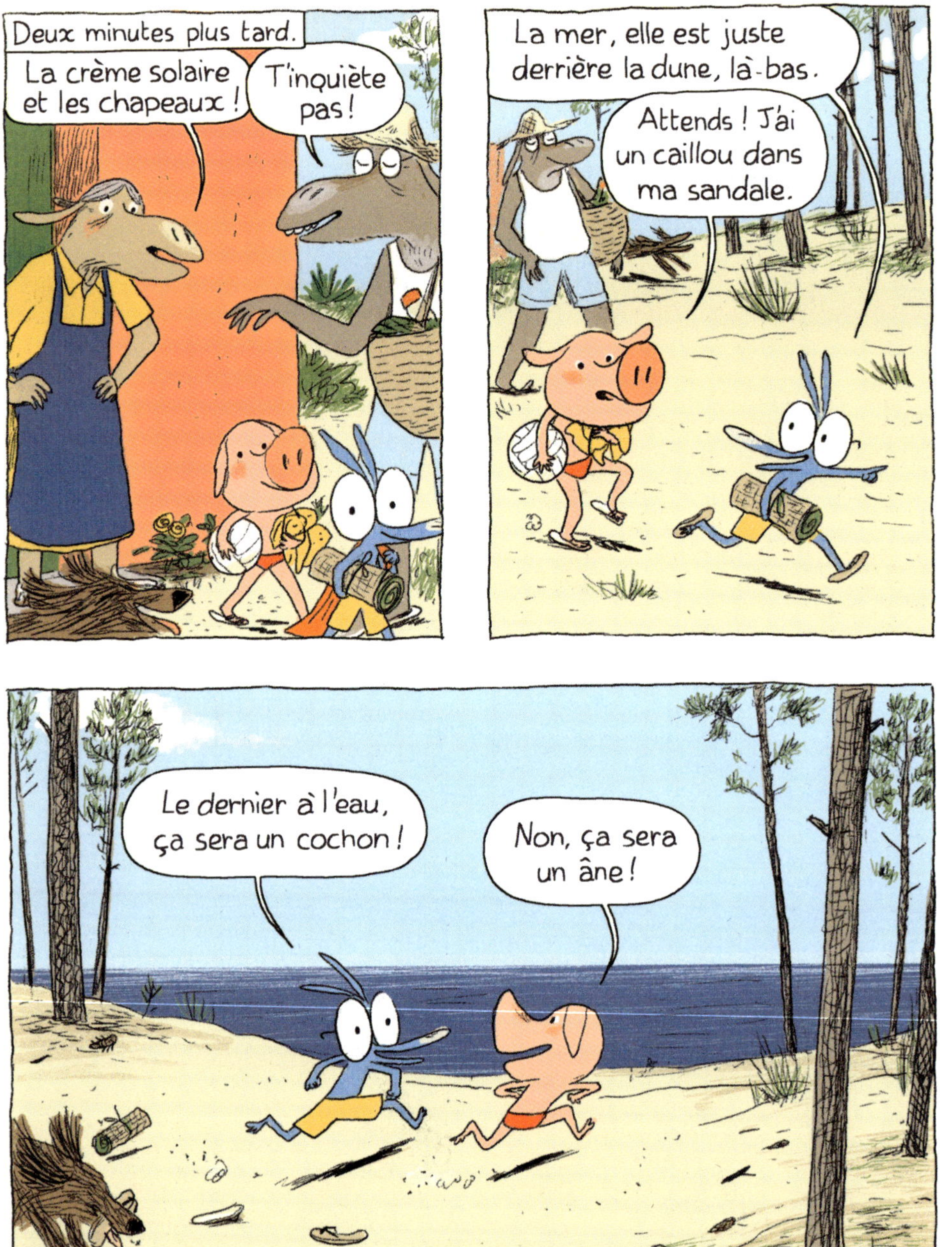
Deux minutes plus tard.
La crème solaire et les chapeaux !
T'inquiète pas !
La mer, elle est juste derrière la dune, là-bas.
Attends ! J'ai un caillou dans ma sandale.
Le dernier à l'eau, ça sera un cochon !
Non, ça sera un âne !
FIN

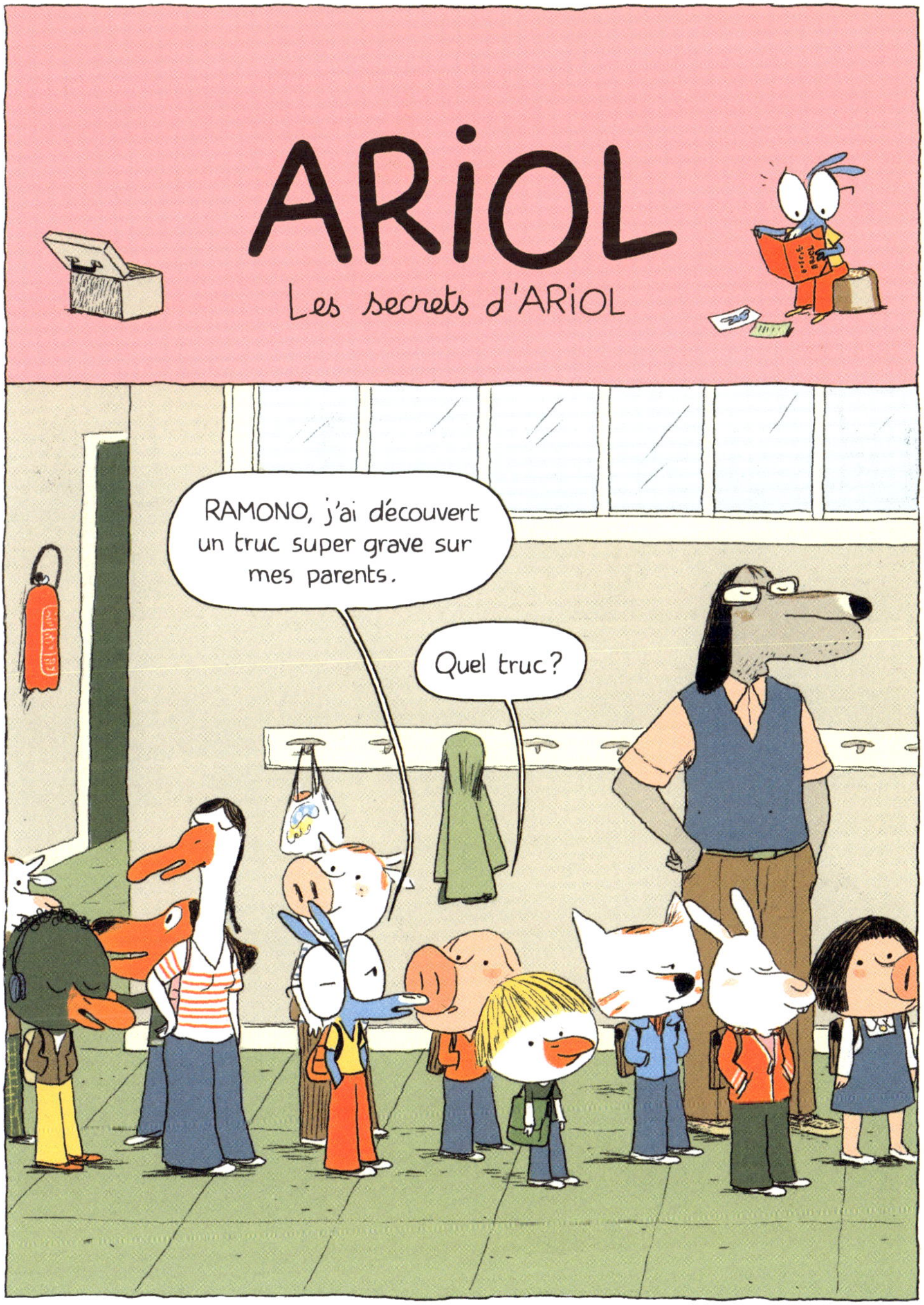
ARiOL
Les secrets d'ARiOL
RAMONO, j'ai découvert un truc super grave sur mes parents.
Quel truc?

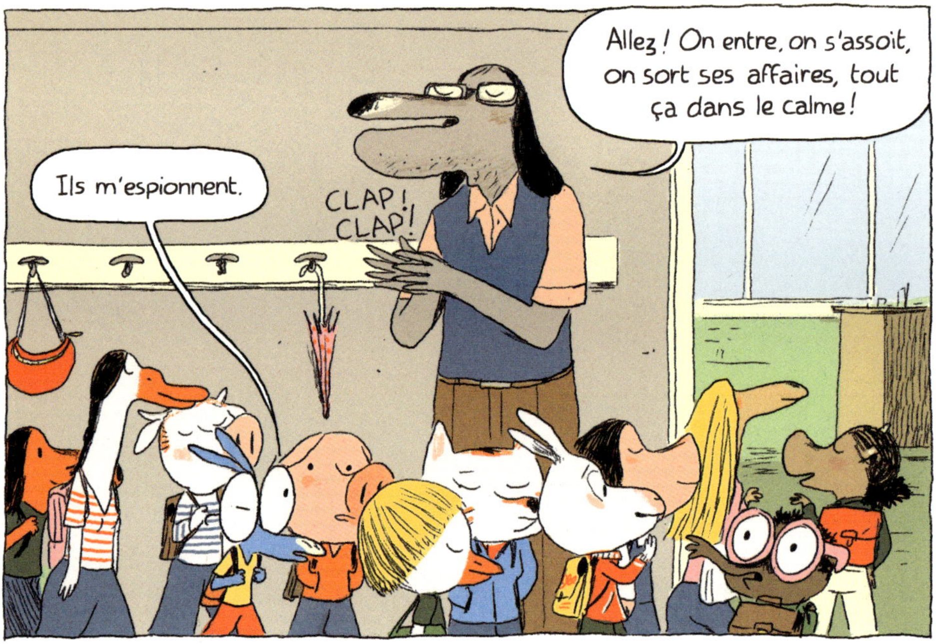
Allez ! On entre, on s'assoit, on sort ses affaires, tout ça dans le calme !
CLAP ! CLAP !
Ils m'espionnent.

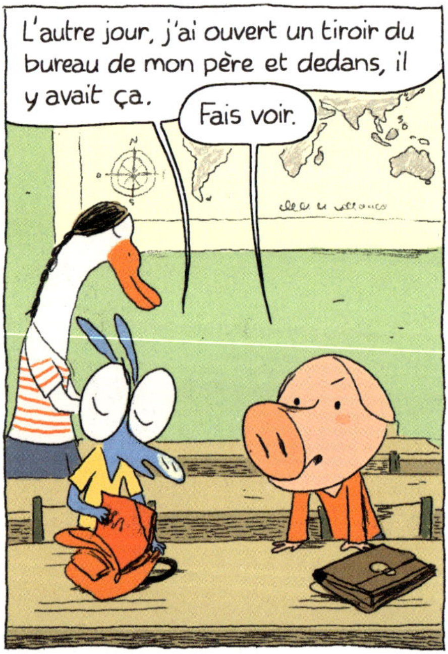
L'autre jour, j'ai ouvert un tiroir du bureau de mon père et dedans, il y avait ça.
Fais voir.

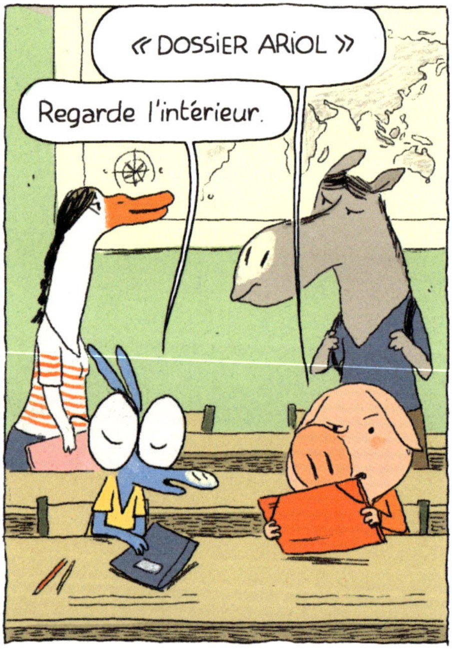
« DOSSIER ARIOL »
Regarde l'intérieur.

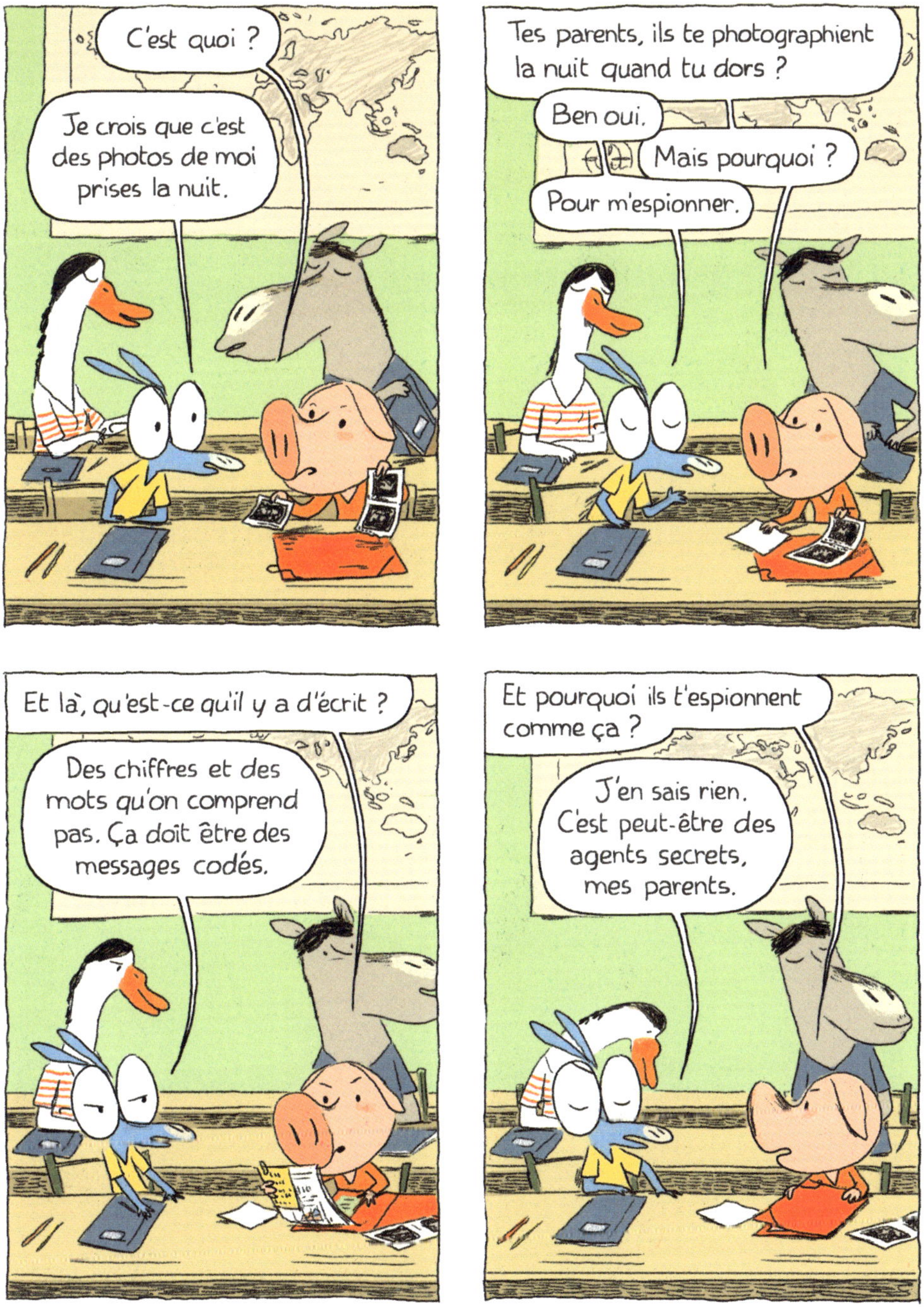
C'est quoi ?
Je crois que c'est des photos de moi prises la nuit.
Tes parents, ils te photographient la nuit quand tu dors ?
Ben oui.
Mais pourquoi ?
Pour m'espionner.
Et là, qu'est-ce qu'il y a d'écrit ?
Des chiffres et des mots qu'on comprend pas. Ça doit être des messages codés.
Et pourquoi ils t'espionnent comme ça ?
J'en sais rien. C'est peut-être des agents secrets, mes parents.

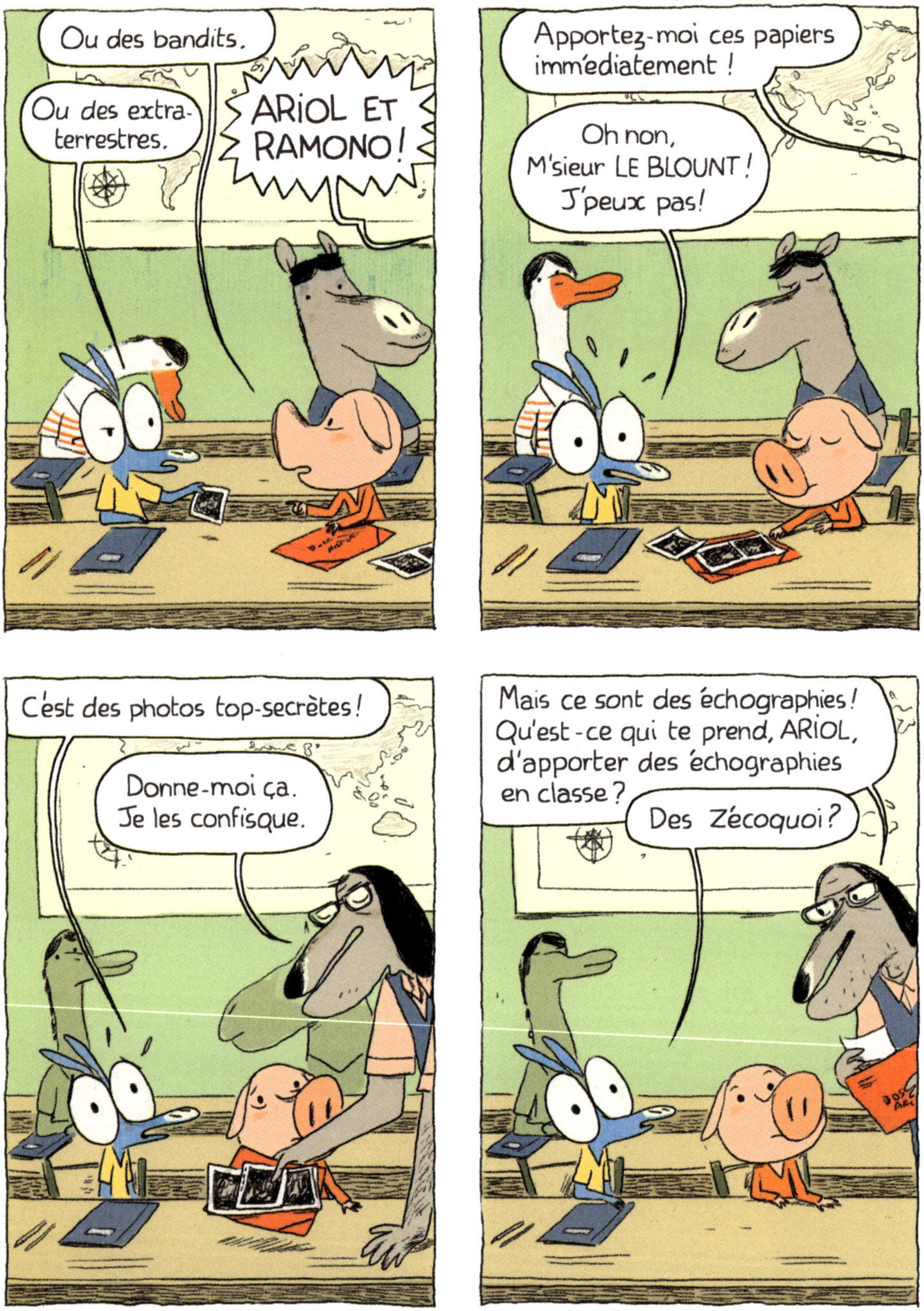
Ou des bandits.
Ou des extra-terrestres.
ARiOL ET RAMONO !
Apportez-moi ces papiers immédiatement !
Oh non, M'sieur LE BLOUNT ! J'peux pas !
C'est des photos top-secrètes !
Donne-moi ça. Je les confisque.
Mais ce sont des échographies ! Qu'est-ce qui te prend, ARiOL, d'apporter des échographies en classe ?
Des Zécoquoi ?

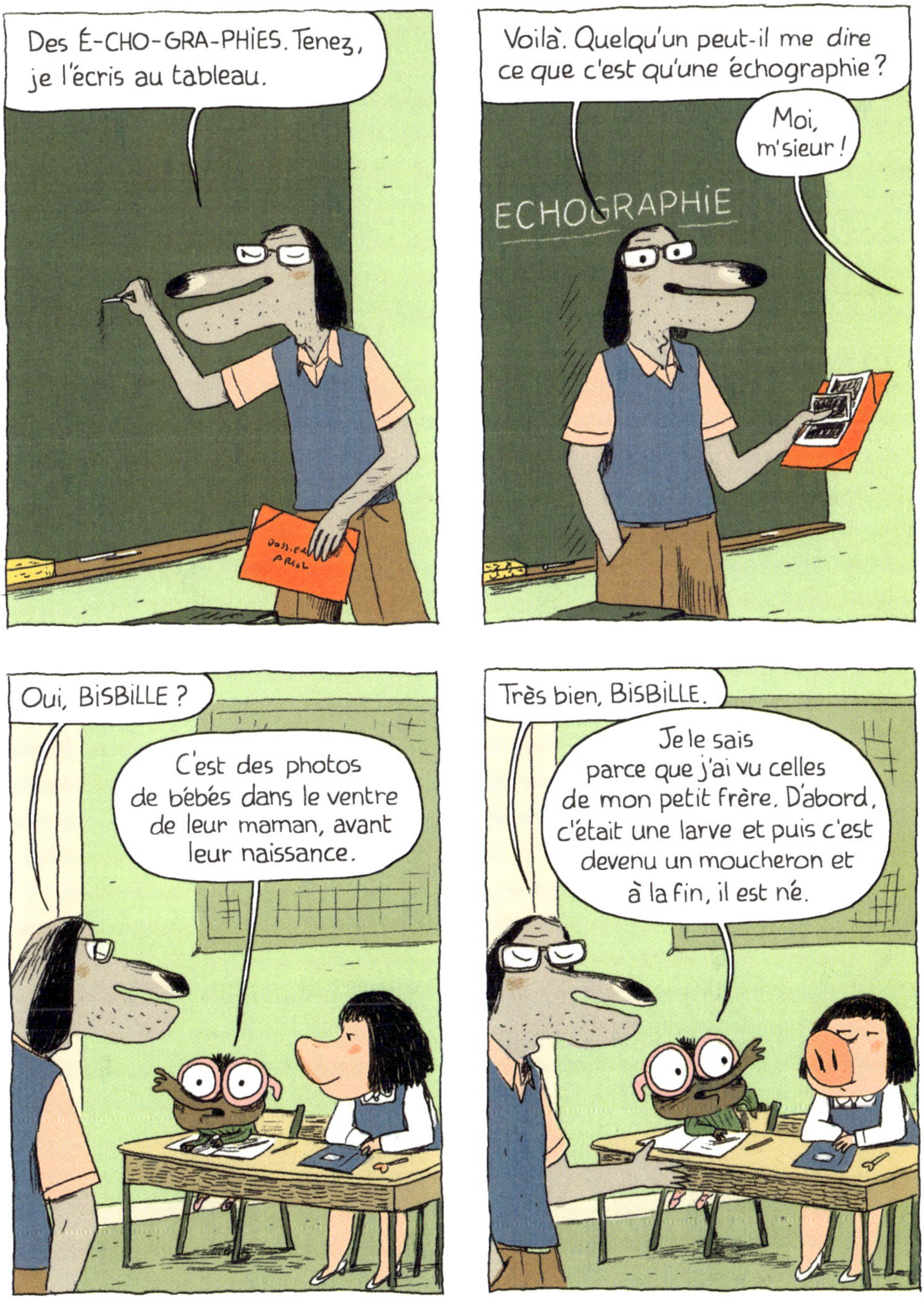
Des É-CHO-GRA-PHIES. Tenez, je l'écris au tableau.
Voilà. Quelqu'un peut-il me dire ce que c'est qu'une échographie ?
ECHOGRAPHIE
Moi, m'sieur !
Oui, BISBILLE ?
C'est des photos de bébés dans le ventre de leur maman, avant leur naissance.
Très bien, BISBILLE.
Je le sais parce que j'ai vu celles de mon petit frère. D'abord, c'était une larve et puis c'est devenu un moucheron et à la fin, il est né.

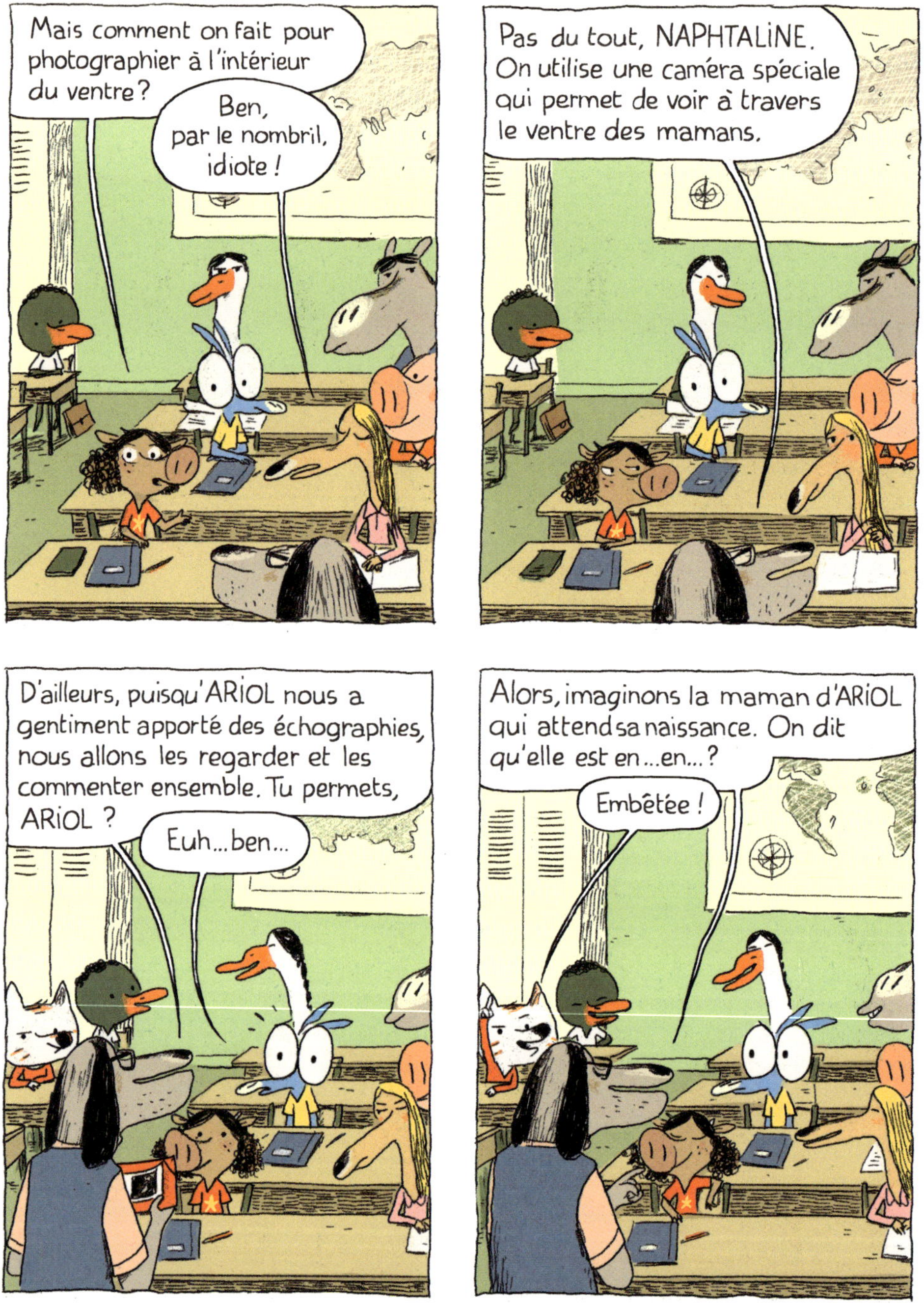
Mais comment on fait pour photographier à l'intérieur du ventre?
Ben, par le nombril, idiote !
Pas du tout, NAPHTALiNE. On utilise une caméra spéciale qui permet de voir à travers le ventre des mamans.
D'ailleurs, puisqu'ARiOL nous a gentiment apporté des échographies, nous allons les regarder et les commenter ensemble. Tu permets, ARiOL ?
Euh...ben...
Alors, imaginons la maman d'ARiOL qui attend sa naissance. On dit qu'elle est en...en...?
Embêtée !

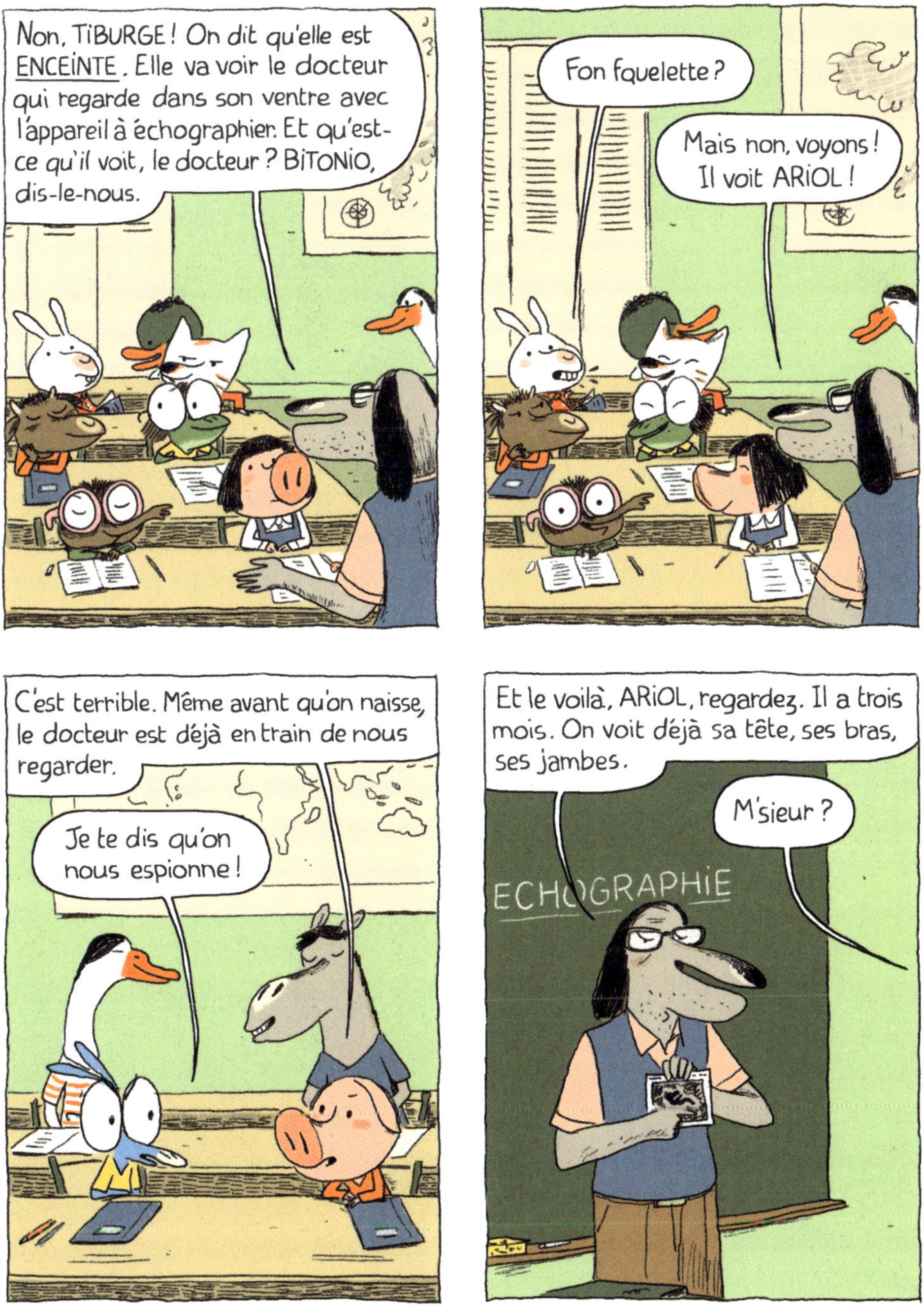
Non, TIBURGE ! On dit qu'elle est ENCEINTE. Elle va voir le docteur qui regarde dans son ventre avec l'appareil à échographier. Et qu'est-ce qu'il voit, le docteur ? BITONIO, dis-le-nous.
Fon fquelette ?
Mais non, voyons ! Il voit ARIOL !
C'est terrible. Même avant qu'on naisse, le docteur est déjà en train de nous regarder.
Je te dis qu'on nous espionne !
Et le voilà, ARIOL, regardez. Il a trois mois. On voit déjà sa tête, ses bras, ses jambes.
M'sieur ?
ECHOGRAPHIE

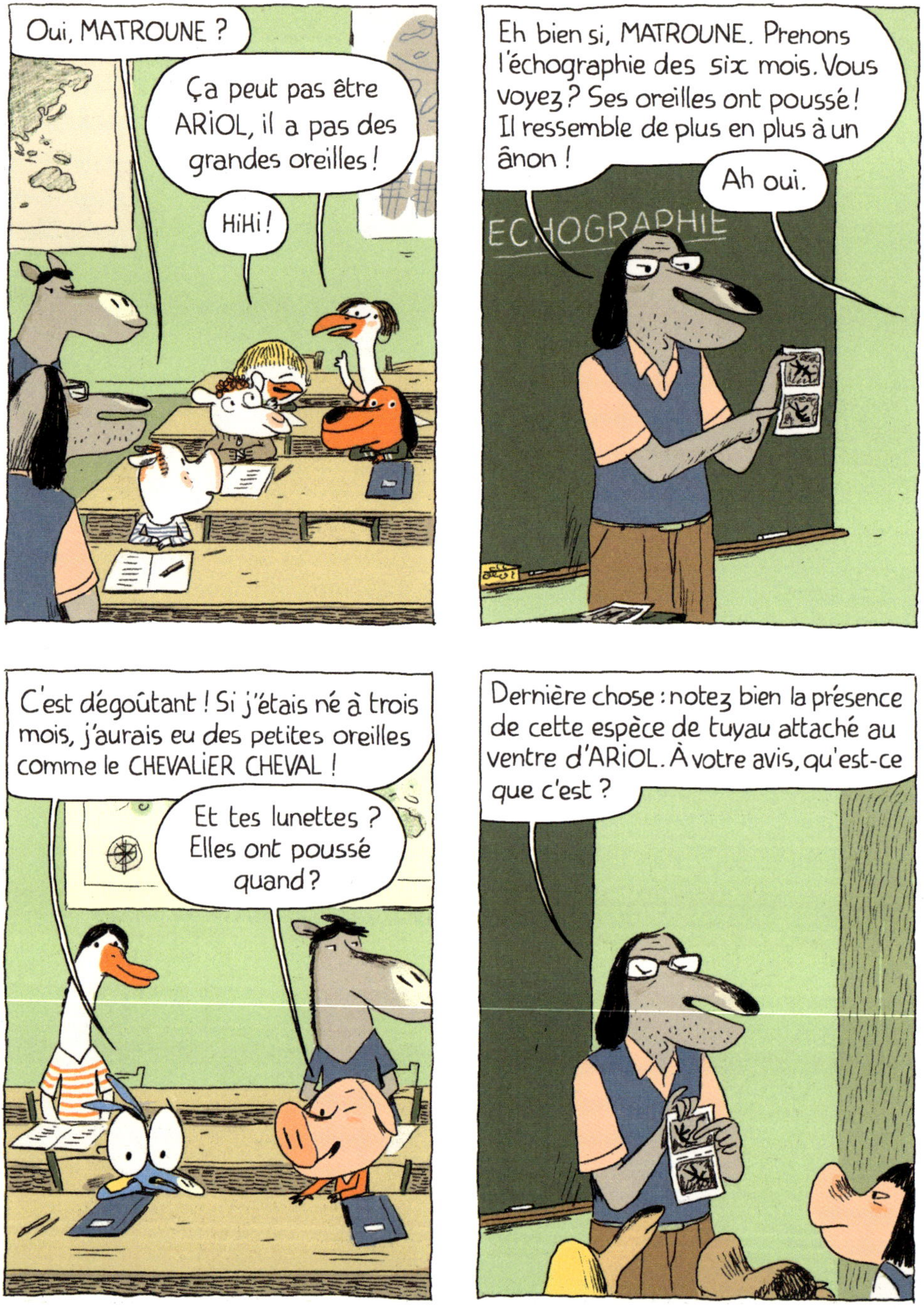
Oui, MATROUNE ?
Ça peut pas être ARIOL, il a pas des grandes oreilles !
HiHi !
Eh bien si, MATROUNE. Prenons l'échographie des six mois. Vous voyez ? Ses oreilles ont poussé ! Il ressemble de plus en plus à un ânon !
Ah oui.
ECHOGRAPHIE
C'est dégoûtant ! Si j'étais né à trois mois, j'aurais eu des petites oreilles comme le CHEVALIER CHEVAL !
Et tes lunettes ? Elles ont poussé quand ?
Dernière chose : notez bien la présence de cette espèce de tuyau attaché au ventre d'ARIOL. À votre avis, qu'est-ce que c'est ?

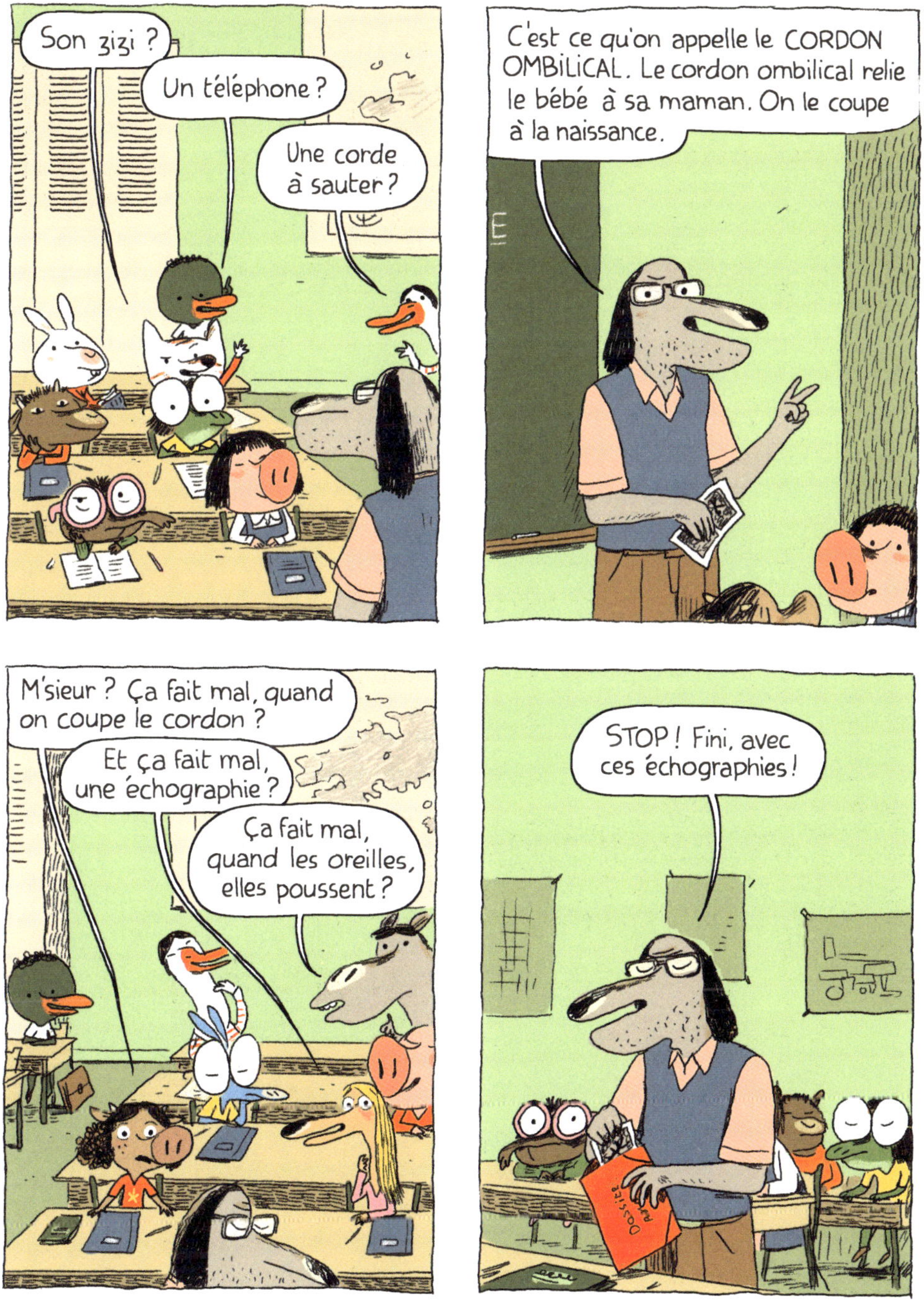
Son zizi ?
Un téléphone ?
Une corde à sauter ?
C'est ce qu'on appelle le CORDON OMBILICAL. Le cordon ombilical relie le bébé à sa maman. On le coupe à la naissance.
M'sieur ? Ça fait mal, quand on coupe le cordon ?
Et ça fait mal, une échographie ?
Ça fait mal, quand les oreilles, elles poussent ?
STOP ! Fini, avec ces échographies !

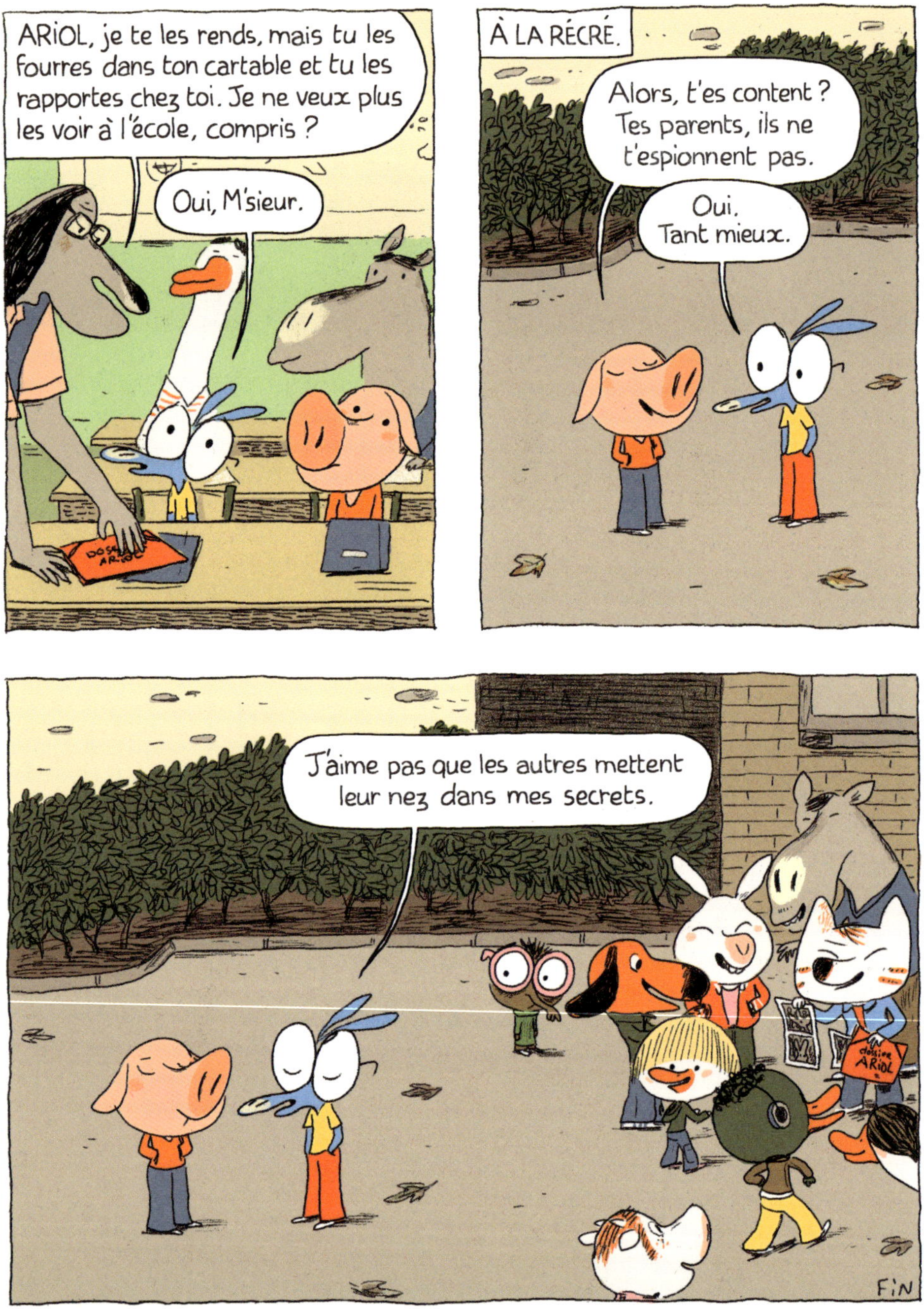
ARiOL, je te les rends, mais tu les fourres dans ton cartable et tu les rapportes chez toi. Je ne veux plus les voir à l'école, compris ?
Oui, M'sieur.
À LA RÉCRÉ.
Alors, t'es content ? Tes parents, ils ne t'espionnent pas.
Oui. Tant mieux.
J'aime pas que les autres mettent leur nez dans mes secrets.
FiN

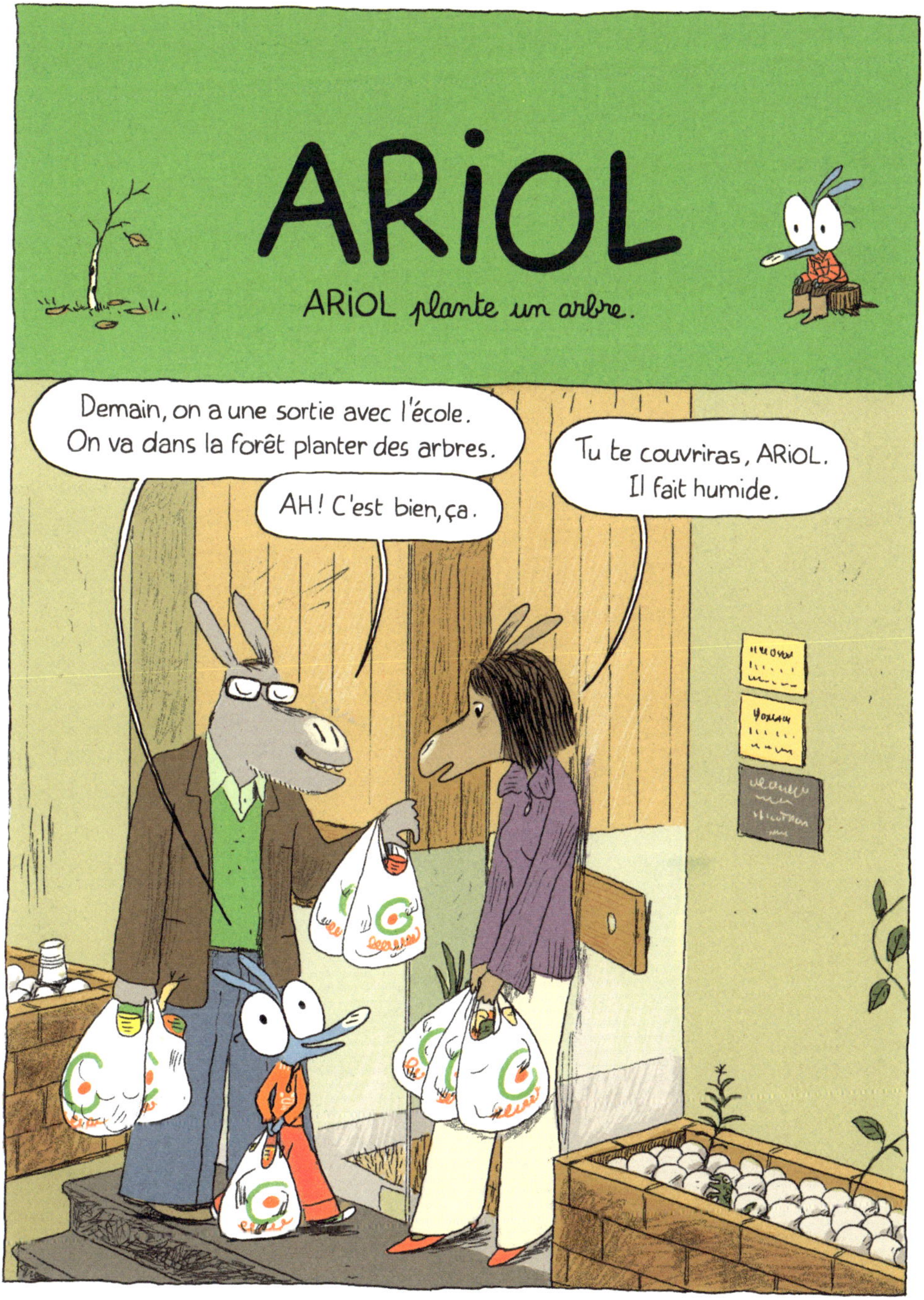
ARiOL
ARiOL plante un arbre.
Demain, on a une sortie avec l'école. On va dans la forêt planter des arbres.
AH ! C'est bien, ça.
Tu te couvriras, ARiOL. Il fait humide.

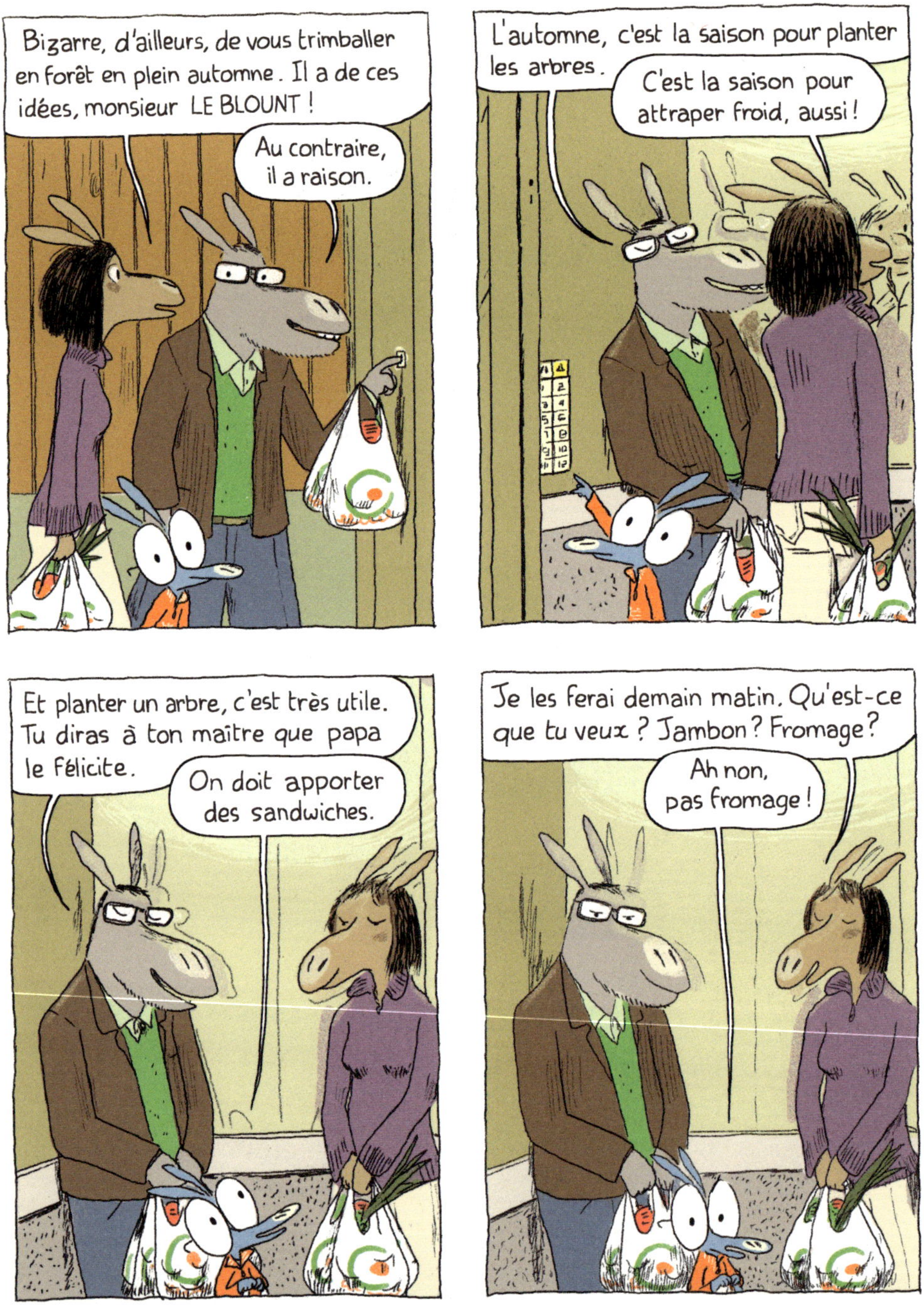

Bizarre, d'ailleurs, de vous trimballer en forêt en plein automne. Il a de ces idées, monsieur LE BLOUNT !
Au contraire, il a raison.
L'automne, c'est la saison pour planter les arbres.
C'est la saison pour attraper froid, aussi !
Et planter un arbre, c'est très utile. Tu diras à ton maître que papa le félicite.
On doit apporter des sandwiches.
Je les ferai demain matin. Qu'est-ce que tu veux ? Jambon ? Fromage ?
Ah non, pas fromage !

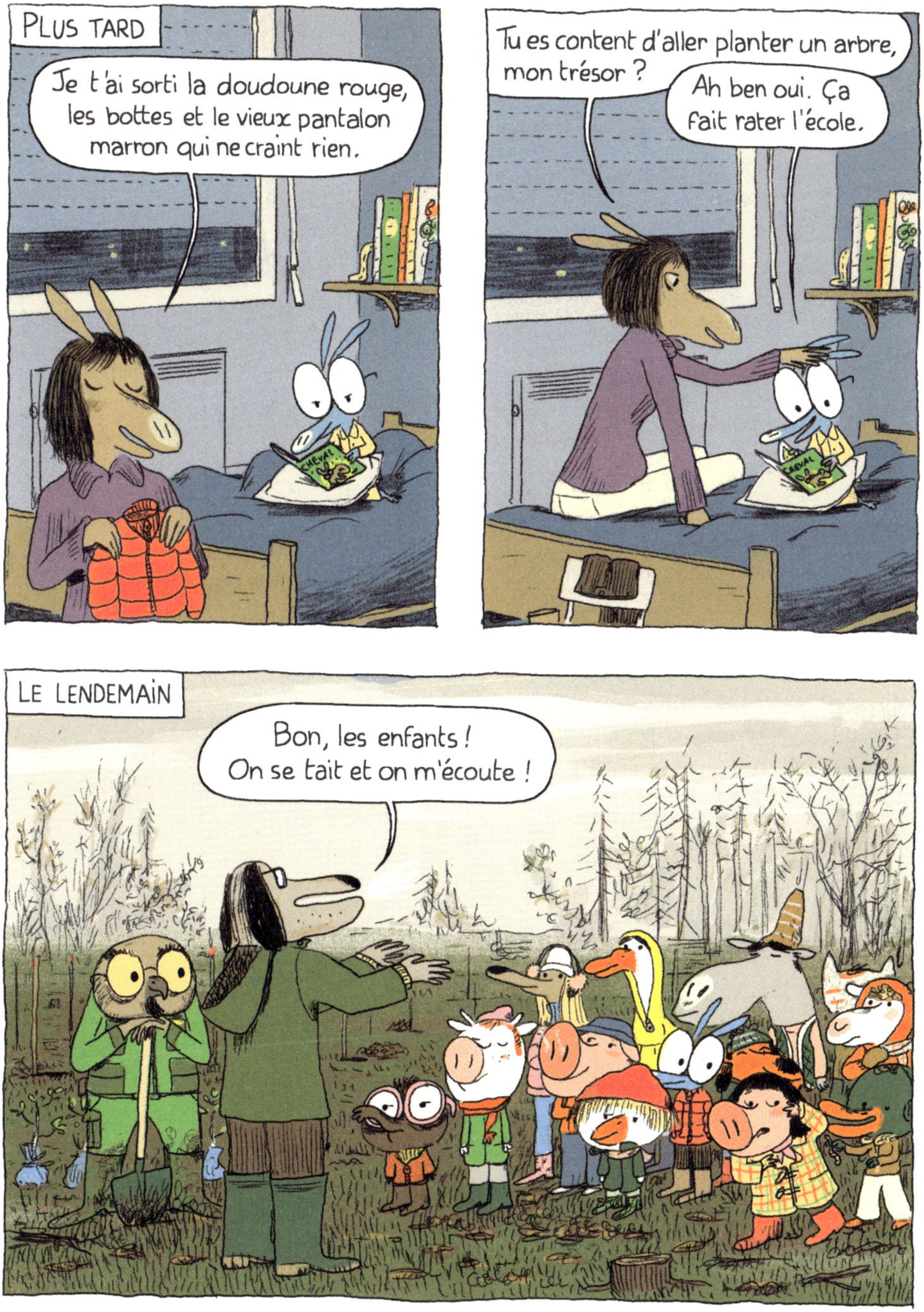
PLUS TARD
Je t'ai sorti la doudoune rouge, les bottes et le vieux pantalon marron qui ne craint rien.
CHEVAL
Tu es content d'aller planter un arbre, mon trésor ?
Ah ben oui. Ça fait rater l'école.
LE LENDEMAIN
Bon, les enfants ! On se tait et on m'écoute !

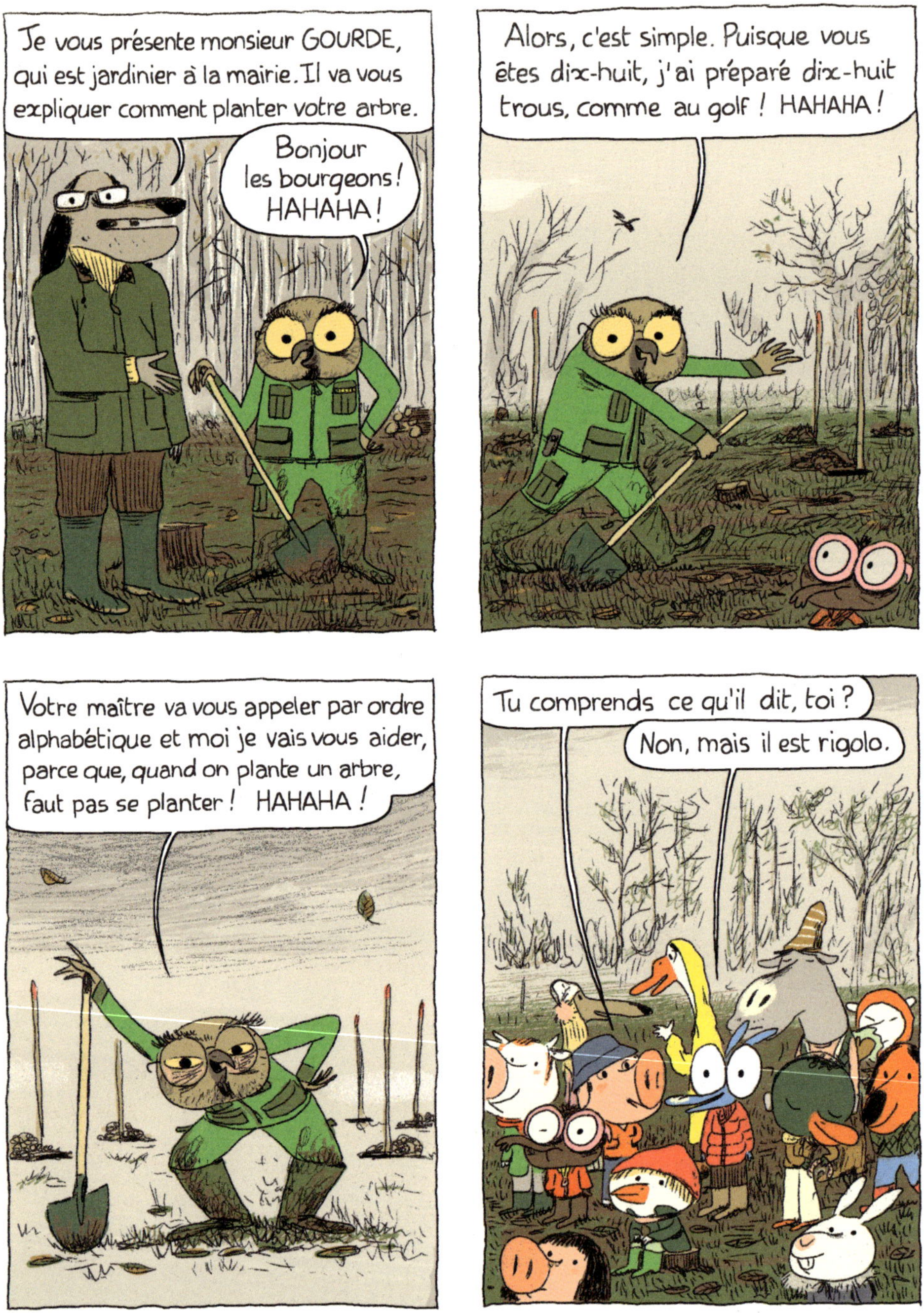
Je vous présente monsieur GOURDE, qui est jardinier à la mairie. Il va vous expliquer comment planter votre arbre.
Bonjour les bourgeons ! HAHAHA !
Alors, c'est simple. Puisque vous êtes dix-huit, j'ai préparé dix-huit trous, comme au golf ! HAHAHA !
Votre maître va vous appeler par ordre alphabétique et moi je vais vous aider, parce que, quand on plante un arbre, faut pas se planter ! HAHAHA !
Tu comprends ce qu'il dit, toi ?
Non, mais il est rigolo.

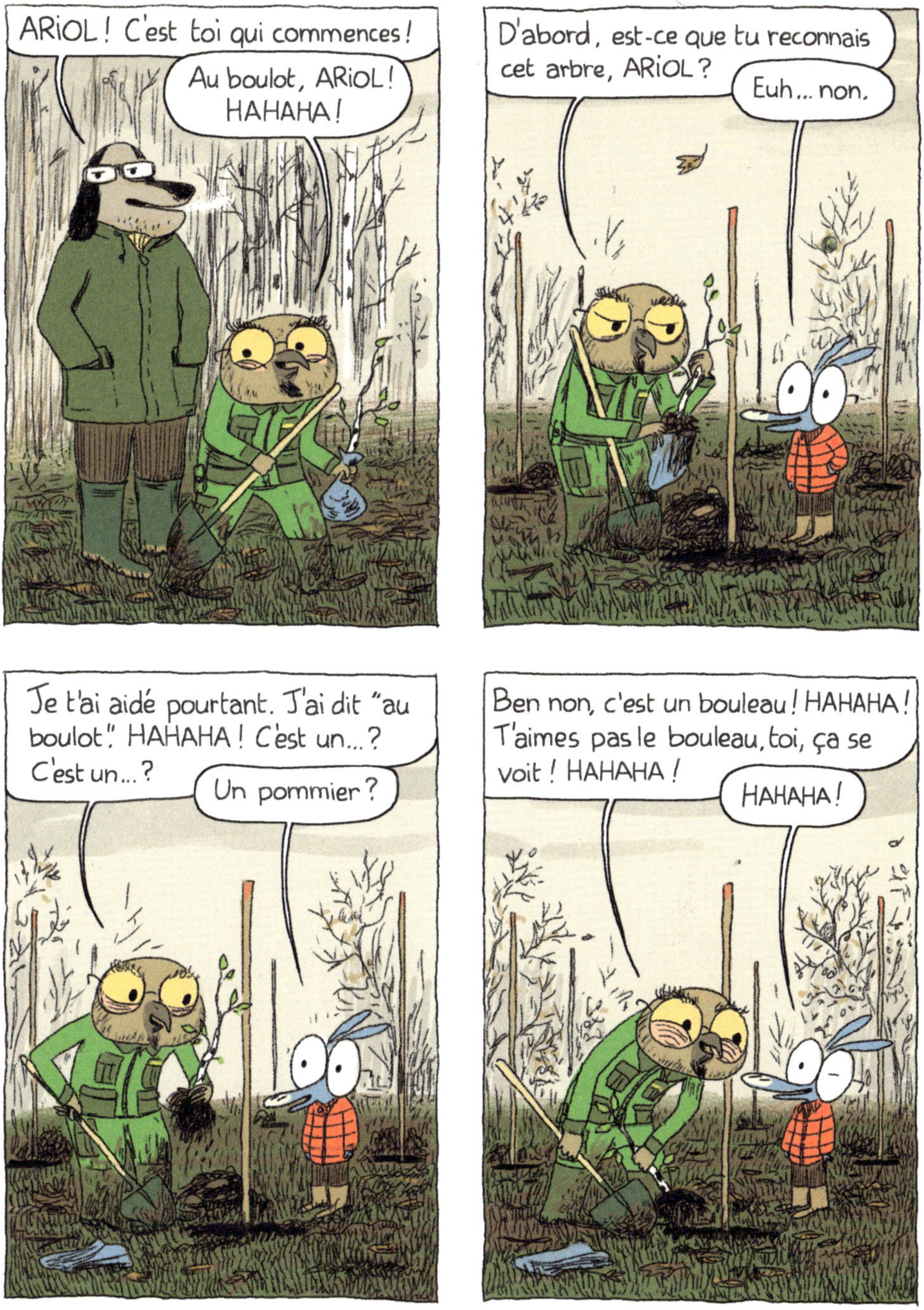
ARiOL ! C'est toi qui commences !
Au boulot, ARiOL ! HAHAHA !
D'abord, est-ce que tu reconnais cet arbre, ARiOL ?
Euh... non.
Je t'ai aidé pourtant. J'ai dit "au boulot". HAHAHA ! C'est un... ? C'est un... ?
Un pommier ?
Ben non, c'est un bouleau ! HAHAHA ! T'aimes pas le bouleau, toi, ça se voit ! HAHAHA !
HAHAHA !

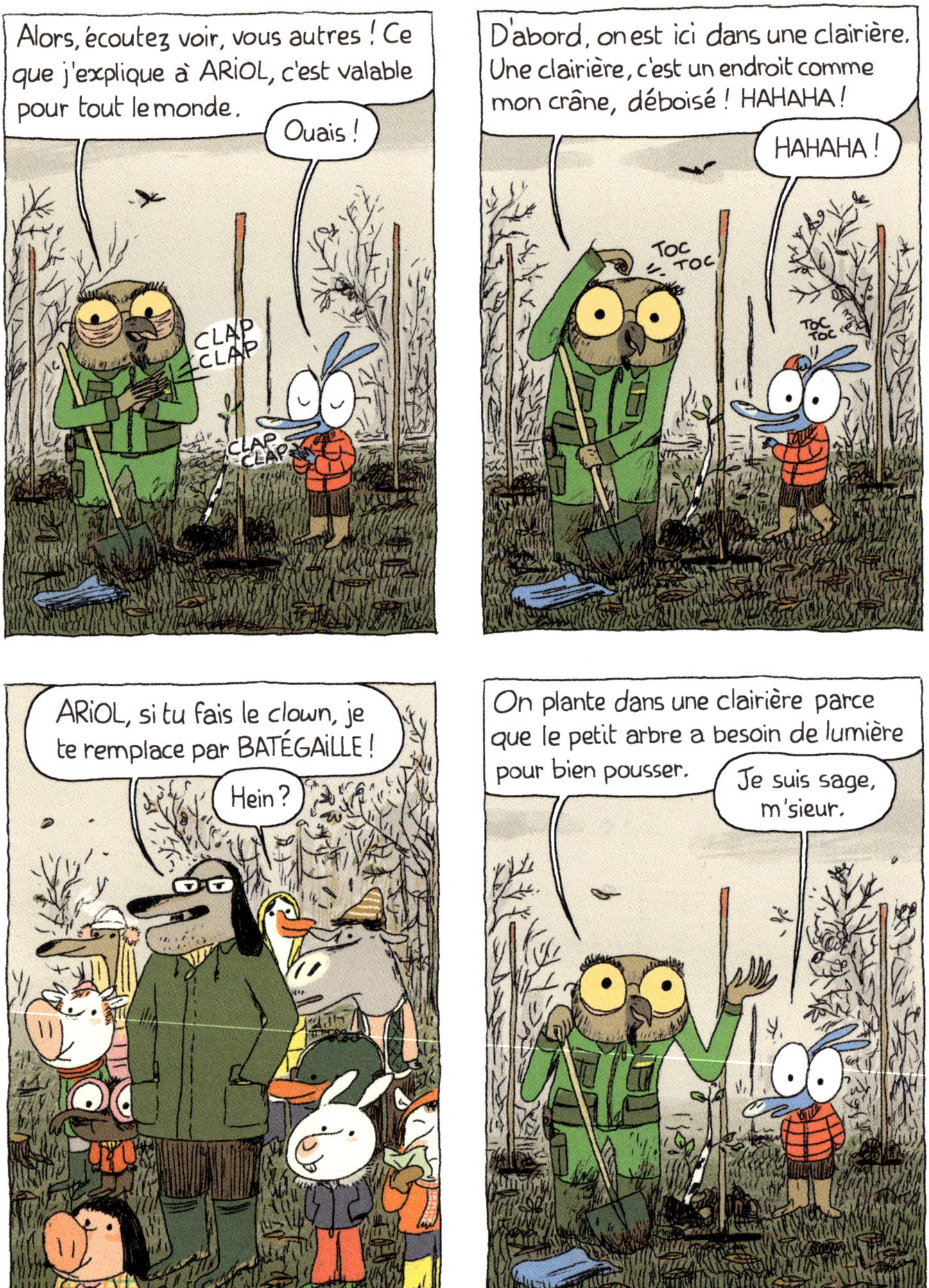
Alors, écoutez voir, vous autres ! Ce que j'explique à ARiOL, c'est valable pour tout le monde.
Ouais !
CLAP CLAP
CLAP CLAP
D'abord, on est ici dans une clairière. Une clairière, c'est un endroit comme mon crâne, déboisé ! HAHAHA !
HAHAHA !
TOC TOC
TOC TOC
ARiOL, si tu fais le clown, je te remplace par BATÉGAILLE !
Hein ?
On plante dans une clairière parce que le petit arbre a besoin de lumière pour bien pousser.
Je suis sage, m'sieur.

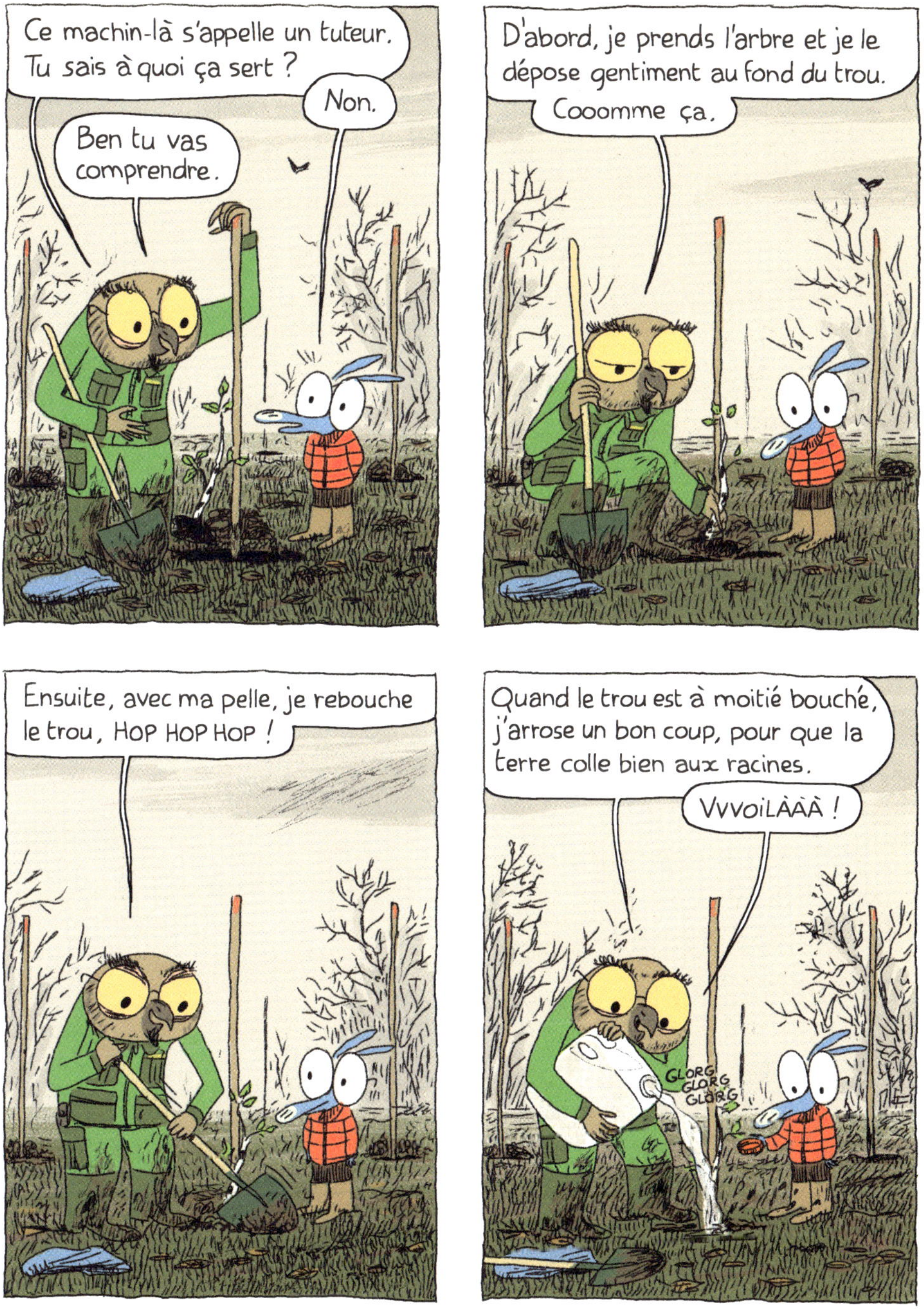
Ce machin-là s'appelle un tuteur. Tu sais à quoi ça sert ?
Non.
Ben tu vas comprendre.
D'abord, je prends l'arbre et je le dépose gentiment au fond du trou.
Cooomme ça.
Ensuite, avec ma pelle, je rebouche le trou, HOP HOP HOP !
Quand le trou est à moitié bouché, j'arrose un bon coup, pour que la terre colle bien aux racines.
VVVOILÀÀÀ !
GLORG GLORG GLORG

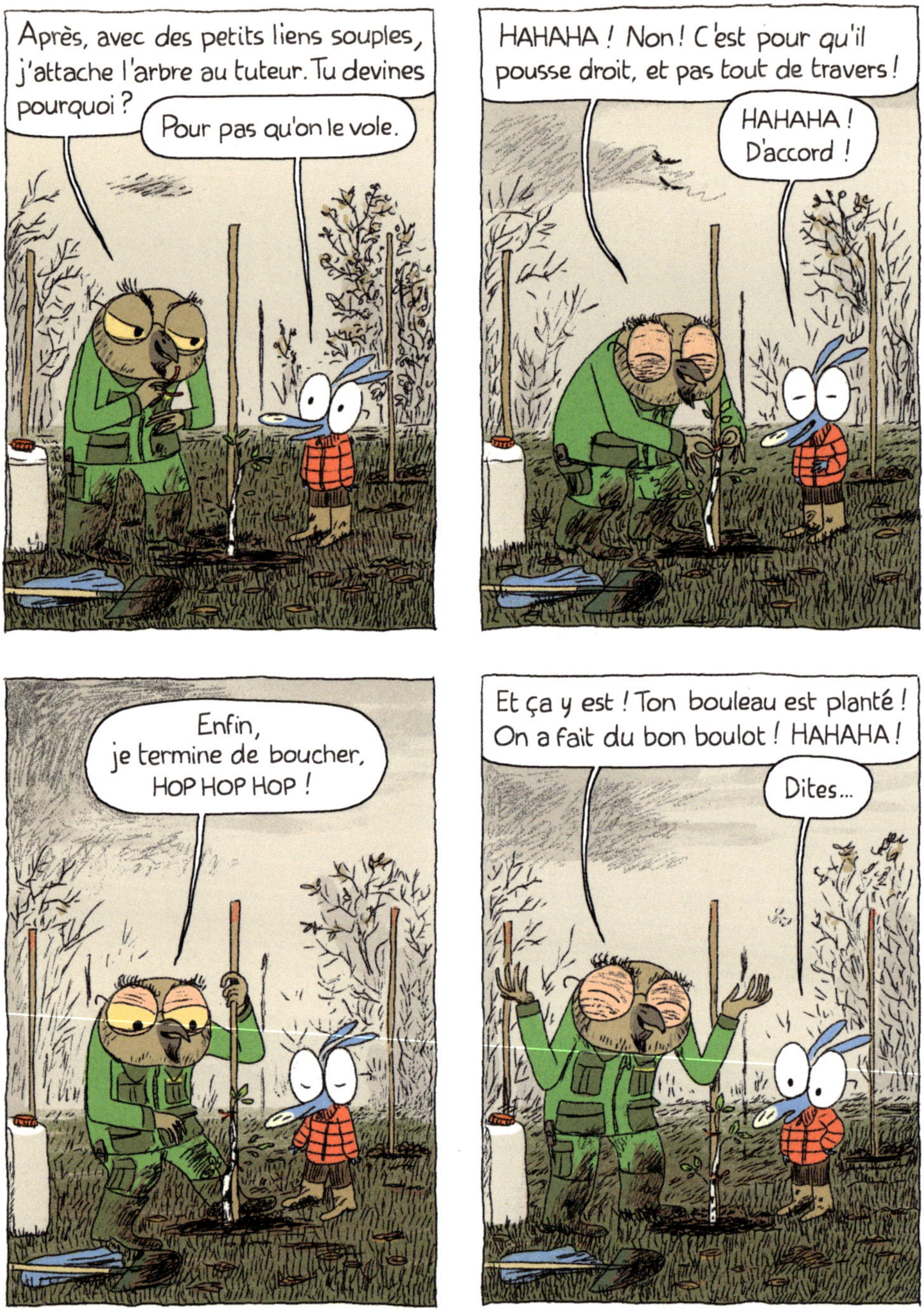
Après, avec des petits liens souples, j'attache l'arbre au tuteur. Tu devines pourquoi ?
Pour pas qu'on le vole.
HAHAHA ! Non ! C'est pour qu'il pousse droit, et pas tout de travers !
HAHAHA ! D'accord !
Enfin, je termine de boucher, HOP HOP HOP !
Et ça y est ! Ton bouleau est planté ! On a fait du bon boulot ! HAHAHA !
Dites...

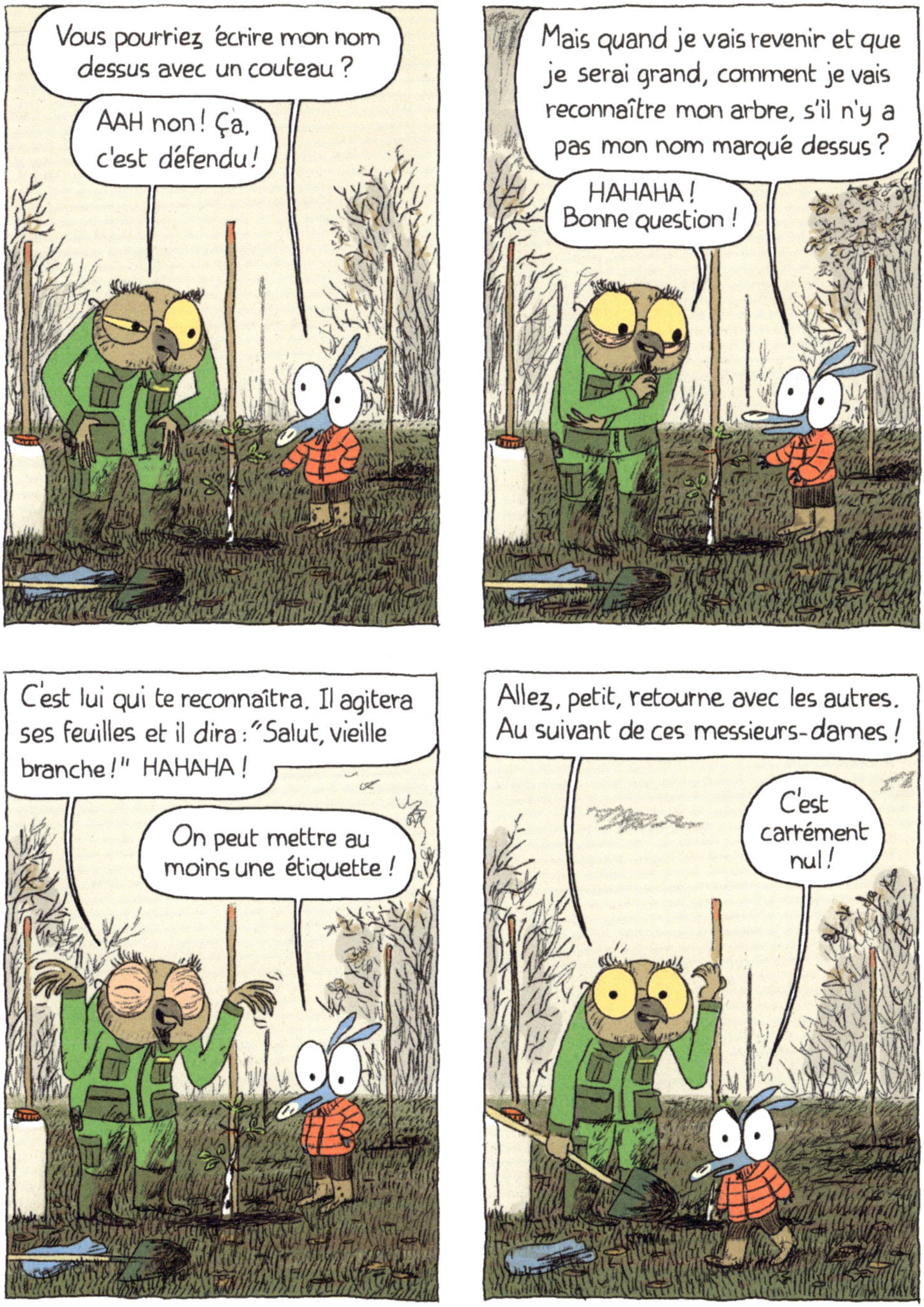
Vous pourriez écrire mon nom dessus avec un couteau ?
AAH non ! Ça, c'est défendu !
Mais quand je vais revenir et que je serai grand, comment je vais reconnaître mon arbre, s'il n'y a pas mon nom marqué dessus ?
HAHAHA ! Bonne question !
C'est lui qui te reconnaîtra. Il agitera ses feuilles et il dira : "Salut, vieille branche !" HAHAHA !
On peut mettre au moins une étiquette !
Allez, petit, retourne avec les autres. Au suivant de ces messieurs-dames !
C'est carrément nul !

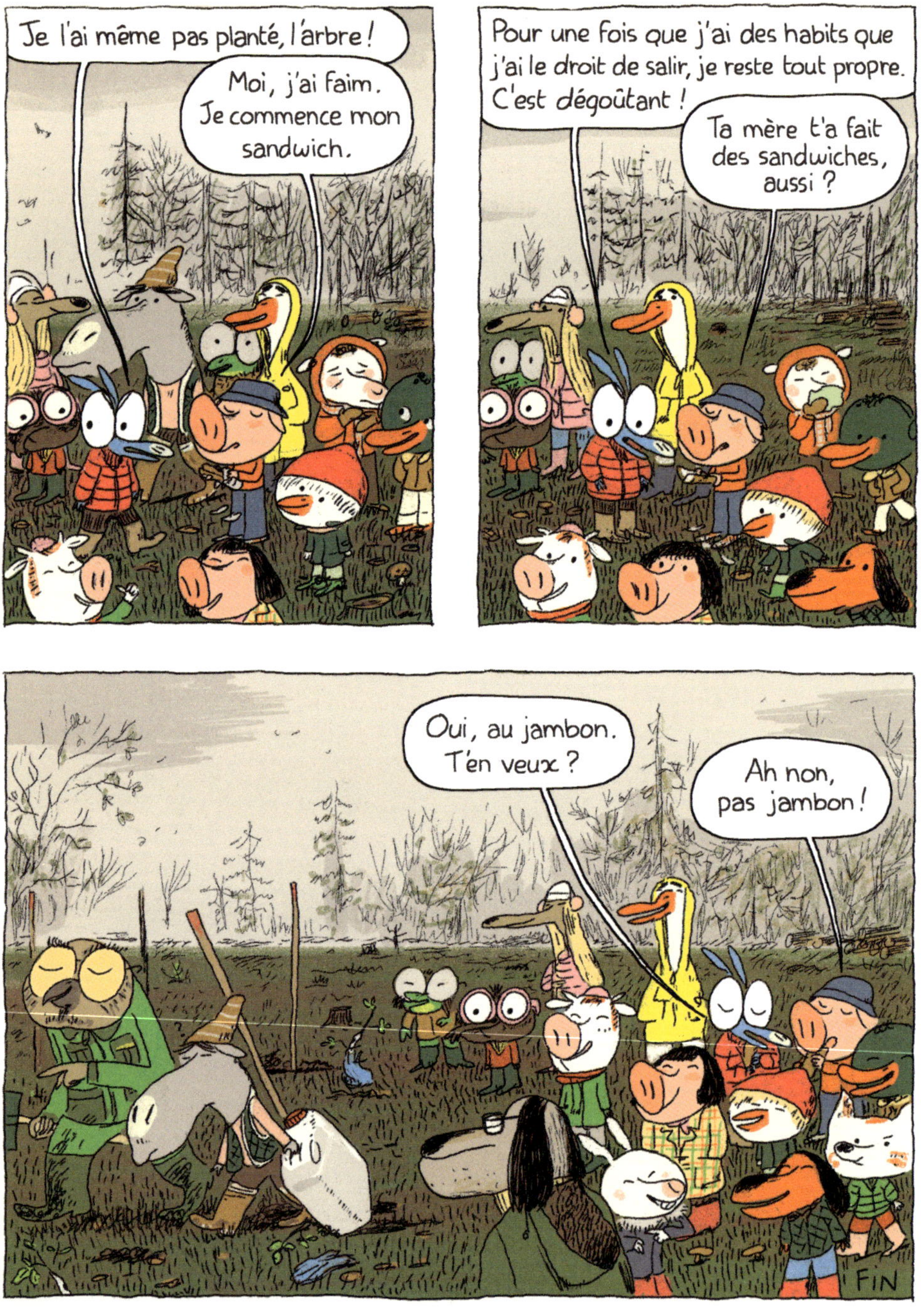
Je l'ai même pas planté, l'arbre !
Moi, j'ai faim. Je commence mon sandwich.
Pour une fois que j'ai des habits que j'ai le droit de salir, je reste tout propre. C'est dégoûtant !
Ta mère t'a fait des sandwiches, aussi ?
Oui, au jambon. T'en veux ?
Ah non, pas jambon !
FIN

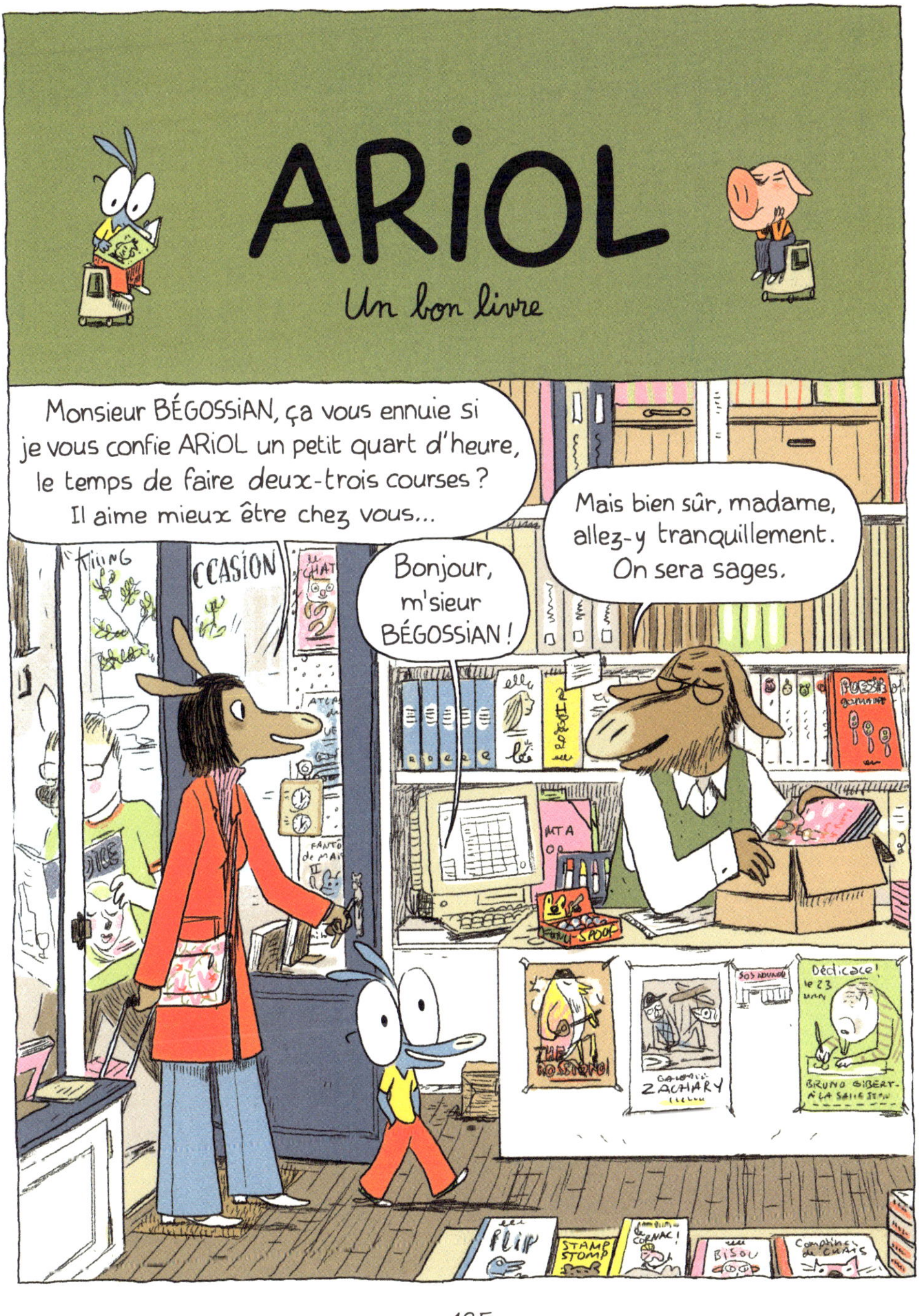
ARiOL
Un bon livre
Monsieur BÉGOSSiAN, ça vous ennuie si je vous confie ARiOL un petit quart d'heure, le temps de faire deux-trois courses ? Il aime mieux être chez vous...
Bonjour, m'sieur BÉGOSSiAN !
Mais bien sûr, madame, allez-y tranquillement. On sera sages.
CCASiON
Dédicace !
ZACHARY
STAMP STOMP
BiSOU

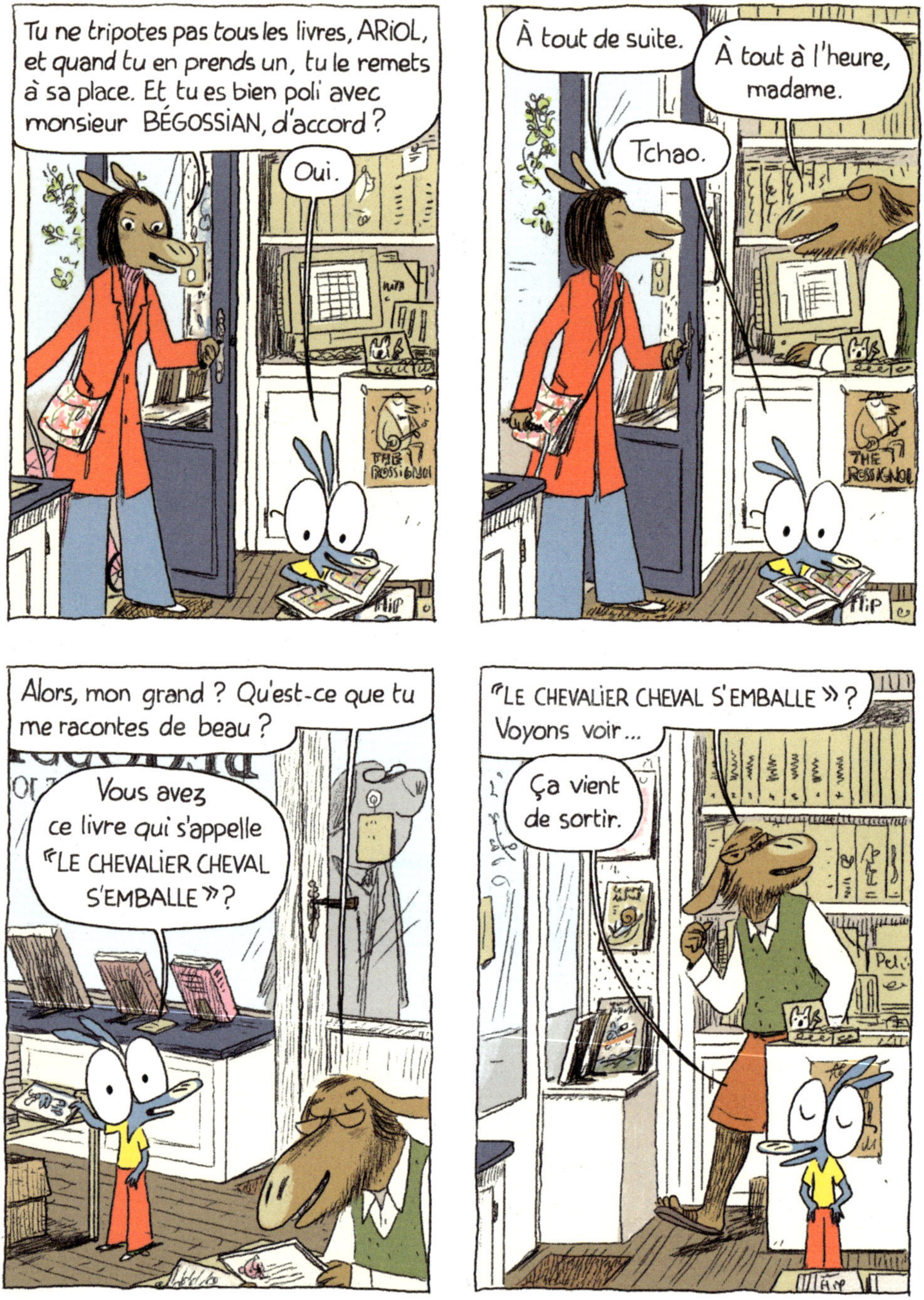
Tu ne tripotes pas tous les livres, ARIOL, et quand tu en prends un, tu le remets à sa place. Et tu es bien poli avec monsieur BÉGOSSIAN, d'accord ?
Oui.
THE ROSSIGNOL
À tout de suite.
À tout à l'heure, madame.
Tchao.
THE ROSSIGNOL
Alors, mon grand ? Qu'est-ce que tu me racontes de beau ?
Vous avez ce livre qui s'appelle « LE CHEVALIER CHEVAL S'EMBALLE » ?
« LE CHEVALIER CHEVAL S'EMBALLE » ? Voyons voir...
Ça vient de sortir.

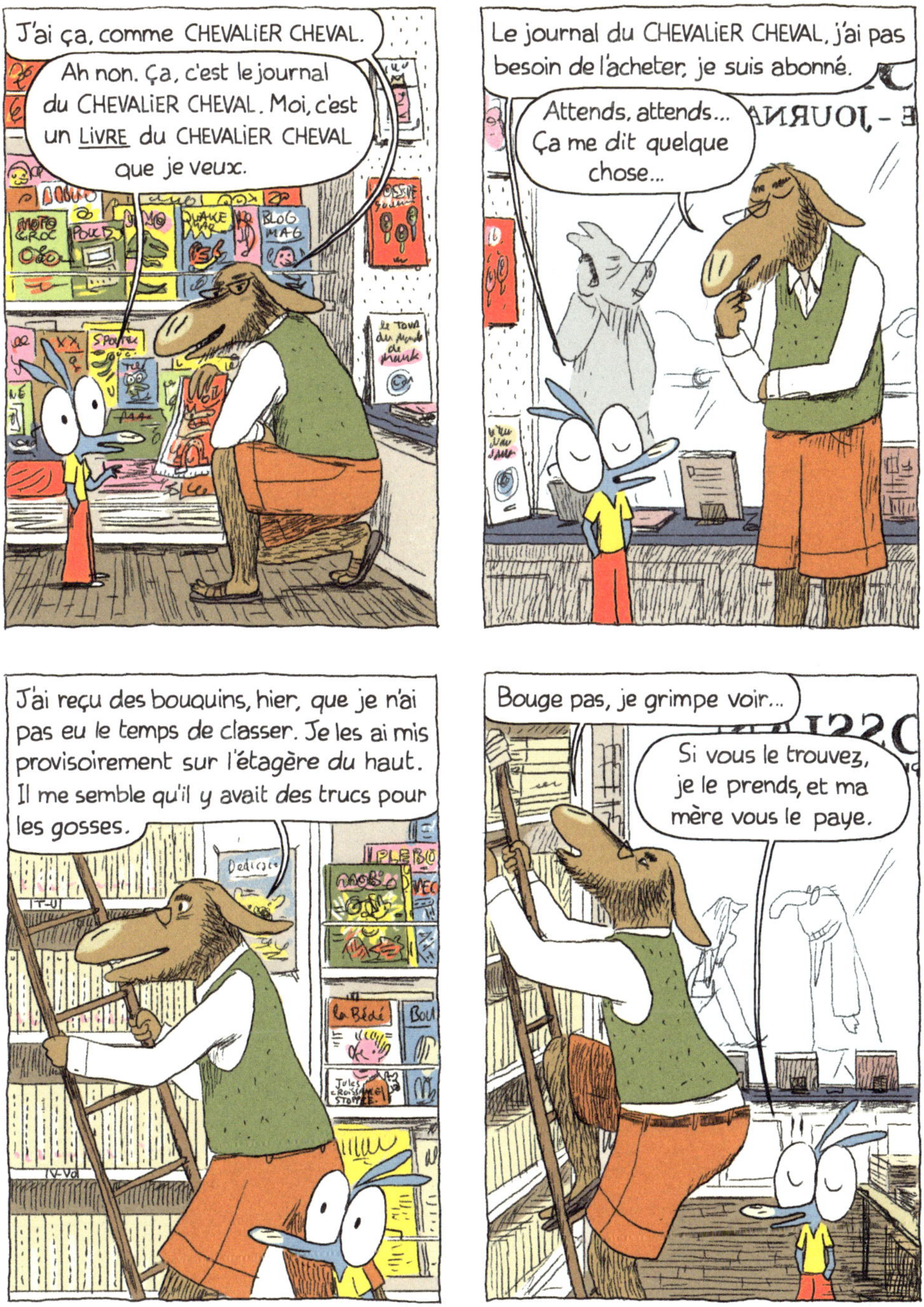
J'ai ça, comme CHEVALIER CHEVAL.
Ah non. Ça, c'est le journal du CHEVALIER CHEVAL. Moi, c'est un LIVRE du CHEVALIER CHEVAL que je veux.
Le journal du CHEVALIER CHEVAL, j'ai pas besoin de l'acheter, je suis abonné.
Attends, attends... Ça me dit quelque chose...
J'ai reçu des bouquins, hier, que je n'ai pas eu le temps de classer. Je les ai mis provisoirement sur l'étagère du haut. Il me semble qu'il y avait des trucs pour les gosses.
Bouge pas, je grimpe voir...
Si vous le trouvez, je le prends, et ma mère vous le paye.

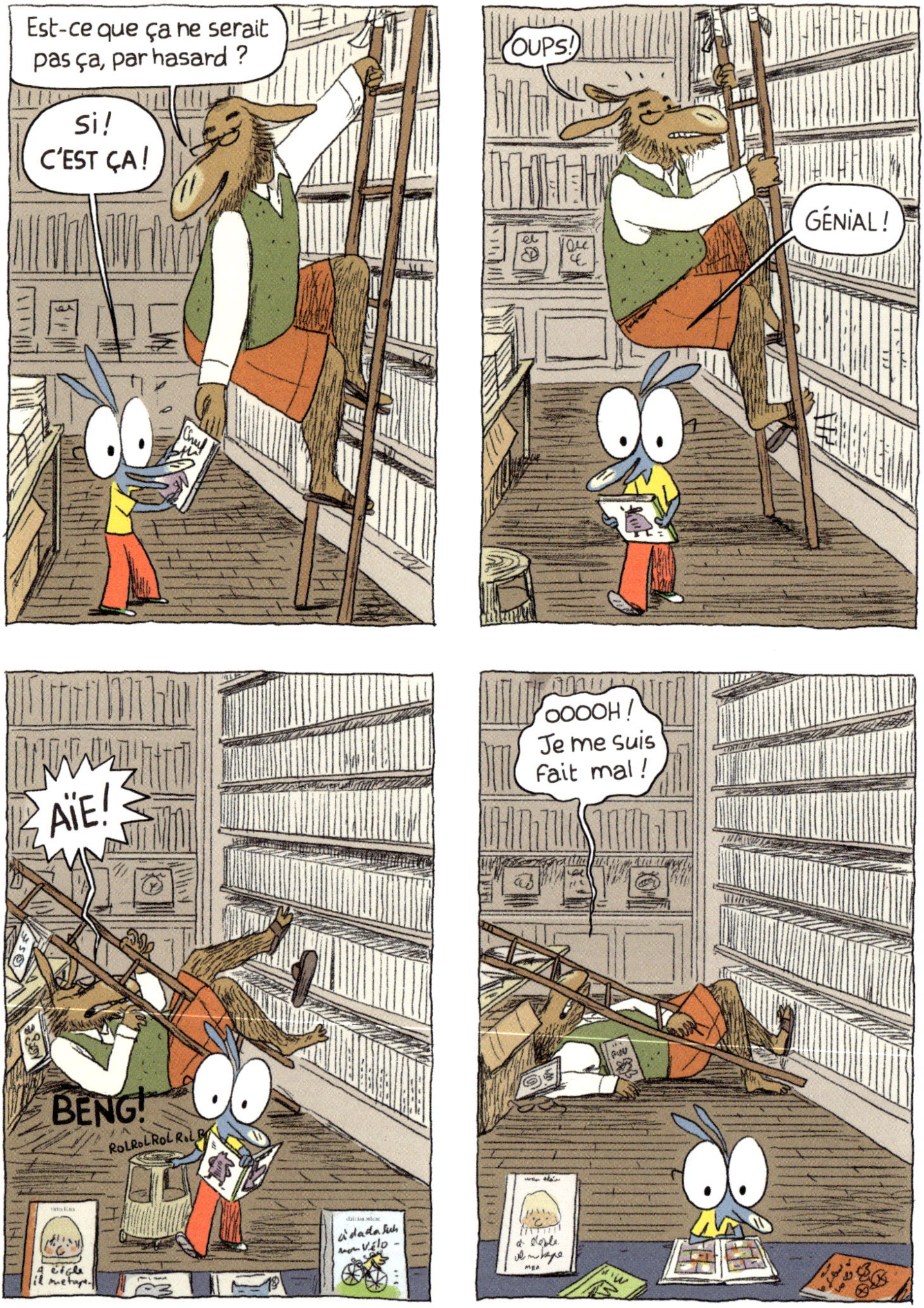
Est-ce que ça ne serait pas ça, par hasard ?
Si ! C'EST ÇA !
OUPS !
GÉNIAL !
AÏE !
BENG !
ROLROLROLROL
OOOOH ! Je me suis fait mal !

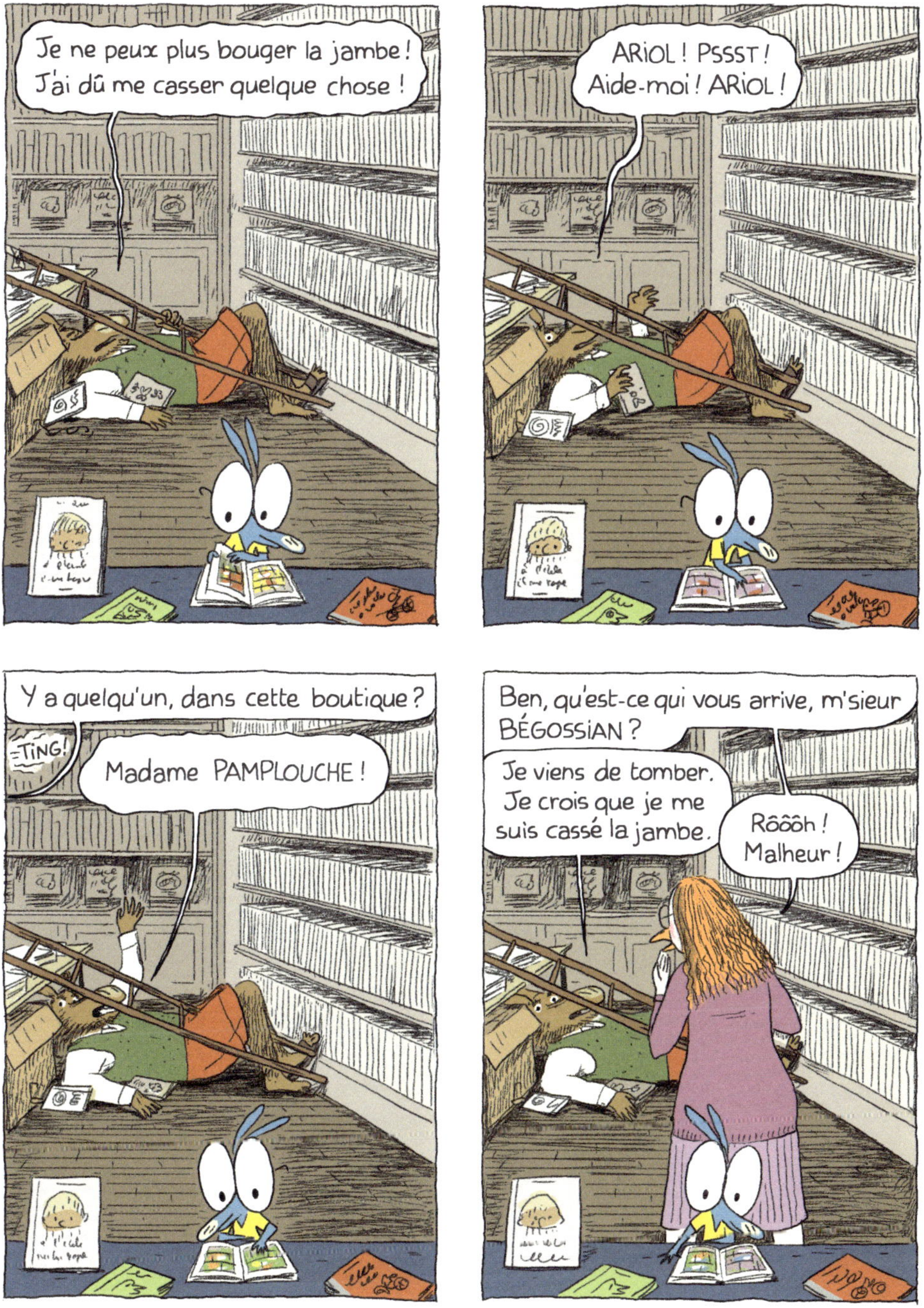
Je ne peux plus bouger la jambe ! J'ai dû me casser quelque chose !
ARiOL ! PSSST ! Aide-moi ! ARiOL !
Y a quelqu'un, dans cette boutique ?
TiNG !
Madame PAMPLOUCHE !
Ben, qu'est-ce qui vous arrive, m'sieur BÉGOSSiAN ?
Je viens de tomber. Je crois que je me suis cassé la jambe.
Rôôôh ! Malheur !

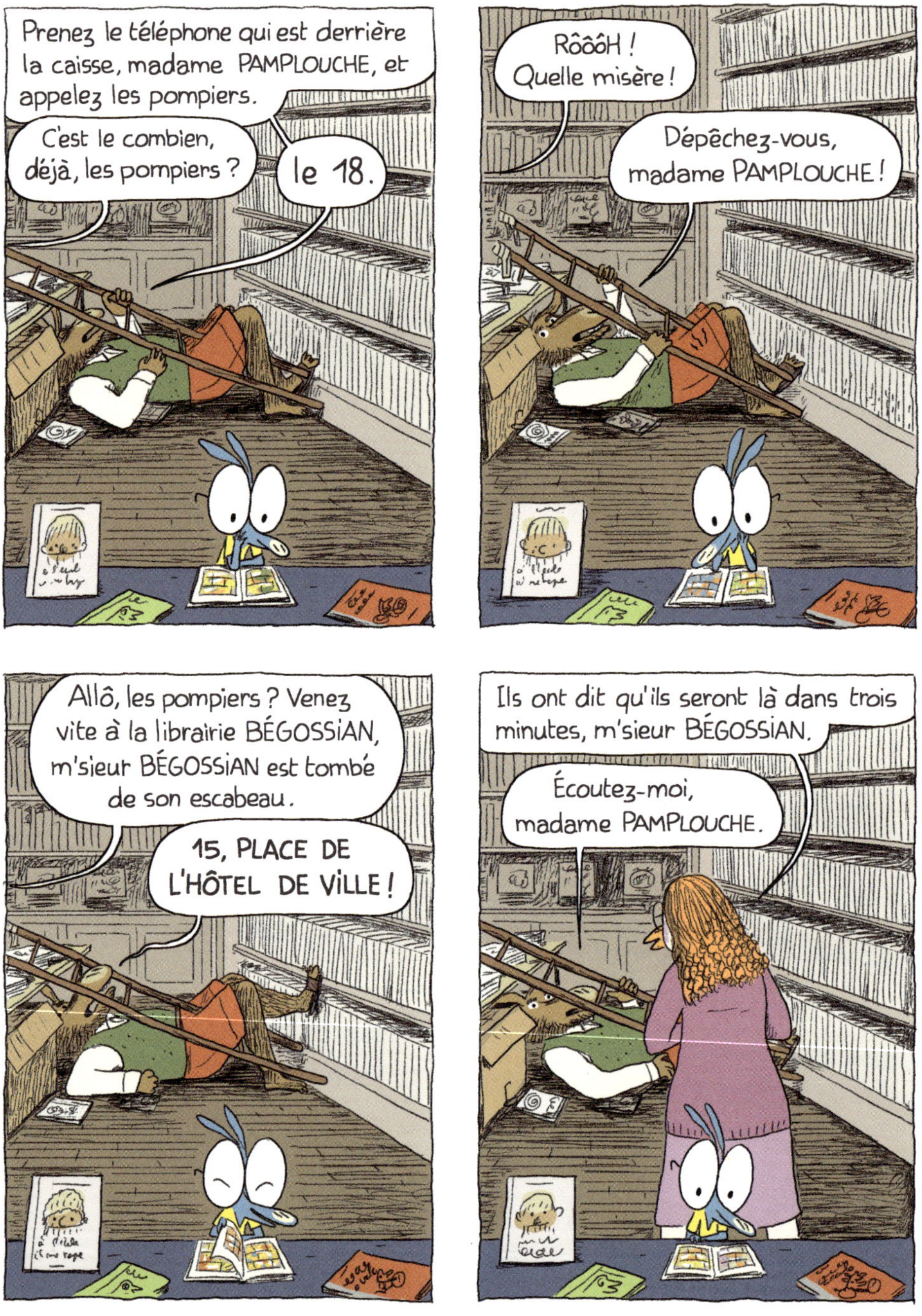
Prenez le téléphone qui est derrière la caisse, madame PAMPLOUCHE, et appelez les pompiers.
C'est le combien, déjà, les pompiers ?
le 18.
RôôôH ! Quelle misère !
Dépêchez-vous, madame PAMPLOUCHE !
Allô, les pompiers ? Venez vite à la librairie BÉGOSSIAN, m'sieur BÉGOSSIAN est tombé de son escabeau.
15, PLACE DE L'HÔTEL DE VILLE !
Ils ont dit qu'ils seront là dans trois minutes, m'sieur BÉGOSSIAN.
Écoutez-moi, madame PAMPLOUCHE.

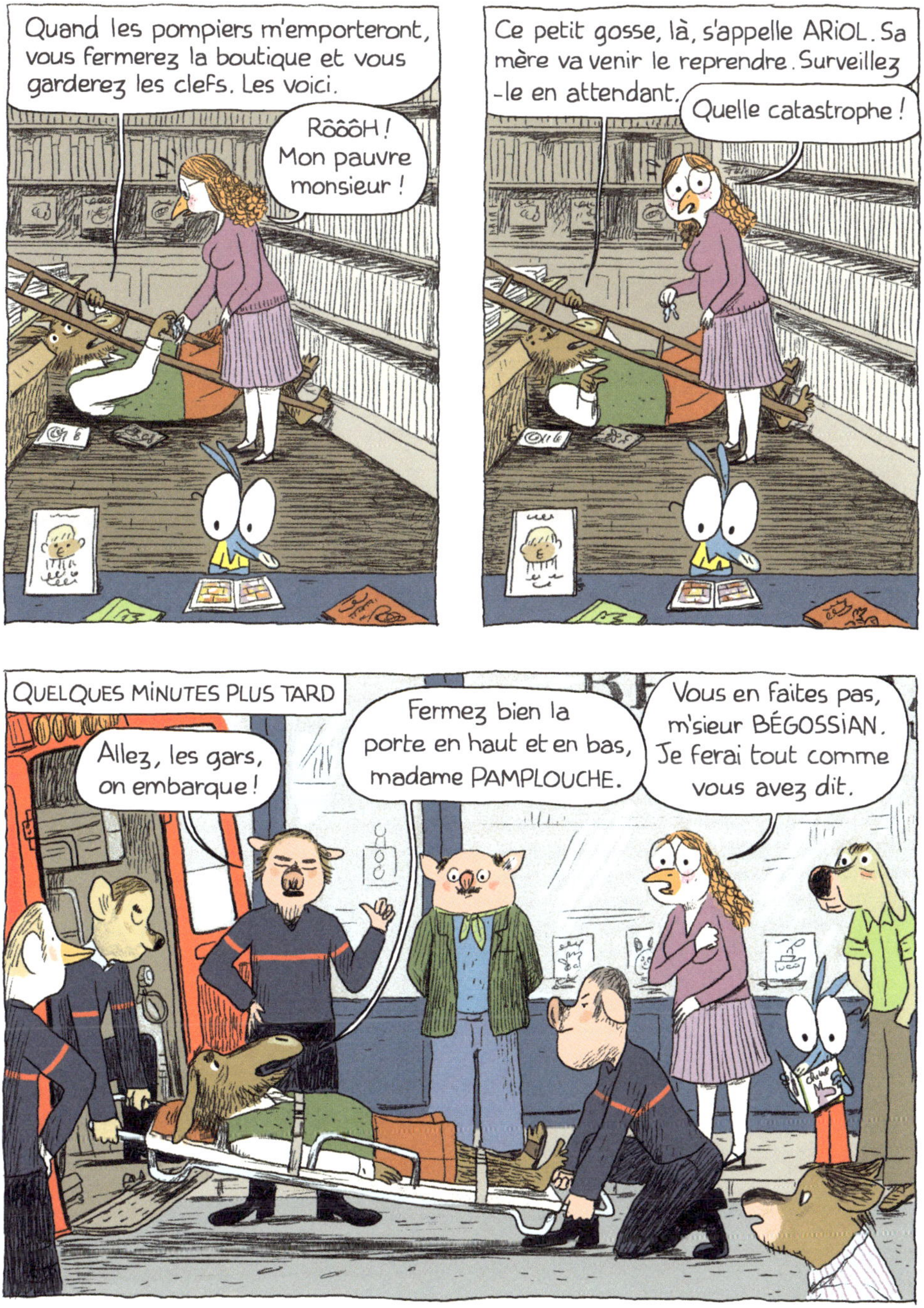
Quand les pompiers m'emporteront, vous fermerez la boutique et vous garderez les clefs. Les voici.
RôôôH ! Mon pauvre monsieur !
Ce petit gosse, là, s'appelle ARiOL. Sa mère va venir le reprendre. Surveillez-le en attendant.
Quelle catastrophe !
QUELQUES MiNUTES PLUS TARD
Allez, les gars, on embarque !
Fermez bien la porte en haut et en bas, madame PAMPLOUCHE.
Vous en faites pas, m'sieur BÉGOSSiAN. Je ferai tout comme vous avez dit.

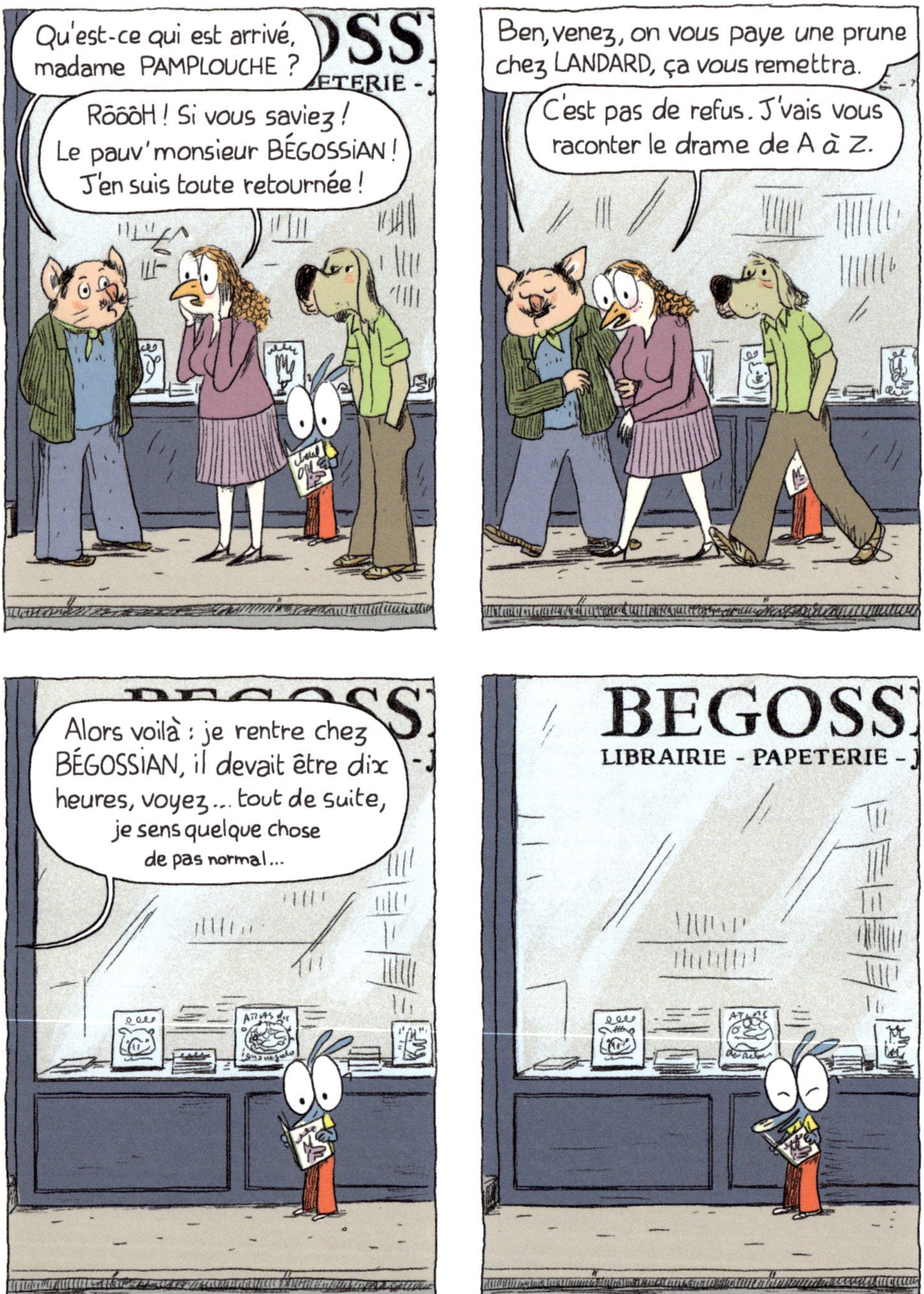
Qu'est-ce qui est arrivé, madame PAMPLOUCHE ?
RÔÔÔH ! Si vous saviez ! Le pauv'monsieur BÉGOSSIAN ! J'en suis toute retournée !
Ben, venez, on vous paye une prune chez LANDARD, ça vous remettra.
C'est pas de refus. J'vais vous raconter le drame de A à Z.
Alors voilà : je rentre chez BÉGOSSIAN, il devait être dix heures, voyez... tout de suite, je sens quelque chose de pas normal...
BEGOSS
LIBRAIRIE - PAPETERIE -

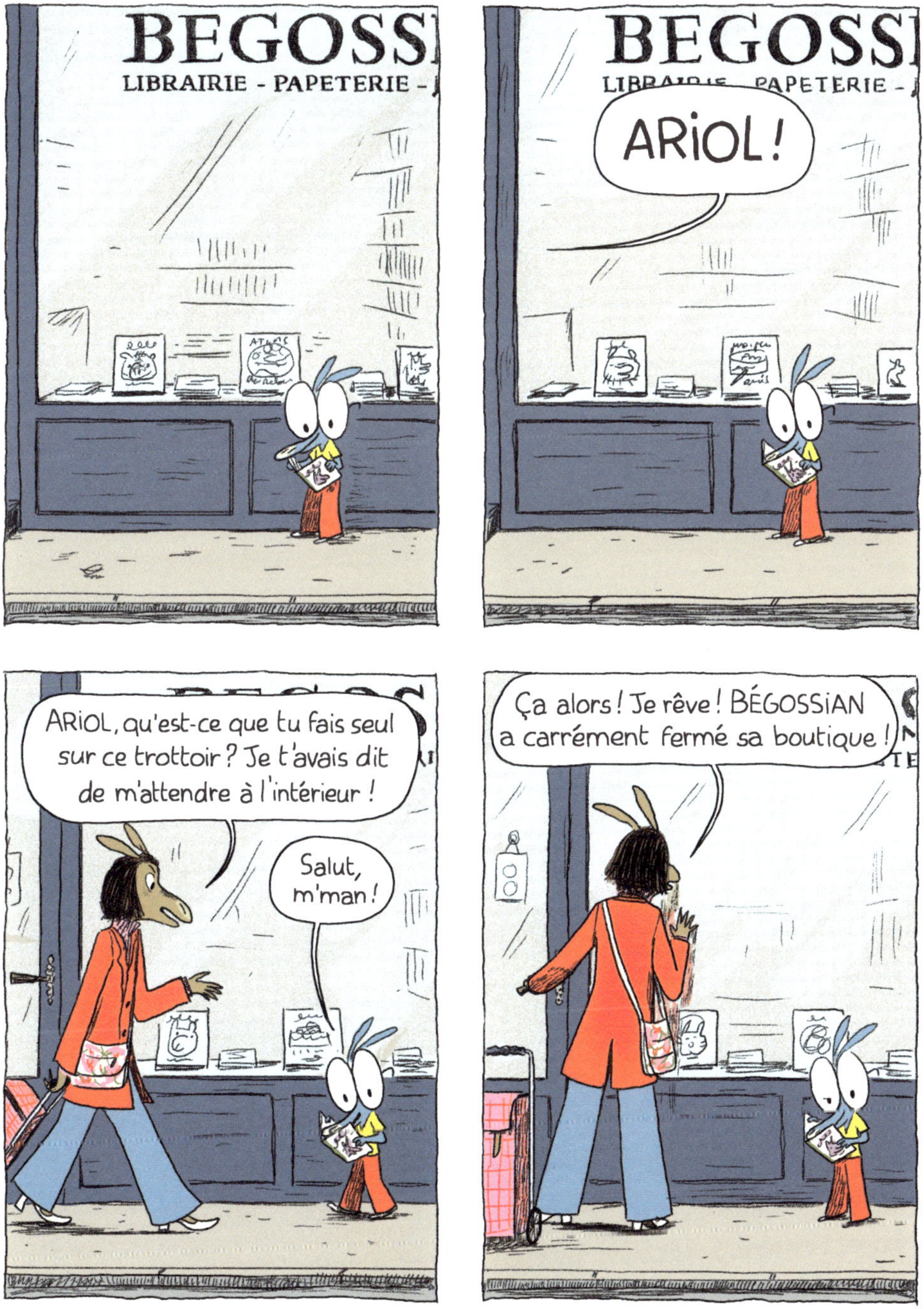
BEGOSS
LIBRAIRIE - PAPETERIE -
ARiOL !
ARIOL, qu'est-ce que tu fais seul sur ce trottoir ? Je t'avais dit de m'attendre à l'intérieur !
Salut, m'man !
Ça alors ! Je rêve ! BÉGOSSiAN a carrément fermé sa boutique !

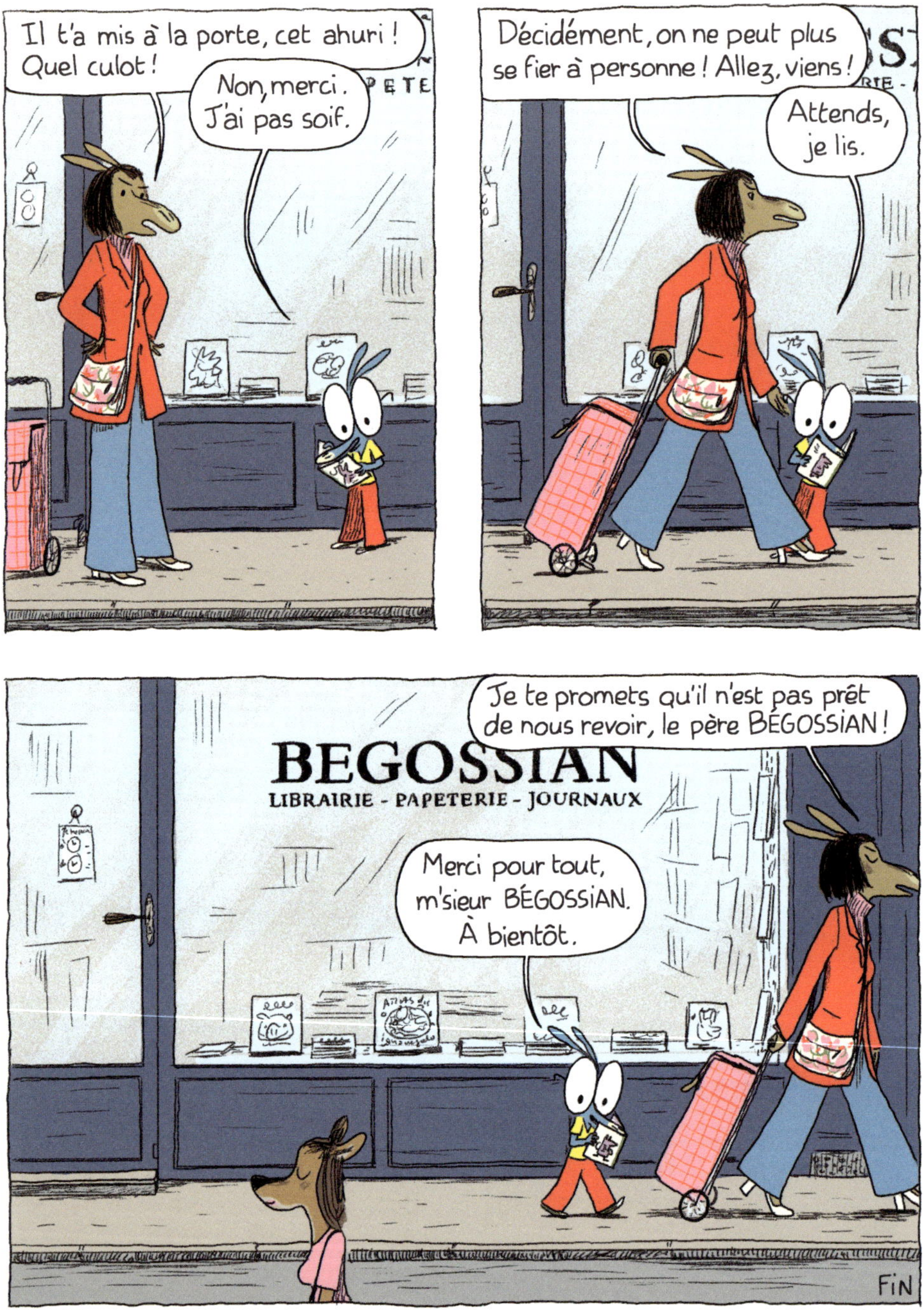
Il t'a mis à la porte, cet ahuri ! Quel culot !
Non, merci. J'ai pas soif.
Décidément, on ne peut plus se fier à personne ! Allez, viens !
Attends, je lis.
BEGOSSIAN
LIBRAIRIE - PAPETERIE - JOURNAUX
Je te promets qu'il n'est pas prêt de nous revoir, le père BÉGOSSIAN !
Merci pour tout, m'sieur BÉGOSSIAN. À bientôt.
FIN

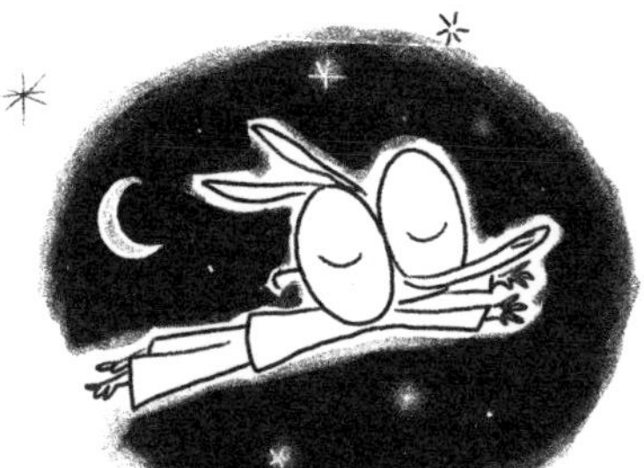